THE UNITED STATES AND WORLD DEVELOPMENT

Acknowledgments

John W. Sewell, *Project Director*
Valeriana Kallab, *Executive Editor*
Nancy J. Krekeler, *Associate Editor*
Rosemarie Philips, *Associate Editor*

Each of the ODC's four preceding *Agendas* has been in some sense a collective effort by the staff of the Overseas Development Council. But *Agenda 1977* more than any previous volume in the series reflects the work and thinking of almost all of the Council's staff. The Project Director would like, therefore, to express his very great appreciation to his colleagues who contributed to the preparation of *Agenda 1977*. Chapters I and II reflect their comments, and many of the policy recommendations contained in Chapter III draw directly upon their work.

The Overseas Development Council wishes to express its gratitude for the generous counsel given to those working on this *Agenda* by several members of the Council's Board of Directors, including particularly the Vice Chairman of the Board, Davidson Sommers, and C. M. van Vlierden and Lincoln Gordon. The preparation and publication of this *Agenda* has been partially supported by a grant from the Edna McConnell Clark Foundation.

The signed chapters in this *Agenda* represent the views of the authors and not necessarily those of the Overseas Development Council, its Directors, or its staff.

THE UNITED STATES AND WORLD DEVELOPMENT

AGENDA 1977

John W. Sewell
and the Staff of the Overseas Development Council

PUBLISHED FOR THE OVERSEAS DEVELOPMENT COUNCIL
PRAEGER PUBLISHERS
NEW YORK/LONDON

Library of Congress Cataloging in Publication Data

Sewell, John Williamson
     The United States and world development, agenda 1977.

     (Praeger special studies in international economics
and development)
     1. Underdeveloped areas. 2. Economic assistance.
3. United States—Foreign relations. 4. United
States—Commercial policy. I. Overseas Development
Council. II. Title.
HC59.7.S4455   338.91'172'4073   76-30725
ISBN 0-275-24440-7
ISBN 0-275-65000-6 Student ed.

PRAEGER PUBLISHERS
200 Park Avenue, New York, N.Y. 10017, U.S.A.

Published in the United States of America in 1977
by Praeger Publishers, Inc.

Printed in the United States of America

THE UNITED STATES AND WORLD DEVELOPMENT

I have chosen the occasion of my inauguration as President to speak not only to my own countrymen—which is traditional—but also to you, citizens of the world who did not participate in our election but who will nevertheless be affected by my decisions.

I also believe that as friends you are entitled to know how the power and influence of the United States will be exercised by its new government.

I want to assure you that the relations of the United States with the other countries and peoples of the world will be guided during our administration by our desire to shape a world order that is more responsive to human aspirations. The United States will meet its obligation to help create a stable, just, and peaceful world order.

We will not seek to dominate nor dictate to others. As we Americans have concluded one chapter in our nation's history and are beginning to work on another, we have, I believe, acquired a more mature perspective on the problems of the world. It is a perspective which recognizes the fact that we alone do not have all the answers to the world's problems.

The United States alone cannot lift from the world the terrifying specter of nuclear destruction. We can and will work with others to do so.

The United States alone cannot guarantee the basic right of every human being to be free of poverty and hunger and disease and political repression. We can and will cooperate with others in combating these enemies of mankind.

The United States alone cannot insure an equitable development of the world resources or the proper safeguarding of the world's environment. But we can and will join with others in this work.

The United States can and will take the lead in such efforts. In these endeavors we need your help, and we offer ours. We need your experience. We need your wisdom. We need your active participation in a joint effort to move the reality of the world closer to the ideals of human freedom and dignity.

As friends, you can depend on the United States to be in the forefront of the search for world peace. You can depend on the United States to remain steadfast in its commitment to human freedom and liberty. And you can also depend on the United States to be sensitive to your own concerns and aspirations, to welcome your advice, to do its utmost to resolve international differences in a spirit of cooperation.

The problems of the world will not be easily resolved. Yet the well-being of each and every one of us—indeed our mutual survival—depends on their resolution. As President of the United States I can assure you that we intend to do our part. I ask you to join us in a common effort based on mutual trust and mutual respect.

JIMMY CARTER
President of the United States of America

Statement to the World
January 20, 1977

Introduction

Theodore M. Hesburgh and James P. Grant

Agenda 1977, the fifth annual assessment by the Overseas Development Council of relationships between the United States and the developing countries, is being published at one of those open moments in history when a series of developments combine to make changes possible on a scale normally not within the realm of possibility. The United States, under the leadership of a President who bears no burden of prior identification with past disputes, has a unique opportunity to contribute to the global leadership that is urgently required if the world is to work more effectively and equitably for people in both the developed and developing countries. The question now is whether or not this opportunity will be seized.

This sense that the next few years will be a period of considerable change in international development is reflected in the unprecedented statement to the world by President Jimmy Carter—reprinted on the facing page—that was broadcast on Inauguration Day. Addressed to those "citizens of the world who did not participate in our election but who will nevertheless be affected by my decisions," President Carter committed his Administration to shaping a world order that is "just" and "more responsive to human aspirations" as well as stable and peaceful. He spoke of the "basic rights" of every human being to be free not only of political repression but also of poverty, hunger, and disease. He further emphasized the need for an "equitable development of the world's resources" and the "proper safeguarding of the world's environment." While stressing the limitations of America's acting alone, he committed the United States to joining with others in addressing these issues and taking the lead in such efforts. His closing words called upon the citizens of the world to "join us in a common effort."

But what is the shape of the "common effort" to which President Carter referred? How far-reaching a response is needed? What is feasible? What might be done now to signal a U.S. will to respond constructively to global problems? Analysis and discussion of these critical issues is the main objective of *Agenda 1977*.

President Carter has come to power in the United States at a time when there is a growing understanding both in the United States and abroad that the world order created after World War II is coming to an end and that another is urgently required. A broad consensus is emerging among the leaders of both the industrialized democracies of the Northern Hemisphere and of the developing countries to their South that the economic, social, and political systems created after World War II require renovation, restructuring, and, in some instances, replacement and supplement. Only through such changes will they once again meet the legitimate needs of the North and, at the same time, become far more responsive to the South's needs and aspirations for greater equality of opportunity. Existing arrangements in areas such as trade and monetary affairs need to be adapted to changed circumstances. Problems such as energy shortages and nuclear proliferation, the deteriorating environment, and growing population require major new approaches if they are to be adequately resolved.

There also is a second and growing area of agreement among citizens and leaders in many countries: the need for increased cooperation to accelerate development in the poorest countries in a way which more effectively addresses the basic human needs of this poorest fourth of humanity. More effective approaches are needed to the problems associated with their poverty—the increased migration from the countryside to the city, growing unemployment, population growth, and the continuing erosion in many countries of basic political rights. It is becoming increasingly apparent that major changes are required in both international and domestic policies if the prospects of the world's poorest billion people are to improve noticeably in the remaining decades of this century and millions are not to continue to die prematurely each year.

Beyond this very general level of awareness of the problem, however, there is no consensus on the goals and means for proceeding on a "common effort." Clearly, a far-reaching response is desirable and, in our view, indispensable. The critical question is how far-reaching a response will be both needed and politically acceptable, and what forms of response are feasible.

This year the format of the Overseas Development Council's *Agenda* has been changed in order to illumine the choices that face the new Administration—and indeed *all* Americans. The opening essay, "The United States and World Development, 1977," by *Agenda* Director John W. Sewell sets the stage for the ensuing analysis of the central issues. It briefly describes global problems, surveys the present state of development progress in the Third World, reviews the record of the past four years of North-South relations, discusses some of the reasons behind the proposals of the developing countries for a "new international economic order," and identifies the need for new policies of global cooperation. This essay also describes the emergence of new international strategies to facilitate the attainment of "basic human needs" on an accelerated basis in all countries, but particularly in the world's poorest nations, and raises the numerous critical questions that must be considered by U.S. policy makers in the years ahead.

The central choices open to the Carter Administration are analyzed in the essay, "Major U.S. Options on North-South Relations: A Letter to President Carter," in which Roger Hansen sets forth the pros and cons on three principal "options" facing the new Administration; from among these, he formulates a preferred proposal which, in effect, represents a fourth possible choice. These four alternative policy "packages" may be briefly summarized as follows.

Option 1 provides for only marginal changes in existing policies—but with more effective implementation. Under this approach, there would be some increased U.S. responsiveness to developing-country concerns, with U.S. *actions* in areas such as aid, trade, commodities, etc., being consonant with the more responsive official rhetoric of the recent past—and especially since the September 1975 Seventh Special Session of the U.N. General Assembly. The prime objective would be to seek to take the heat out of the North-South confrontation. This would reduce the adverse impacts that this confrontation is having on the operation of various aspects of the present international system and would increase the capacity for collective action on a range of global issues.

Option 2 calls for a policy of "accelerated reform." In contrast to the "marginal change" approach of Option 1, this package of policies emphasizes the *active search* for a broader and more significant range of reforms of existing international political and economic systems. It suggests using the present North-South debate as an opportunity to not only examine and hopefully resolve some conflict-ridden North-South issues but also as a chance (similar in scope to that which confronted the Bretton Woods and subsequent negotiations in the post-World War II era), to lay the basis for the new, more relevant world order that so many believe is required for the balance of this century.

Option 3, which could be carried out in combination with either of the first two options, provides for greatly increased support for a "basic human needs" strategy of development designed to virtually eliminate, by the end of this century, the worst consequences of absolute poverty—including widespread malnutrition, mass underemployment, high birth rates, and low productivity of the poor.

Hansen's preferred proposal for the United States and the new Administration would combine early implementation of those "incremental" reforms of Option 1 which do not foreclose more far-reaching actions together with active exploration (with the developing countries) of the potential for the "accelerated reform" proposals of Option 2, as well as with a limited version of the basic human needs of Option 3. Any other choice, he concludes, would amount to selling ourselves short—for the future as well as the present.

Two major conceptual differences divide the proponents of Option 1 and the proponents of the more far-reaching proposals. The first is their differing assessment of the seriousness of the current predicament of mankind—an assessment which can differ in part depending on one's values. The second is a divergence of views over what is politically feasible. Clearly, far more than ad hoc pragmatic responses is required if the increasingly dangerous situation in which humanity now finds itself is to be avoided. Yet it is generally acknowledged that it is considerably more difficult to address world problems today than it was in the late 1940s. There now are far more national actors and a far greater diversity of interests represented on the world scene (the number of independent countries has nearly tripled since World War II). The United States is no longer the overwhelmingly dominant power among the market-economy countries; and domestic expectations of governmental action to provide jobs and protect human welfare are far higher among the developing countries than ever before.

Responsible and knowledgeable persons will take different positions on these two questions of need and feasibility. Our own personal judgment is that something considerably more substantial than marginal changes is required, and that such changes can be made politically feasible. But these are only *our* conclusions; the analysis in the "Letter to President Carter" is, we think, sufficiently comprehensive and balanced that others may reach different conclusions from the same information.

The third chapter of this *Agenda*, "Recommendations for U.S. Policy," presents a series of specific proposals—within a broader, long-term framework—for early U.S. action on issues relating to trade, commodities, developing-country debt, technology transfer, energy, oceans, food, basic human needs, population, human rights, development assistance, arms transfers, and decision-making processes on interdependence issues. The policy recommendations are of several different types. Some call for decisions which can be taken in the immediate future to signal a constructive intent on the part of the United States to reshape its policies toward the developing countries; others set forth actions which can be taken in the next two to four years. Still others identify major areas on which further studies and discussion should be initiated now to permit early decisions on a range of far-reaching reforms of various global systems and on a cooperative effort to address basic human needs so that the worst aspects of absolute poverty might be largely eliminated during the remaining years of this century.

An important addition to this *Agenda*'s Statistical Annexes is the introduction of a "Physical Quality of Life Index" (PQLI) designed to complement per capita gross national product (GNP) in measuring development progress. This index is described in the introductory note to the Annexes; in Table A-3 of the Annexes, it is shown—along with other economic and social indicators—for 160 countries. The increased attention paid in recent years to addressing basic human needs more effectively has only strengthened the need for the development of an indicator that would parallel the GNP measure of output of goods and services and could be used to measure progress in terms of human well-being. The PQLI demonstrates that individuals in some areas (which differ widely in other respects)—for example China, Taiwan, Sri Lanka, and the Indian state of Kerala—have a far higher level of physical well-being than would be expected from an assessment of their per capita GNP figures alone—and that the reverse is true in other countries, including Algeria, Brazil, Iran, and South Africa.

Four final points merit mention in this introduction. First, the development of a coherent strategy for addressing the global problems of today will require a great deal of analysis and discussion among the developed countries, between developed and developing countries, and among developing countries. The atmosphere in which these discussions and negotiations are undertaken is critically important. Is the underlying assumption that where one party to negotiations gains, the other must necessarily lose? Or are negotiations undertaken with the commitment to address major problems in such a manner that there may be direct or indirect benefits to all principal parties? If the former, then it is highly likely that the confrontational atmosphere of the last three years will continue; if the latter approach is adopted (as already has been done in the mid-1970s on questions of world food policy), then the prospects for global solutions to these pressing problems will improve greatly.

If the United States were to take an active lead in implementing present policies on which there already is substantial agreement in principle—such as the partial lowering of trade barriers, noticeably increased aid flows to the poorest countries, and establishment of world food reserves—such actions should create a constructive atmosphere for the active exploration in 1977 and 1978 of the possibilities for greatly increased cooperation in reshaping the international system.

Second, analysis and discussion of the more far-reaching changes that will be required should be launched in many forums. Some will encompass both the public and private sector—as does the January 1977 proposal by World Bank President Robert S. McNamara for a commission of eminent persons to examine North-South issues. Action by the private sector is particularly important in the years ahead. Much of the progress that has been made in recent years in this country and internationally in such areas as environment, population, women's rights, and a more effective approach to solving the world food problem has resulted from private initiatives and leadership.

Third, more serious attention needs to be given to those individuals and groups within the United States who suffer losses even though our economy as a whole gains. Trade policy provides the best example of this problem. In the long run, freer trade will benefit all Americans by providing more efficient and higher-paying jobs and less costly consumer goods. But liberalized trade also will mean allowing the developing countries greater access to our markets for their manufactured goods. Is the total price for these benefits to society as a whole to be paid by, for example, a Hispanic worker in the garment industry or a Southerner working in a textile mill who lose their jobs due to competition from other countries? Clearly we will need policies that not only accommodate the needs of the developing countries but also assure all Americans of just treatment in accommodating to changed circumstances.

Fourth, in the mid-1970s we are witnessing a tremendous increase in awareness and concern among Americans about human political and economic rights. It seems increasingly likely that an effective combination of international and domestic policies could overcome the worst aspects of absolute poverty by the end of this century. But far more analysis and thought is required on what might be considered minimum political rights and on how their acceptance can best be advanced, on the degree to which progress on political and economic well-being is associated, and on what goals—if any—we should seek to attain in these areas by the end of this century. Most studies to date have treated approaches to advancing political and economic well-being as two separate topics. President Carter, however, has quite properly encompassed both under the common heading of "basic rights."

The ideas and proposals contained in this *Agenda* may not find agreement among all or even a majority of Americans. They have been designed, however, to stimulate thinking about actions needed a year ahead as well as forward planning of the kind of world we want by the end of the century. A majority of those who read this *Agenda* will still be in their working lives by the year 2000. They have a stake in seeing to it that a reshaping of international institutions and structures begins now if they wish to glean any of the benefits of such changes in their lifetimes.

The industrial democracies should resist the temptation to see the current North-South dialogue as a situation in which losses are inevitable and negotiations are primarily designed to gain time or preserve the status quo. Rather, they should treat it as an extraordinary opportunity for initiating, in the words of President Carter, "a common effort"—which, by the end of this century, could create a world that not only better serves the already advantaged, but also is free of the worst aspects of absolute poverty and repression.

Contents

AGENDA 1977

CHAPTER I

The United States and World Development, 1977

John W. Sewell

A Rapidly Changing World Setting

The world Americans face in 1977 is in a state of rapid change. Global economic growth and expanding population have placed severe strains on the economic and political institutions that were created in the post-World War II years and that contributed so greatly to growth and progress among the industrialized countries. At the same time, the world political environment has changed drastically, and the developing countries are now demanding a greater share in decision making on international economic and political issues as well as more equitable returns for their contributions to the international economy. There is also a growing realization that the situation of the nearly one billion people living in extreme poverty in the developing world may even worsen unless special measures are taken at the international level as well as within these countries themselves to make it possible for the majority of their people to obtain their most basic economic and social needs within a reasonable period of time.

It has also become increasingly clear in the last several years that treating U.S. policy toward the developing countries as a derivative of American interests in some other part of the world is no longer possible; relations with the developing countries are becoming a major concern of American foreign policy—joining relations with our industrial partners, the Soviet Union, and China as one of the major policy concerns of the United States. A more coherent and comprehensive U.S. policy approach toward the developing countries is urgently needed.

1

Increasing Interdependence

The last decade has been marked by the emergence of global political and economic interdependence on a scale hardly imaginable only twenty-five years ago. This interdependence has been manifested in such seemingly unrelated phenomena as continued "stagflation" in the industrialized economies, the depletion of the world's fisheries, the continuing threat of a world food shortage, and the impact of a fourfold increase in the price of oil.

These developments have led many observers in both rich and poor countries to conclude that global problems will not be resolved unless they are addressed by most, if not all, nations working together. Such attempts are already in progress in a number of areas: reform of the world monetary system, negotiation of a new regime for the oceans, organization of a network of both altered and new institutions for increasing the world food supply and stabilizing grain prices, and growing awareness that a cooperative international approach is needed in the energy field. Many Americans now also perceive that the social costs of problems such as population growth, terrorism, and narcotics traffic cannot be handled unless there is cooperation between most nations, rich and poor.

An aspect of increasing interdependence that is still insufficiently recognized in the United States is the reality that the economic growth and progress of the developing countries is in the U.S. interest. At present, 27 per cent of our exports—more than we sell to the members of the European Communities, Eastern Europe, and the Soviet Union combined—now go to the non-OPEC developing countries. These exports have increased from under $6 billion in 1955 to nearly $28 billion in 1974.[1] If the developing countries were to grow at the same rate in the next decade as in the 1960s, and if the U.S. share of developing-country imports also were to at least remain the same as in the past decade, the developing countries could be expected to import an *additional* $27 billion of goods per year from the United States by 1985. That total could mean as many as two million additional jobs in this country's export industries. The developing countries will also continue to grow in importance as producers of raw materials and exporters of consumer goods and thus can contribute significantly to limiting inflation in the United States. Moreover, their economic growth will be necessary if they are to meet debt obligations that will be coming due in the next few years.

Dramatically Altered Development Prospects

In early 1973, the *growth* prospects of most developing countries for the 1970s appeared good. The countries in the Middle East, Latin America, East Asia, and most of Africa were well on the road to exceeding the Second Development Decade target of increasing gross national product by 6 per

---

[1]See Statistical Annex C of this volume, Tables C-7 and C-8, for data on U.S. trade.

cent annually. The notable exceptions were the sparsely populated, drought-ridden countries of the African Sahel and the densely populated countries of South Asia—India, Pakistan, Bangladesh, and Sri Lanka. Even then, however, it was apparent that—despite the unprecedented increases in output—social problems of population growth, unemployment, income maldistribution, and rural stagnation were worsening in most countries other than China and some of the smaller nations of East Asia.

By early 1974, however, even the admittedly limited goal of increasing economic growth rates was jeopardized in a majority of the poorer developing countries—with the striking exception of the OPEC countries—by the jolt of sudden, massive price increases in their essential imports (primarily oil, food, and fertilizers), and by the global economic slowdown, which severely decreased their earnings from exports to the industrialized countries. The development prospects of some of the most populous poor countries, notably those of South Asia, were thus even more gravely endangered for the balance of the decade.[2]

Most developing countries have dealt with these economic shocks better than was expected. They did so, however, by cutting back imports where possible, by using their own financial reserves, and by borrowing extensively from both private banks and government and international agencies. The current account deficit of the non-oil-exporting developing countries was about $37 billion in 1975; their debt grew from $89.2 billion in 1973 to an estimated $138.6 billion in 1975.[3] Although the developing countries have been able to cope with the *worst* financial aspects of these crises—both through their own efforts and by the creative response of a variety of private and public institutions in the developed world—the question now is how much longer they can continue to do so if the industrial countries do not resume growth and if changes are not made in various international economic systems.

Both the price rises and other economic "shocks" of recent years have greatly widened differences among the developing countries in terms of the state of their economies and their development prospects. Among the market-economy developing countries, two distinct groups of countries have emerged—groups with quite different needs in terms of their external economic relationships: the "middle-income" developing countries, consisting mostly of the countries of Latin America, North Africa, the Middle East, parts of the rest of Africa (notably Nigeria), and the countries of East Asia and having a total population of approximately 900 million; and the poorest

---

[2]In the ODC *Agenda* series, these problems received detailed coverage in 1974 and 1975. See James P. Grant, "Energy Shock and the Development Prospect," in James W. Howe and the Staff of the Overseas Development Council, *The U.S. and the Developing World: Agenda for Action, 1974* (New York: Praeger Publishers, Inc., 1974), pp. 31-50; and Helen C. Low and James W. Howe, "Focus on the Fourth World," in James W. Howe and the Staff of the Overseas Development Council, *The U.S. and World Development: Agenda for Action, 1975* (New York: Praeger Publishers, Inc., 1975), pp. 35-54.

[3]Tables E-1, E-2, and E-3 in Annex E provide indication of the current account and debt problems of the developing countries.

countries, concentrated primarily in South Asia, Sahelian Africa, and much of sub-Saharan Africa and having a total population of approximately 1.2 billion.

The middle-income developing countries as a group are among the fastest-growing countries in the world. Over the past decade, they have achieved an overall growth rate for the decade of 6.8 per cent—about 4 per cent in per capita terms. Some of these countries are demonstrably better off than others because of their rich endowment of natural resources. Most conspicuous within this group are the countries which export petroleum, but others, such as Malaysia, which is virtually self-sufficient in oil as well as in tin and rubber, also fall into this category. Another group of middle-income developing countries consists of those countries which have been able to increase their exports of processed and manufactured goods. Countries as diverse as Taiwan, the Ivory Coast, Brazil, and Mexico fall into this category. In many of these countries there is still a great deal of poverty. However, with sufficient national political will, economic recovery in the industrialized world, and supportive reforms in the international economic systems (none of which can be assumed as certainties), these countries should prove to have resources adequate for addressing their poverty problems. Per capita income differences between these middle-income countries and the developed countries appear to be narrowing (at least in relative terms); perhaps even more important is the likelihood that these countries may be able to greatly narrow the "gap" in terms of many of the most basic indicators of economic and social well-being (such as life expectancy, infant mortality, and literacy) during the remaining years of this century.

On the other hand, the more than forty nations that constitute the poorest or "low-income" group have the slowest growth in output of any group of countries in the world. Average per capita incomes in the poorest nations grew at an annual rate of only 1.5 per cent, or $2 per year, during the past decade, in contrast to annual per capita increases of $30 in the middle-income countries and $130 in the high-income countries. The future prospects of these poorest countries are not bright. The World Bank estimates that, over the ten-year period 1975–1985, the per capita income of the 1.2 billion people living in these poorest nations will increase by only 20 per cent (from $150 to $180), even under the most optimistic circumstances. And even if the per capita income in these countries were to grow at the rate of 3 per cent annually until the end of this century—which is unlikely—it would only then begin to approximate that of England and the United States in 1776.[4]

Not only is the gap between the developed countries and the developing countries widening; income disparities between rich and poor people *within* most developing countries are also growing. The ratio of income

---

[4]See Annex A, Table A-7.

received by the top 20 per cent of the income recipients to that received by the bottom 20 per cent is about 6:1 in the United States and the United Kingdom, and 4:1 in Poland; but it is 29:1 in Ecuador, 20:1 in Brazil, and 15:1 in Mexico.[5] In most developing countries, moreover, this ratio is worsening.

The result of all of these trends is that, despite the trebling of world output since the late 1940s, nearly one billion people today subsist in chronic poverty in the developing world. The economic and social indicators included in the Statistical Annexes of this volume show all too clearly the condition of this large proportion of the planet's population. Stark as these numbers are in themselves, they do not fully convey that in human terms they mean a vicious circle of widespread illiteracy, unemployment or underemployment, malnutrition, hunger, ill health, and short life expectancy.[6] A person born in the United States can expect to live nearly twice as long as a child born in Upper Volta; a child born in Mali is ten times as likely to die in its first year of life as a child born in the United States.

Why have the development strategies—both national and international—of the past twenty-five years failed to reach this vast portion of the world's population? In general, the development policies of the post-World War II period were based on the principle that a high rate of investment would produce rapid growth in the gross national product (GNP). But the rapid growth of productive capacity and the equitable distribution of its benefits were seen by most economists as *contradictory* objectives. It was assumed that the benefits of accelerated growth, would ultimately (but not immediately) "trickle down" to the entire population in the form of growing per capita income, which in turn would improve the living standards of the poor.

In the 1960s, many developing countries did indeed achieve high rates of growth—rates higher than those in the industrial countries. But the "trickle-down" strategy of expecting increased growth to gradually take care of the well-being of the poor has shown itself to be both too slow and inadequate in political and ethical as well as economic terms. In many other developing countries, moreover, including several of the most populous, GNP has risen so slowly that there have been few benefits to "trickle down" to the majority of the people. And even where growth has increased, the benefits have flowed largely to a minority of the population.

New Development Strategies

This experience of recent years has led to an intensive rethinking of development theories and strategies among economists and development

---

[5]See Annex A, Table A-11.

[6]Annex A Tables (pp. 155-79) provide data on economic and social dimensions of poverty within and between countries.

practitioners in both developed and developing countries. A new under-standing is now emerging concerning development strategies that could be effective in alleviating poverty in the developing countries in a relatively short time. Recent academic studies and the experience of several countries indicate that it is possible to achieve greater equity and growth *simultane-ously*. A direct improvement in the condition of the very poorest groups constitutes an investment in human capital which, along with labor-intensive development policies, can itself contribute to the growth process. The application of strategies focused along these lines would, however, require most poor countries to allocate their resources differently in the future and in ways much more appropriate to countries which lack capital but not labor.

These concepts were much debated at the World Employment Confer-ence held in Geneva in late spring 1976 under the auspices of the Interna-tional Labour Organisation (ILO). The basic document prepared for this Conference by the ILO secretariat is the most comprehensive elaboration prepared to date of the new "basic needs" strategy against global poverty,[7] The policy conclusions of the World Employment Conference included a call for an international "basic needs strategy" that would assign first priority to meeting certain minimum human requirements for jobs, food, shelter, and clothing, as well as to providing access to basic health, education, and other services to all people. The program of action adopted by the Conference—which won the endorsement of both developing- and developed-country participants—is an important first step in the acceptance of these new development strategies.

The new equity-oriented approach to development does, however, face many problems whose resolution requires far more attention in 1977 and the years ahead. First among these is the fact that the success potential of the new strategies depends on many factors, including the capacity of the poor societies to make more effective use of their indigenous organizations and traditional values. This finding underlines the need for a thorough re-examination by the poorer countries themselves of their development concepts and by donor countries of the form and content of their develop-ment assistance policies.

The second and closely related problem confronting the new develop-ment approach relates to the question of whether the major objectives of an equity-focused strategy—the wide dispersion of improvements in the basic quality of life, such as low death and infant mortality rates and high life expectancy and literacy rates—*can be achieved at relatively low levels of per capita gross national product*. The experiences of a few widely different societies (notably Sri Lanka, South Korea, Taiwan, China, and the Indian

---

[7]ILO International Labour Office, *Employment, Growth and Basic Needs: A One-World Problem*. Published for the Overseas Development Council in cooperation with the International Labour Office (New York: Praeger Publishers, Inc., 1977).

state of Kerala) all now suggest that this is possible even at per capita income levels that are still extremely low by the standards of the more developed countries.

Third, the implementation of equity-oriented strategies clearly encounters complex political problems. The adoption of any of the potential forms of these strategies will involve difficult measures such as land reform and an emphasis on rural development that will be opposed by various powerful groups within the developing countries. Therefore the implementation of these strategies will have substantial political costs for important segments of the elites within the developing countries. And in most cases, far-sighted, comprehensive "basic needs" policies are unlikely to be launched in the poorer countries without either the catalyst of great social upheavals—with all of their attendant social costs (including the possibility of widespread violence)—or, alternatively, the inducement of increased political, moral, and financial support from outside.

A fourth problem of particular importance in designing and implementing "basic needs" strategies is the present relatively disadvantaged position of women—a problem almost totally ignored by planners in both developed and developing countries until it began to receive attention during International Women's Year in 1975. Women in many developing countries play a major role in food production and in a wide variety of other economic activities that are crucial to the actual delivery of the most essential requirements of daily living to all individuals in their societies. Evidence is increasing that past development strategies not only have often failed to enhance the quality of women's contributions but have actually hampered women in the performance of both traditional and new roles—to the detriment of all groups, not women alone. Awareness of the present and potential roles of women in development must be an important factor in the design and implementation of any successful "basic needs" strategy.

Finally, the problem of implementing the new development strategies is increased by the fact that there is no accepted way to measure whether or not the *minimum human needs* of the majority of people within the world's poorest countries are being met. The conventional measure of economic progress—per capita gross national product—does not purport to measure the extent to which basic *human* needs are being met. What is needed for this purpose is an index that is a composite of other indicators of well-being, such as nutrition, health, life expectancy, and greater access to opportunity. A usable index of this type has been developed; it is both described and shown for all countries in the Statistical Annexes of this volume.[8] This "physical quality of life" index (PQLI) may provide a useful measure of a country's general progress toward meeting the basic human requirements of the majority of its population.

---

[8]See pages 147-54 for a description of this indicator and Table A-3 for the "PQLI" of all countries.

A New Political Environment

Clearly the world in which U.S. foreign policy must be developed in 1977 is very different from that in which the United States found itself at the end of World War II. The role of the United States remains crucial in international affairs—in economics and politics alike—but the present period is one in which no one nation is dominant. Even while we are experiencing increasing global interdependence, recognizing inadequacies in the operation of existing international economic systems, and witnessing dramatic shifts in the development prospects of specific groups of developing countries, the international political environment in which changes must be negotiated is being transformed.

The current political situation is in fact only a stage in the process of continuous adjustment in the international system that has been going on for most of this century. The disappearance of colonial empires, the emergence of new nations, and the evolution of a new relationship between the Soviet Union and the industrialized countries are all part of a process of bringing new states into the international system and adjusting relationships among already participating states.

One major aspect of this situation is that the developing countries are currently pressing for major changes in the economic and political structures that have governed international relations since 1945. Their demands for greater participation and decision-making power have many precedents, both international and domestic, in the actions of countries and groups that considered themselves disadvantaged in the past. It is analogous, for instance, to Japan's drive prior to World War I, and then in the interwar period, for equal standing in the international system. It also bears some similarity to the emergence of organized labor in this country in the late 1920s and 1930s. In each of these cases, it became apparent, after much resistance by those in power and after prolonged struggle and strife, that accommodating the reasonable demands of those on the outside for effective participation within the system paid both political and economic benefits to all concerned.

Inherent in the present drive of the developing countries for increased status and influence is another major characteristic of the world of 1977: the continuing post-colonial upsurge of nationalism and the consequent emphasis on national sovereignty. At a time when many are beginning to realize that the nations of the world are becoming increasingly interdependent, this strong insistence on national sovereignty is a complicating factor in developing new cooperative mechanisms to deal with the world's pressing economic and social problems.

This emphasis on nationalism and sovereignty both reinforces and is reinforced by growing developing-country interest in the principles of *national*—as well as *collective* "self-reliance"—that is, the measures that developing countries themselves, individually and collectively, can take in support of their national or collective development. Their interest in self-reliance stems from the desire to fashion economic policies according to what they see as their own needs, problems, and historical experience. It is also partly an expression of frustration with the lack of development results derived from two decades of applying conventional development strategies patterned after those conceived and followed in the industrialized world.

Neither "self-reliance" nor "collective self-reliance" are new concepts; indeed, collective self-reliance was implicit in the shaping of the European Communities and the Atlantic Community. There also have been many attempts at economic cooperation among *developing* countries, usually with relatively little success, partly because one vestige of the colonial era is the continuing close economic linkage of many of these countries with specific developed countries, and partly because a considerable number of developing countries perceive their best prospects for development to lie in greater integration into the world's trading and monetary systems. Both developing and developed countries might benefit from some varieties of developing-country "self-reliance"—for example, from expanding trade among developing countries and, equally important, from the lessening of the "psychology of dependence" through increased interdependence among developing countries. Collective "self-reliance" approaches pose choices for *both* developed and developing countries. The latter will have to decide the degree and the manner of their integration into the world's various economic systems, and the former must decide whether or not to encourage increasing autonomy on the part of the developing world.

A further important aspect of the present world political situation is the fact that pressures in the *developed* countries for governmental action to ensure full employment and to address the social welfare needs of all citizens have grown steadily since the late 1940s. These pressures have led to a variety of domestic social welfare programs that in many cases were overdue; at the same time, however, they have limited the negotiating freedom of governments on foreign policy issues which touch the welfare of their own citizens. Thus trade negotiations, for example, have become increasingly difficult as organized labor, fearing the loss of U.S. jobs, has opposed tariff-cutting measures that would permit the increased import of low-cost consumer goods—including imports from developing countries.

Finally, the issues of new political and economic relationships between the rich and poor countries intersect with the traditional concerns of foreign policy in ways that are still only dimly perceived. For instance, our policies toward the developing world will have to be meshed with our policies toward our industrial partners in the Organisation for Economic Co-operation and Development (OECD). The European countries and Japan, for example, all depend to a far greater degree than the United States on the developing countries for markets and for raw materials.[9] But they are split in their

---

[9]See Annex B, Table B-12, for U.S., European Communities, and Japanese dependence on imports of a selected list of raw materials.

reactions to the demands for a "New International Economic Order." Some of these nations—for example the Netherlands and the Scandinavian countries—are willing to accommodate many developing-country demands for change and have also stepped up their aid to the poor countries. Others—particularly Germany, but also Japan—generally oppose reshaping the international economic system; their aid as a percentage of GNP is declining. Coordination and advance consultation among the industrial countries has been notably weak in the past few years, with the result that cohesion among the OECD countries often has been lacking at various international meetings.

U.S. policy on North-South relations clearly will have to take account of the traditional American goals of minimizing international conflict and maintaining international stability. In recent years, many of the areas of potential "superpower" confrontation have been in the Third World. The points of tension have not been Berlin or Eastern Europe, but areas of turmoil in Southeast Asia, the Middle East, and Southern Africa. Considerable political and social turbulence can be expected in many developing countries in the years ahead. Contrary to the conventional wisdom of the 1950s and early 1960s, it now is generally accepted that development progress in and of itself will not bring peace and stability. Indeed, it may even have the opposite effect in the short run as the process of development itself creates stresses and strains within heretofore largely traditional societies. Yet in the *long run*, the *lack* of development progress is likely to give rise to even greater conflicts within these societies which may also intensify tensions between the superpowers. The prospects of conflicts within the developing world are further complicated by the likelihood that many developing countries will be turning to nuclear power as a source of energy, with all of the attendant risks of proliferation of nuclear weapons. An additional issue of critical importance to the goal of minimizing conflicts is the future of U.S. programs that transfer arms and military equipment (through either aid or sales) to the developing countries. Arms orders from these countries have grown from under $1 billion in 1970 to nearly $8 billion in 1974 and $6.2 billion in 1975. These transactions have been carried out almost completely independently of any overall assessment of real American political and security interests in the developing countries.

U.S. bilateral relations with some countries also have had an impact on U.S. relations with developing countries generally. For instance, the close U.S. ties with Israel have been used by the OPEC and other Arab nations in their relations with African, Asian, and Latin American countries. Similarly, U.S. policy on the issue of majority rule in Southern Africa has been a factor in the official stance of many African countries on U.S. initiatives in the economic field; and the current state of the negotiations between the United States and Panama over a new status for the Panama Canal is perceived by many Latin Americans as a bellwether of future North American relationships with the Southern Hemisphere.

The Past Four Years of Negotiations

The involvement of the United States in a wide-ranging series of international negotiations has steadily increased to a point where the number and complexity of the discussions now going on, or about to commence, between the rich nations of the North and the poor nations of the South may be unprecedented.

In brief, what the developing countries are demanding is a "New International Economic Order" that includes: a) nondiscriminatory and hopefully preferential treatment for their manufactured goods in the markets of the industrialized world; b) more stable and higher prices for their commodities; c) renegotiation of their external public debt, which has grown by more than 50 per cent in the last two years; d) curbs on the activities of multinational corporations and greater access (on more favorable terms) to the technology of the industrialized countries; e) a growing share in producing the world's industrial goods; f) a greater voice in the management of the world's monetary system and a greater share of any new reserves created in the future; and g) a new, less demeaning aid relationship that increasingly provides for greater financial resource transfers on a more automatic basis.

The central complaint of these countries is that they are subject to the rules of international economic institutions and systems that they feel have long discriminated against them, but about which they in the past never have had any significant say. The current demands of the developing countries did not emerge *de novo* in late 1973 and 1974 following the Arab-Israeli War and the subsequent oil embargo and the dramatic price increase of petroleum; they were the predictable outcome of more than a decade of largely fruitless efforts to evoke a significant response from the developed countries on issues crucial to developing countries. Indeed, they have evolved over the past two decades at a series of international meetings and discussions mainly within the group of Non-Aligned Countries and UNCTAD.[10] What the events of 1973–74 did generate, however, was a new belief on the part of the developing countries that they finally had at their disposal new bargaining power (because of their unity and alliance with the OPEC countries) and that placing all their demands in one package—a "New International Economic Order"—could also add to their bargaining strength. The continuing unity of the OPEC and other developing countries, a unity that has been maintained despite the very heavy adverse effects of higher oil prices on many developing countries, has been one of the generally unforeseen developments of the past two years. It is unlikely for a variety of reasons that any other group of raw-material producing states will be able to effectively emulate the OPEC countries in so drastically increasing prices or in using an embargo for political purposes. Nevertheless, the political and psychological

---

[10]See Chapter II, pp. 28-29.

impact of the events of the past several years will remain very great, and the developing countries recognize that their strength vis-à-vis the industrialized world lies in their unity and in their alliance with OPEC.

Initially, the United States opposed most of the demands of the developing countries, hoping that the increasingly serious economic difficulties of the oil-importing developing countries would lead them to pressure the OPEC countries to reduce oil prices. This policy held until the spring of 1975, when some officials within the U.S. government concluded that the OPEC and other developing countries could not be split easily and that a number of pressing problems could be addressed and solved only on the basis of greatly broadened participation. A major speech by former Secretary of State Kissinger at the Seventh Special Session of the U.N. General Assembly in September 1975 appeared to signal a new willingness within the U.S. government to begin to negotiate on a variety of North-South issues. This apparent shift in U.S. policy engendered generally positive and moderate responses on the part of the developing countries and hence a more promising atmosphere for negotiations.

The seeming lack of any dramatic progress since 1975 has led some to conclude that the opportunity to create a new relationship between the developed and developing countries has been missed. Yet in the past year the United States has been involved in negotiations at the Conference on International Economic Cooperation (CIEC), the fourth session of UNCTAD, the Law of the Sea Conference, the World Food Council, ILO's World Employment Conference, and within the International Monetary Fund and the World Bank. In addition, North-South relations were discussed within the OECD and in the preliminary sessions of the multilateral trade negotiations. Indeed, these issues assumed such importance that former Secretary of State Kissinger participated personally in both UNCTAD IV and the Law of the Sea Conference. Never before had a U.S. Secretary of State committed his intensive personal efforts to negotiations with the developing countries on issues previously perceived to be primarily in the "economic" domain.

However, the pace of these negotiations has been slow—often reflecting the lack of a coherent Northern approach to the issues and generally proceeding in fits and starts, particularly at UNCTAD and CIEC. At the fourth session of UNCTAD, for example, the developing countries arrived with a carefully prepared set of proposals and a coordinated negotiating position on several key issues: developing-country debt, raw-material prices, an integrated commodity scheme, and the transfer of technology. The industrialized countries, particularly the United States, did not come prepared or willing to talk in any detail about the debt problem or to enter into serious discussion of commodity prices. Instead, the United States wanted to discuss the issue of access to raw materials; it proposed an International Resources Bank to stimulate investment in and mobilize private capital for raw-material production in the developing countries. In addition, the United States made a range of other proposals, in some cases reiterating or extending those made the previous fall at the United Nations. In the course of the four-week meeting, the developing countries received only lukewarm support at best from the rich for their demands on debt and technology transfer; they did, however, attain somewhat reluctant acquiescence to the holding of a conference in March 1977 to discuss commodity issues. The U.S. proposal for an International Resources Bank was turned down by a narrow margin, mainly because its precise objectives and potential were not sufficiently clear and many delegations were suspicious of American intentions. In effect, neither side was willing to negotiate on the issues considered crucial by the other.

A similar pattern marked the developed-country approach to the Conference on International Economic Cooperation in Paris (CIEC). The four separate CIEC commissions—on energy, raw materials, development, and financing—began meeting in December 1975, but so little progress had been made by the time they recessed in July 1976 that the entire process threatened to break down. The stalemate arose because the industrialized countries, led by the United States, were seriously interested in discussing energy problems only; the developing countries and their OPEC allies, for their part, would not consider energy issues unless the industrialized countries also were forthcoming on their debt and commodity-price problems. A face-saving compromise was worked out to enable the Conference to reopen discussions in September, but when the stalemate continued throughout the fall of 1976, both sides agreed at year-end to postpone the Conference's final meeting, scheduled for December, to spring 1977. The postponement was due in large part a) to the continued reluctance of the United States to negotiate seriously on the proposals of the developing countries, and b) to the developing countries' desire to test whether a new U.S. Administration would be more forthcoming. The U.S. reluctance apparently was based on the belief of many in the Executive Branch that no package of proposals that might conceivably be agreed upon by the industrialized countries would provide a sufficient inducement to OPEC to refrain from a substantial increase in the price of oil. In addition, many felt that compromise proposals would be dangerous because they would strengthen the linkage between OPEC and the oil-importing developing countries in CIEC—a linkage that would neither moderate decisions on oil-price increases nor weaken the ties between OPEC members and other developing countries.

Other discussions held during 1976 between developed and developing countries also had mixed results. The Law of the Sea Conference failed to reach agreement on the critical issue of rules to govern exploitation of the mineral resources of the deep ocean. On monetary reform, in contrast, the developed and developing countries reached compromises on a series of useful reforms at the January meeting of the Interim Committee of the International Monetary Fund. The Committee agreed to increase the resources available to developing countries experiencing balance-of-payments difficulties and to establish a new Trust Fund that would provide the developing countries with a portion of the funds raised by selling some of the IMF's gold holdings. On another front, a $1 billion International Fund for Agricultural Development (IFAD)—funded jointly by the industrialized and OPEC countries—was established to support increased food production in the developing countries; IFAD is the first major instance of an effort jointly financed by the OECD and OPEC countries.

During 1976, the United States continued to grope for a new policy toward the developing countries. Some individuals in the Ford Administration concluded that relationships between the developed and the developing countries must be placed on a new basis. Too often, however, the recognition was present only at the rhetorical level. As a result of bureaucratic differences among competing agencies, promising proposals often were unenthusiastically followed up, and, as a consequence, the few U.S. initiatives that were taken generally came too late and without adequate consultation with even our closest industrial partners. Although the negotiations did not break down, by the end of 1976, when the inauguration of a new Administration in the United States was also generally awaited, a stalemate had been reached in many areas of negotiation.

What Have We Learned?

What lessons can the United States draw from its experience with North-South negotiations during the past year? *First*, there is a growing conviction that there no longer is a choice about whether or not to negotiate with the developing countries on a myriad of issues. From their different points of view, both developed and developing countries now seem to recognize that the international economic and political arrangements developed after 1945 no longer are adequate in many respects; consequently they have begun tentative negotiations that could lead to far-reaching changes.

Second, despite the fact that, in today's world, neither the United States nor any other nation is as dominant as the United States was in the post-World War II period, the role of the United States remains highly important to the outcome of these negotiations. When, for example, the United States seeks compromise with the developing countries, as it has done (albeit reluctantly) at various forums, compromise is possible. When it opposes any comprehensive action, as it has done on the debt issue, for instance, none is possible. But when the United States provides leadership, as it did at the World Food Conference in Rome in 1974, considerable progress may result.

Third, the pace and progress of the negotiations is likely to be much slower than some initially expected. A "New International Economic Order" will not be created overnight to be ratified by some glorious international gathering reminiscent of the Congress of Vienna. Rather, it will be hammered out in a multiplicity of forums encompassing many different countries

14

negotiating on what may often seem to be unrelated issues. This fact alone will make the management and monitoring of the negotiations very difficult both for governments and for nongovernmental observers. Yet these difficulties, though considerable, should not lead to the conclusion that negotiations should be avoided; the discussions may well be important simply in that they avoid confrontation and eventually may allow gradual agreement to emerge.

Fourth, the cohesion of the developing nations has remained surprisingly strong, given that *specific* developing country interests often diverge. It would be unwise, therefore, to discount the possibility that the developing countries will stay united. It is in any case impossible to estimate with any assurance how long this cohesion can be maintained. However zealously the developing countries guard it, their unity clearly is vulnerable in at least two respects. First, if confrontation between developing and developed countries (such as the clash at the 1974 Sixth Special Session of the U.N. General Assembly) is resumed, then individual countries may diverge on tactics. On the other hand, if serious negotiations do begin between the developed and developing countries, the differing economic interests of the various developing countries will quickly become apparent. Differences already are emerging among the developing countries on the issue of a debt moratorium (which is opposed by some better-off countries because it would affect their ability to borrow in the future) and on the issue of whether to emphasize demands for better prices for their commodity exports more than demands for significantly increased market access for their manufactured exports. Similar splits have been evident during the law of the sea negotiations, where the interests of the coastal states have differed sharply from those of countries which are landlocked or otherwise geographically "disadvantaged." In fact, some observers maintain that the pace of negotiations in 1976 slowed down primarily because of differences among the developing countries stemming from their diverging interests. To some degree, the unity of the developing countries has been enhanced by the continuing unwillingness on the part of the developed countries to produce comprehensive responses. If that changes, "Southern" cohesion may be more difficult to maintain.

Fifth, the evolution of the developing-country positions on economic issues has been marked by considerable moderation. Shrill rhetoric often has continued, but the actual negotiating positions of the developing countries have been more measured. The concept of "indexing"—linking the prices of raw materials to the prices of manufactured goods—which is such anathema to the industrialized countries, has been honored by the developing countries mainly in rhetoric. And the developing countries' threat to block international monetary reform unless it included the creation of new monetary reserves linked to development needs was dropped when both developed and developing countries compromised on a package of reform measures. Despite the seemingly far-reaching nature of their proposals, the developing

15

countries by and large have been demanding not that the existing world economic systems be radically transformed but rather that they be reformed to permit their greater participation and sharing of the benefits of growth.

The Choices Ahead

The United States will be faced with a number of pressing policy choices in the months ahead as it moves to set relations with the developing countries on a new basis and hopefully begins to address in a more comprehensive fashion the pressing problems of the world's poorest people. The range of unresolved questions that the new Administration will need to consider in formulating a U.S. policy on North-South issues is suggested in the following summary.

What Overall Strategy Should Be Followed by the United States?

A more comprehensive and effective mix of U.S. policies is required if a steady worsening of North-South relations is to be avoided and if the international economic and political orders are to be reshaped to better meet the urgent needs of both developed and developing countries. Should the new Administration essentially continue present policies, making only incremental changes? Should it take only the minimum steps necessary to meet the most compelling demands of the world's "South" on the grounds that domestic economic and political forces will not allow more?

Or should the United States seek a new policy of accelerated and far-reaching reform which carefully considers each of the issues in contention between the countries of the North and those of the South and, where possible, seeks those solutions, compromises, and alternatives that can benefit both sides either directly or indirectly—by providing substantial gains for *world* development?

And to what extent should the United States, together with both the other developed countries and the developing countries seek to *jointly* devise and carry out policies that would make it possible for the world's poorest people (the majority of whom live in the world's poorest countries) to acquire within the foreseeable future at least the minimum physical requirements for basic human life and dignity?

How Far-Reaching Should Specific Policy Choices Be?

The choices to be made on specific issues obviously will depend in considerable part on the strategy chosen for overall American policy on world development and North-South relations. In the field of *energy*, for instance, a choice will have to be made between a global policy which seeks to encompass the energy needs of the developing countries and which comes to grips with the manifold problems of relying on oil and nuclear power to meet the energy needs of the world, or a fragmented policy which treats energy as an issue to be decided between the industrialized and OPEC countries but does not include consideration of the needs of the developing countries.

16

Similarly, in the area of *food security*, a choice will have to be made between full implementation of the agreements reached at the 1974 Rome World Food Conference (including the early establishment of a world food reserve system), or continued reliance on a partial approach to these urgent issues until they no longer can be ignored.

In each of the areas being discussed in the various international forums—trade, commodities, monetary reform, debt, technology transfer, food, energy, and a regime for the oceans—similar choices between incremental approaches and more far-reaching solutions will have to be made. The temptation will be to choose those policies which respond to a problem at the lowest possible immediate economic and political costs. Yet following this path may mean missing the opportunity to resolve many problems in a manner more congruent with the needs of the future than of the past. In the field of trade, for instance, the tendency will be to reduce tariff barriers only to those products that do not affect many U.S. jobs—particularly at a time when large numbers of Americans already are unemployed. Yet the potential *gains* from trade liberalization—including *overall* increases in employment, higher wages, and easing of inflationary pressures for both the United States and the developing countries—are so great that the short-run costs make a renewed commitment to lowering tariff barriers to the maximum degree possible both far-sighted and realistic.

What "Packages" of Bargains Can Be Assembled?

In the next few years, the developed and the developing countries will be involved both in negotiating changes in a variety of global systems and hopefully also in a concerted address of absolute poverty within the world's poorest countries along the lines suggested in this *Agenda*. But the short- and long-run gains, both tangible and intangible, from specific policy changes will vary greatly depending on the particular issue and on the countries most involved.

The development of "packages" of agreements cutting across issues may make compromise on individual issues more attractive for both rich and poor countries. For example, the developing countries need greater access to the markets of the industrialized world; the developed countries need greater assurance of access to adequate amounts of raw materials. The linkage of these two concerns might make a potential package of agreements more politically acceptable for a considerably greater number of countries than if each of these issues were considered separately.

What Form of Cooperation for Addressing
the Basic Human Needs Problem?

Even while a consensus is beginning to take shape on the need to focus development policies on meeting the minimum basic human needs of the world's poorest billion people, a host of new questions is emerging on how such an approach should be implemented. What specific development strategies would best enable the developing countries to meet the needs of the majority of their population? To what extent should external aid be concentrated on meeting basic human needs and shifted away from the prevailing pattern of supporting economic development in general? How much can or should basic human needs strategies be supported by outsiders —whether other countries or international organizations? To what extent does the whole approach of a concerted address of minimum human needs involve "intervention" from the outside? (This issue arises at a time when the developing countries are more protective than ever of their sovereign prerogatives.)

If a minimum human needs approach to development cooperation were accepted, a host of operational questions still would need to be resolved. How much aid would be necessary either to achieve certain economic goals (such as a specific growth rate in gross national product) or social goals (such as targeted reductions in illiteracy, infant mortality, birth rates, or malnutrition)? What should be the "fair shares" of the donor countries? Should the United States adhere to some existing standard (such as the objective of the International Strategy for the U.N. Second Development Decade that each "donor" nation should provide 0.7 per cent of GNP in the form of development assistance), or should the United States continue to eschew any formula for participation?

Through what channels and to what countries should aid be provided? The argument between the proponents of bilateral aid and multilateral aid has a long history, and no conclusion as to a desirable balance between the two forms has been reached. What should be the relative roles of private and governmental channels of development assistance? And should concessional aid concentrate primarily on the poorest countries while reforms of international economic systems are relied upon to provide the middle-income countries with the resources necessary to address their poverty problems? Or should aid be provided to any country and program which is seriously committed to ensuring that the benefits of its developmental effort reach the poorest people? To what extent should such a strategy include special measures to assist women, whose contributions and needs often have been neglected by past strategies? Finally, how can a basic human needs approach contribute to an earlier stabilization of the world population? These are not easy questions to resolve, but they must be addressed if the effectiveness of development assistance is to be improved in the years ahead.

What Kinds of Equity?

Among the most crucial of all the questions to be resolved concerns the relationship between the issues of a) equity between states, and b) equity among people *within* states. The question of equity between states is at the base of the demands of the developing countries for changes in existing international economic and political systems. But the question of equity *within* states will grow increasingly important as it becomes apparent that certain states—or important groups within states—may have to pay costs, at least in the short run, to increase equity between states. Even short-run political costs to the developed countries of changes in political and economic systems may become impossibly high if it is not apparent to the public in these countries that major efforts are being made by the developing countries to ensure that the benefits of development reach their poor majorities.

The evidence is increasingly clear that changes in the external economic order as well as in the internal structures of the developing countries themselves will be necessary if the problems of the world's poorest people are to be alleviated in the foreseeable future. But what commitments will the developed and the developing countries be prepared to assume to achieve this end? Are the developing countries willing to undertake difficult domestic reforms? And can the developed countries be relied upon to offer enough help from the outside to permit developing-country leaders to make the far-reaching, politically difficult changes required to provide a greater degree of equity within their own societies? Some will conclude that the past record indicates that no major changes are likely; others will argue that the growing costs of inaction may be so great as to impel changes, and that the present circumstances provide an opportunity for both rich and poor countries alike.

How Best Advance Human Rights?

The United States may well find that it must give more comprehensive attention to the human rights issue in the near future. This issue area poses many difficult questions. To what extent should the United States attempt to protect human rights in other countries? What are the most appropriate ways to do so? What is the relationship between *human political rights* and *human economic rights*? The industrial democracies tend to give higher priority to the former, and the developing countries tend to give higher priority to the latter. Can a common ground be found?

How Best Organize for Global Cooperation?

How should the United States organize itself to effectively handle both the international and domestic aspects of global issues? At the international level, there will be a need to determine which existing or new forums that include both the developed and developing countries can best undertake the multiplicity of negotiations and discussions now needed. Many observers had hoped that the Conference on International Economic Cooperation would provide a central forum for these purposes. Yet for a variety of reasons, including the lack of results to date, there is widespread disillusionment with the CIEC. There is likewise considerable dissatisfaction with the various organizations of the United Nations system on the grounds that most of these bodies, as now constituted, are too large and unwieldy for negotiating purposes.

Another major question is the extent to which the Soviet Union and China need to be brought into these discussions. The Soviet Union, the Eastern European countries, and China have remained on the sidelines in most of the international economic discussions that have taken place over the past several years. Soviet and East European aid to the developing countries also has diminished during the same period. Is the involvement of these countries in North-South negotiations essential only on global problems which their actions affect greatly (e.g., the world food problem and nuclear proliferation in the case of the Soviet Union), or on all issues?

The United States also must decide how to organize the federal bureaucracy to deal more effectively with all of these (and other) issues. Currently aspects of these issues are handled by many departments, with the result that decisions on both North-South and "global agenda" issues are difficult to reach and perhaps even more difficult to carry out.

These unresolved questions, which will be the central issues of American foreign policy concerning the developing countries in 1977 and the remainder of the decade, are the focus of *Agenda 1977*. Many of them are analyzed in Chapter II, which outlines the broad policy options from among which the new Administration needs to select its own preferred approach to North-South issues. These questions are also addressed in specific terms in the final chapter of this volume, "Recommendations for U.S. Policy: Agenda 1977."

Major U.S. Options on North-South Relations: A Letter to President Carter

Roger D. Hansen

Since the authors of all the memoranda you have received, Mr. President, are no doubt personally convinced that the issues they raise are of fundamental importance to an appropriate and desirable evolution of U.S. policy, that argument alone might not be sufficient to merit your consideration of this letter in the first months of your incumbency. Three closely related and compelling reasons *other* than personal conviction guide the timing of this submission.

The *first* is that your Administration will be called upon to make some specific decisions concerning relations between the industrial countries of the Northern Hemisphere and the developing countries in the South long before you have the time to analyze fully the complex bundle of issues which constitutes the entirety of the interactions between the United States and its industrialized-country allies on the one hand and the developing countries (OPEC members included) on the other. For example, you will probably be forced very quickly to make a host of policy decisions relating to a spring meeting of the Conference on International Economic Cooperation (CIEC). Similar decisions will have to be made shortly concerning U.S. policies regarding a potentially lengthy list of commodity agreements and a "common fund" to finance international commodity schemes. You will have to examine present policies related to U.S. arms sales to developing countries. And you will quickly want to explore with our allies the issue of nuclear proliferation, both in general and specifically with regard to the potential spread to the developing countries.

Furthermore, you may well be faced with some problems relating to North-South issues the timing of which you cannot control: initiatives in

Congress to cut off economic aid and/or arms sales to certain developing countries because of what it sees as human rights violations by their governments; emerging differences between the United States and its OECD allies on responses to developing-country demands for international economic reforms (in CIEC, UNCTAD, and other forums); or unilateral developing-country actions (e.g., major oil price rises, disputes over new nationalizations of U.S. foreign direct investment, default on foreign debt, or the voiding of agreements providing for U.S. military installations within particular developing countries). For all these reasons, North-South relations simply cannot await a lengthy and leisurely review.

The *second* compelling reason for laying these thoughts before you early in your Administration, Mr. President, involves my concern that, while all the issues I want to bring to your attention will be presented to you *seriatim* by your own White House staff and Cabinet members, they may be presented in such a way that what seem like very logical policy options in a case-by-case or issue-by-issue approach may well prove to be—at a point too late to reverse their aggregate impact—mutually inconsistent, neutral if not negative in their overall impact on U.S. relations with the developing countries, and severely lacking in guiding principles against which to judge U.S. policy formulation and implementation in the "North-South" arena.

The *third* reason that I submit this letter now rather than later is one that you and many members of your Administration may find far less compelling than I do. Such potential disagreements can result from both practical and value considerations. The proposals eventually set forth toward the end of this letter will seem rather sweeping. They are that, I suppose—even if viewed as part of a process which may take a full eight years to launch in its entirety. Therefore the approach must be viewed as a *priority* item by you and the members of your Administration if it is to have any chance of success. And herein lies the potential for honest differences on two points: 1) differences over the *feasibility* of various approaches to the easing of North-South tensions and to the optimizing of Southern opportunities for economic growth and meaningful political and cultural participation in the present international system; and 2) differences over *value preferences*.

It is obvious that for one or both reasons your Administration might decide not to grant to North-South issues the degree of priority which I believe would be required to make substantial progress, however that progress is to be measured. Some international and domestic issues might seem more important to you, both normatively and prudentially. Still others might seem to be of equal or lesser intrinsic importance, but their resolution might seem much more feasible. In either case, the result would undoubtedly be that your Administration would devote less time, energy, resources, and political capital to the growing number of political, economic, and security issues generally encompassed under the heading of "North-South" relations.

Fully recognizing the possibility—indeed, the rather high probability —that my third reason for raising these issues will not be widely accepted within your Administration, I will state it as concisely as possible at this point and hold further elaboration for a later section of this letter. As a matter of sheer prudential statesmanship, I believe you should expect that almost all of your foreign policy initiatives will be significantly affected by the North-South issue. And I further suspect that an altered U.S. foreign policy vis-à-vis the developing world, shaped to the greatest extent possible in collaboration with other members of the OECD and with the developing countries themselves, can significantly increase the prospects for concrete progress in most *other* areas of U.S. foreign policy initiatives.

Moreover, at the level of values and norms central to our Western heritage, it is hard to imagine a set of issues more deserving of priority attention than those presently touched, directly or indirectly, by the North-South conflict. Starvation? Malnutrition leading to permanent debilitation? Infant mortality? The right to increasing opportunity to improve life chances for self and family? Human rights? Civil liberties? Concrete progress in these areas can, of course, be made domestically by individual states. And the adoption of inappropriate policies at the international level might actually exacerbate some of these problems while making marginal if any progress with others. But if statesmanship, Northern and Southern, were to produce 1) a *mutual* recognition of the moral imperative which such problems together represent; 2) a *shared* attempt to redefine the very empirical content of that moral imperative (e.g., the delicate balance between the often conflicting concepts of "basic human needs," "human rights," and "civil liberties"); and 3) the beginnings of a *jointly constructed* attack on these problems, then the achievements at the international level clearly could surpass individual national efforts in the aggregate.

Public opinion polls, recent congressional actions, and your own campaign statements, Mr. President, provide clear signs that there is a marked desire within this country to infuse American foreign policy with a greater sense of "justice" and "moral purpose." We all know how infinitely complex that infusion actually becomes in practice. Should we continue to sell billions of dollars in sophisticated arms to developing countries? If not, why not? Don't we need to "stabilize" regional balances of power? Should we continue to supply military and economic forms of foreign aid to countries which consistently violate human rights and civil liberties as we define them? If not, why not? Don't the regimes receiving such aid often help us to support a "stable structure of peace," and don't they often promote policies of rapid economic growth?

The point is accepted; it would be nice to have a "moral" foreign policy, but the past and present workings of the international system often turn "morality" into an unaffordable luxury if not, as in the case of Vietnam, a grotesque mockery of original intent.

The remainder of this letter will explore the major options concerning U.S. policies toward the developing countries in a manner which gives more than adequate consideration to all of the harsh realities which international politics inevitably and inextricably imposes upon the making of foreign policy. To offer less would not only waste time; it would inevitably suggest that the policies eventually prescribed in this letter could not withstand the harsh scrutiny they must endure before they can invoke any support from your Administration.

In summary, Mr. President, I submit this letter early in your Administration for these crucial reasons:

(1) Already scheduled resumptions of ongoing negotiations in several forums will require your action on the issues addressed in them shortly after you have taken office.

(2) The very nature of the negotiating calendar and the normal functioning of the federal bureaucracy produce constraints from which no Administration is exempt. The danger, of course, is that of *partial* analyses and step-by-step responses to this set of issues which, however adequate for each venue and each functional aspect of the nexus of North-South issues, produce an untargeted pattern of "eclectic incrementalism" unimbued with *either* longer-range prudential or normative vision.

(3) The full range of so-called "North-South" issues is far more likely to receive the high priority in your Administration's outlook that it in my view deserves only if you personally share the persuasion that according it high priority a) can significantly increase the probabilities of success in other major foreign policy initiatives, and b) can once again infuse U.S. foreign relations with that degree of *normative purpose* necessary to make the United States an enlightened and credible articulator of a global vision—a vision capable of engaging national leaders both at home and abroad in a constructive debate concerning purposes and programs appropriate to the present stage of evolution of the nation-state system.

If these three arguments are unconvincing, then there is little reason to make North-South relations a priority issue during your Administration. For success in this area will come only at considerable cost in terms of time, energy, and political capital spent in convincing skeptical domestic constituencies of the potential longer-term gains to be reaped when those very constituencies are more likely to be focusing their attention on the shorter-run dislocations entailed and the lack of anything resembling immediate progress. But such cost reflects the nature of any attempt by a democratic government to implement a long-run foreign policy strategy unlikely to be accompanied by major short-term payoffs.

Four Predominant Perspectives on North-South Issues

Although it will—like all "action" memoranda—conclude with a discussion of "issues and options," this unsolicited letter will follow the standard approach in a somewhat relaxed fashion. It would be difficult not to ease some of the usual constraints on the author of an action memorandum to the President in this instance, since neither Cabinet Secretaries nor their proxies are leaning over my shoulder to cry "foul" if I fail to do justice to one option or the other. Nevertheless, I will endeavor to present without bias the four currently fashionable ways of looking at North-South relations in this section and then to examine the three predominant policy options with an equal degree of detachment.

In the interests of candor and credibility, I will depart from the usual "options paper" approach in one major regard. I will attempt to label all editorial comments as such rather than to "tilt" a "dispassionate" piece of policy analysis toward the author's preferred option. I do this not because I am a particularly honorable fellow but because of the very nature of the subject matter. The individual issues involved in the present North-South dialogue—whether concerned with security, political, economic, or "equity" matters—are so complex, their "natural" linkages are so little understood, and the capacity of the policy maker to create and manipulate "synthetic" linkages for national advantages is so novel and perplexing that only a very wise individual or a very foolish one could point the way out of present and predictable North-South dilemmas with much self-assurance. This in itself is reason enough to reject the role of the Pied Piper of the Planetary Bargain.

The "Southern Unity Won't Last" Perspective

Many observers simply deny that a "South" exists as a "real" entity in international relations. At best, they would argue, this somewhat mystifying agglomeration of states into a serious bloc to be reckoned with in international politics is a superficial phenomenon, one that will soon disappear as the radically differentiated members of the present developing-country coalition recover from the psychological euphoria induced by the 1973-74 OPEC actions in quadrupling oil prices. Their differing levels of economic development create divergent needs; their differing political systems, religious beliefs, and ethnic conflicts defy the capacity for continued diplomatic cooperation; and within Latin America, Africa, the Middle East, and Asia, bids for regional hegemony and other forms of bilateral security threats will soon remove the "South" as an actor in the international system.

Surely there is a great deal of truth in the empirical observations made by those who doubt that the "South"—or the now-common triptych of the oil-rich countries, the Third World (the middle-range developing countries with per capita incomes often exceeding $500 per year), and the Fourth World (the world's poorest countries, concentrated in South Asia and Black

Africa, in which annual per capita incomes revolve around the $150–$200 range)—can much longer retain their present diplomatic cohesion. And behind the common front of Southern "solidarity," the strains are increasingly apparent. At the Law of the Sea Conference, the landlocked and shelf-locked LDCs are at the throats of their coastal neighbors. At UNCTAD and the joint World Bank/International Monetary Fund meetings, those developing countries which rely on international capital markets for substantial borrowings refuse to back the demands of their poorer brethren on issues such as international debt moratoria. At the CIEC meetings in Paris, the smaller developing countries become increasingly suspicious of the major role being played by such Third World-OPEC giants as Brazil, Iran, and Saudi Arabia. Finally, how long can the "artificial" alliance between the OPEC nations and other developing countries last? Facing rapidly escalating debt burdens, low growth rates in the OECD countries, and therefore steadily increasing constraints on growth, can the oil-importing developing countries withhold criticism of the OPEC nations through any more oil-price increases? Will not the very OPEC successes of 1973-74 that "launched" the North-South conflict, the resolutions calling for a New International Economic Order, and the U.N. Charter of Economic Rights and Duties of States eventually destroy Southern solidarity by contributing to Northern stagflation and Southern inflation, markedly slowed developing-country growth, rapidly escalating debt burdens, and ever increasing rates of developing-country unemployment?

This may well be the inevitable result. It certainly appears to be the outcome upon which U.S. diplomacy has been betting, if one is to judge from the "leaked" Kissinger telegram of November 22, 1976, which referred to the "relative success" of the industrial countries in intensifying restraints placed upon OPEC by other developing countries. At the urging of the United States, the countries of the European Communities agreed to a postponement of the December 1976 CIEC ministerial meeting, at which some Northern concessions or counterproposals to developing-country demands for international economic reforms had been expected to surface as the result of one year's joint North-South meetings. This postponement was in part an attempt to exacerbate relations between the OPEC countries and the rest of the developing world.

U.S. attempts to drive a wedge between the OPEC and other developing countries have been widely evidenced throughout the world for three years now. Thus far, however, common front Southern unity has prevailed. This raises an interesting question. If this is so, then *is* the description of OPEC and all other developing countries—both Third World and Fourth World—as a "Southern bloc" an example of "false concreteness" or a fairly accurate description of a grouping of well over one hundred nations that exhibits enough cohesiveness to be considered a serious actor in international relations? This issue has been analyzed ad nauseam, Mr. President, and will not be detailed here. Suffice it to make three simple but fundamental points.

First, developing countries have psychic needs, wants, and desires as well as economic, political, and security needs. Indeed, major and convincing studies have produced interpretations of developing-country foreign policies that are built around the former types of needs as Southern elite groups attempt to "build nations" as well as construct foreign policies. When examined in this light, the general developing-country support of OPEC oil-price actions is far more "rational" than is usually noted by most Northern analysts. The crucial question then becomes, when will the psychic gains to the LDCs which result from watching another group of developing countries (OPEC) twist the tail of the rich, the ex-colonial masters, and the major benefactors of the present international economic and political systems (i.e., the OECD countries)—when will these psychic gains become outweighed by the material costs to the non-oil-exporting developing countries stemming from increased oil prices? Since we are dealing with immeasurables, I submit that we cannot easily tell if and when the magic moment of ultimate "Southern" fragmentation, so assuredly predicted by Northern governments and analysts, will arrive.

The second point to be made increases the speculative nature of any such estimate concerning the "end of Southern solidarity." It concerns the fact that this solidarity is a function not simply of psychic needs but also of a deeply held conviction among many Southern governments that *only* through unity can the international economic and political changes which they view as essential ingredients of their development be achieved. Their *perception* is that the present international economic rules and norms are stacked against their developmental prospects and that more than twenty years of painstaking, issue-by-issue negotiations with Northern states have produced, at best, extremely marginal results. Their perception of the biases in the present system may be inaccurate, and their assessment of the value of years of incremental change incorrect, but national leadership more often than not acts upon such perceptions, not upon the latest and most erudite economic analysis flowing from think tanks and planning agencies. As long as these perceptions reflect the views of the political leadership of a large majority of Southern states, then psychic rewards and material interests will be considered consonant rather than contradictory. This is especially true since, given Northern unwillingness to compromise on almost all Southern demands (in many instances such unwillingness is warranted), OPEC is viewed, for better or worse, as the overwhelming source of Southern strength in the present North-South conflict. Unless and until this perception changes and/or the OECD countries agree with the majority of the developing countries about the implementation of reforms in the international economic system which benefit the process of the latter's development, the "South" will constitute a diplomatic reality, not a fantasy.

This tentative judgment is reinforced by the third and final point to be made concerning Southern cohesion. One would be very ill-advised to characterize this apparent unity as a creation of OPEC actions in 1973-74. No one, of course, doubts that the OPEC successes at that time provided the major impetus for Southern rhetorical demands and the strategic and tactical maneuvers in the Sixth and Seventh Special Sessions of the U.N. General Assembly, at UNCTAD IV, at the CIEC meetings in Paris, at UNESCO meetings over the last two years, and in many other venues.

What is often overlooked, however, is the twenty-year history preceding 1973, during which time the developing countries slowly constructed a network of institutions, communications, and norms of diplomatic behavior that prepared them to react so instantly and with such unified precision in the final months of 1973 and thereafter. Two separate institutional networks with initially disparate agendas provided the base for the 1973-74 diplomatic explosion. The first network, constituted by the so-called Non-Aligned Countries, which met for the first time officially in 1961, was really inaugurated by the Bandung Conference in 1955. Initially the meetings of the Non-Aligned Countries were politically motivated, and the group's political concerns and goals were reflected in its agendas and conference resolutions. By 1970, however, the group had undergone a rather dramatic evolution of interests: the issues of economic development, Southern "collective self-reliance" in the development process, and the demand for major international economic reforms—expressed in the landmark "Lusaka Manifesto" adopted by the Third Conference of Heads of State of the Non-Aligned Countries in September 1970—had replaced the older political issues and goals.

Thus by 1970 the issues, agenda, and goals of the "political" voice of the developing countries came to resemble in great part the issues and goals which had always served as the raison d'être of their "economic" voice, the so-called Group of 77 developing countries that constituted itself during the first UNCTAD in Geneva in 1964 and now includes over one hundred members. Prior to the 1973 oil crisis, UNCTAD met twice again, in New Delhi in 1968 and in Santiago in 1972.

As a result of the work of these two institutions, the conceptual groundwork, the programmatic elements, the diplomatic contacts, and the norms of Southern bargaining behavior vis-à-vis the OECD countries were so far advanced, that one month *prior* to the outbreak of hostilities in the Middle East in 1973 the Fourth Summit of the Non-Aligned Countries (held in Algiers) had already called for "the establishment of a new international economic order" and a special session of the U.N. General Assembly to re-examine the role of the U.N. system in assisting the development process. This linking of developing countries from every continent to a philosophy, a program of action, and a diplomatic method of operation provided these countries with the necessary machinery and mentality to use the OPEC success for all it was worth. But it would be folly to forget that the development of the machinery and the mentality preceded the emergence of OPEC. To reverse the order is to run the risk of seriously underestimating the "reality" of developing-country solidarity *especially when faced by intransigent Northern solidarity.*

Undoubtedly, Mr. President, Southern psychological needs as well as Southern developmental problems would have produced a minimal degree of cohesion regardless of developed-country policies. But a close examination of the history of both the Non-Aligned group and the Group of 77 reveals that time and again Northern unwillingness to discuss or compromise on developing-country requests for alterations in international economic rules and norms *added strength* to what is in many ways an unnatural alliance. What do Iran, Peru, Zambia, and Sri Lanka have in common? Perhaps only a shared sense of relative deprivation vis-à-vis the OECD countries. Is that enough to hold together an "unnatural alliance"? It may be, Mr. President, if no other card is played at the bargaining table.

The "Global Agenda" Perspective

A second major perspective on North-South relations is exhibited by those government officials, scholars, and other observers whose major concerns are the need for increasingly effective forms of multilateral diplomacy in a world characterized by declining U.S. hegemony, a growing dispersion of power and influence among an ever broadening number of state and non-state actors in the international system, and the increasing number of global problems that can only be solved by means of collective action at the international level. Among the problems presently high upon the so-called global agenda are such issues as international rules covering the use of the seas and the seabeds, international environmental problems, population growth and control, a global food "regime," nuclear proliferation, and several others of equal or slightly lesser importance.

The most novel aspect of many—though certainly not all—of these and similar problems is that they *cannot* be resolved by unilateral, bilateral, or even small-group actions. Their resolution requires the collective consent and action of the majority of states; the smaller the number of nations willing to abide by new rules and norms of behavior, the lower the probabilities of the rapid appearance of successful international problem-solving mechanisms.

Perhaps the classic example of a global agenda item before us at the present moment concerns the issues which have come together in the complex and seemingly endless negotiations over a new "law of the sea" treaty. The third U.N.-sponsored Law of the Sea Conference (LOS III) has been struggling for over three years to come to grips with such issues as the extension of territorial waters, national "economic zone" boundaries, fishing rights, deep-seabed mining rights, environmental standards, and a host of others.

29

During the process of multinational negotiation, three trends have emerged which have troubling implications for other "global agenda" problems. The first has been the steady erosion of general "global interest" and "international interest" themes in favor of specific "special interest" and "national interest" proposals. Perhaps the outstanding example of this trend is evidenced by the ever expanding territorial claims by coastal states and the ever outward extension of national boundaries. If this trend is legitimized in a new law of the sea treaty within the next year or two, the initial theme of a "common heritage of mankind"—which was grounded in the concept of narrow territorial waters and narrow national economic zones, with the vast majority of the riches of the seas and seabed mineral deposits to be harvested and used for development purposes in the world's poorer countries—will have been all but lost in the national- and special-interest scramble for those same sources of wealth.

The second trend concerns the continuing conflict between developed and developing countries. The degree of developing-country distrust of U.S. foreign policy initiatives has become so strong that an initial U.S. proposal on ocean issues that contained many elements supportive of the "common heritage of mankind" concept was automatically rejected by the developing countries, which—in LOS III as elsewhere—have continually caucused and (with but a few exceptions) acted as a remarkably solid unit. Many developing countries with coastal waters rich in fisheries and with continental margins rich in minerals have been able to effectively use automatic developing-country distrust of U.S. policy initiatives in order to enhance their own national interests at the expense of the "common heritage of mankind" approach.

The final trend, implicit in the first two, concerns the extraordinary difficulties of reaching optimal solutions—indeed, *any* solutions—to this particular "global agenda" item. Can close to 150 countries successfully conduct multilateral diplomacy? Or does the particular problem in this arena lie with the sheer volume of distinct issues raised by the law of the sea discussions? Finally, does the role of domestic interest groups—which have formed both national and transnational alliances to support, modify, and/or defeat national positions in such negotiations—suggest ever growing problems with the present mode of multilateral negotiations and force a fundamental reconsideration of the linkages between domestic interest groups, national governments, and the process of multilateral diplomacy?

These are among the major concerns of those who see the United States moving into a period in which collective action via multilateral diplomacy will form an increasingly dominant mode of international relations. From this perspective, they are deeply concerned with the potentially destructive effects of continued North-South conflict on "global agenda" issues. If the conflict continues at its present level of intensity, optimal outcomes from international negotiations will be impossible to realize in sphere after sphere. Not only will talk of a "global community" be dangerously misleading insofar as it suggests a minimum of shared values and norms of international behavior; it will be next to impossible to make progress toward the formulation of those one or two commonly accepted superordinate goals among states which might form the foundation of a slow but steady move toward a "community" of nations.

The "Global Equity" Perspective

An apparently increasing number of observers are coming to the view that the issue of "equity" and the manner in which the issue is managed internationally will to a large degree determine the course of North-South relations for many decades to come. It has been argued that global politics is becoming more "egalitarian" than "libertarian," that most states in today's world appear to have far more interest in material equality than in the more abstract concept of liberty. The fear has also been expressed that America's emphasis on liberty rather than equality as a superordinate value may lead the United States into a position of philosophical and diplomatic isolation unless this nation becomes more responsive to "a value that has not been central to the American experience" and begins to take into account the philosophical dimensions and political realities of a growing international emphasis on equity issues.

These prudential concerns with the issue of international equity are echoed by governments and private groups throughout the OECD countries as well as the developing countries and international organizations. It is quite apparent, however, that the "equity" issue covers many different, and often divergent, concerns. First among these is concern about equity in *interstate relations*. Most supporters of the "new international economic order" concept are persuaded, in varying degrees, that the present international economic system does not work in an "equitable" fashion. That is to say, the system is not structured in a way which gives most developing countries an "equal opportunity" to benefit from the operation of the system. The charges are legion and are catalogued in the U.N. General Assembly resolution calling for a New International Economic Order: the workings of the present system limit developing-country access to international monetary reserves, to private international capital, to Northern consumer markets, to industrial technology, etc.

The belief that the present international economic system operates in such a way as to benefit primarily the developed countries, often to the detriment of the still developing, is clearly spreading. Within developing countries, it is by now an article of faith; within developed countries, supporters of the view appear to be multiplying rapidly. Empirical evidence for this assertion can be found in a host of recently published analyses of North-South issues by individuals and groups from many OECD countries. Perhaps the most publicized among these are the Aspen Institute's *The Planetary Bargain*, the Dag Hammarskjöld Foundation's *What Now?*

Another Development, and the just-published "Tinbergen Group" or "RIO" report to the Club of Rome, entitled *Reshaping the International Order*.

In these and similar reports and studies produced by Northerners, the conclusion that the present system is inequitable and should be rapidly modified to assist the developing countries results from an uncertain mix of scientific analysis and normative judgment. Some lean toward scientific analysis of different aspects of the present international economic system in reaching their conclusions; others clearly base their conclusions on the value judgment that the gap between rich and poor countries is morally indefensible, and that the present international economic (and political) system must be altered to begin to moderate present extremes in the distribution of income and wealth. The conclusions of still others are prudential in nature. Within this category are observers who note growing North-South antagonisms linked to the international equity issue and, without further analysis of the empirical or normative issues involved, suggest that Northern policies should make much more of an attempt to "accommodate" the desires of developing countries. Finally, the work of certain European groups resonates with feelings of guilt, which quite possibly are linked to the historical period of European colonialism.

A second and very different equity theme concentrates not on interstate but on interpersonal equity comparisons. This focus on individuals often leads observers to radically differing empirical, normative, and policy conclusions than does the concern with interstate equity issues. There is generally a clear recognition that changes in the international system such as those espoused in the New International Economic Order (NIEO) proposals may have *little if any* effect on the distribution of income, wealth, or life chances *within* developing countries. Indeed, one of the most prominent "Southern" spokesmen on these issues has quite recently written that unless governing elites within developing countries are committed to internal equity goals, "foreign donors are completely helpless" to assist in their achievement.

A third equity theme, analytically linked to the equity issue as it affects individuals, is the concern with human rights issues. Clearly, Mr. President, this may be the most insoluble of all issues presently troubling North-South relationships. Indicative of the potential magnitude of the problem is the fact that those very groups most committed to radical restructuring of the international economic (and even political) system to aid the developing countries are very often the very ones who make the observance of human rights the sine qua non of system restructuring for development. For example, it is the Dag Hammarskjöld Foundation's *What Now? Another Development* that states most precisely the linkage: "Countries which do not respect human rights should not benefit from financial transfers"; this statement follows a section which constructs the report's entire strategy for greater equity upon the foundation of "financial transfers" from North to South.

If a "left-leaning" group within a "left-leaning" country in the North feels this strongly about the overriding value of human rights as defined during the evolution of Western civilization, and if developing-country elites in general have far less regard for that particular ordering of values, the potential strains for North-South relations on this issue could quite easily become the major obstacle to an easing of North-South tensions. Whether or not it does depends upon 1) whether or not the renewed Northern concern for human rights is a superficial phenomenon or an irreversible trend, and 2) the capacity of North-South discussions to discover a *mutually satisfactory* "definition" of minimum human rights. Unless and until they do, Mr. President, you may find that your best efforts in the North-South field are victimized by an issue which presently appears to be the single most "nonnegotiable" issue from both sides of the governmental bargaining table.

The "Basic Human Needs" Perspective

The final major perspective on North-South relations has blossomed recently, but fully. While it falls under various labels, the most fashionable at the moment is "basic human needs." Holders of this perspective are concerned above all else with developing new international and national institutions and norms of behavior which assure, within as short a period as possible, the emergence of a minimum standard of living for all the world's people. The approach most generally adopted is to set minimum targets in terms of per capita standards for food, nutrition, health services, and basic education. The more ambitious the program, the longer the list; some include such elements as housing, clothing, water, sanitary facilities, etc. Nevertheless, the basic minimum is generally limited to nutrition, health care, and basic education. Descriptions of the problem and the approach to its resolution can be found in many recent writings, including the already mentioned reports by the Aspen Institute, the Dag Hammarskjöld Foundation, and, most recently, the study entitled *Employment, Growth and Basic Needs: A One-World Problem*, prepared by the ILO International Labour Office for the 1976 World Employment Conference.

The basic propositions set out in support of this approach are the following:

(1) Difficult problems of measurement aside, there seems to be general agreement that close to one billion of the world's population of over four billion are presently receiving so little food, nutrition, basic health care, and basic education that they are fundamentally deprived of what might best be called "equality of opportunity" to enhance their own life chances. Whether the deprivation results from a lack of health care and nutrition during the earliest years, or of basic education slightly later in life, the result is to severely handicap (if not kill in early years) close to one quarter of the globe's population.

(2) The costs of providing these "basic human needs," insofar as they have been estimated, are not very large. One recent estimate suggests that $12.5 billion per year over a (probably unrealistically short) ten-year period could, if properly invested, eliminate absolute poverty throughout the world and meet the basic human needs standards discussed above.

(3) Much of the population involved, in quantitative terms, is located in South Asia and in the African countries south of the Sahara. Where such concentrations exist, *international programs* which transfer resources to the poorest countries could be of major assistance.

(4) In most other developing countries, the problem could be managed by *domestically financed programs* which restructure development priorities. But governing elites and political systems in the majority of these countries—as in almost all countries—are not inclined to attach high priority to "basic human needs" programs. Indeed, programs with this intent are of fairly recent vintage within the United States itself and have not yet achieved total success, despite major progress in the last two decades. Therefore the attack on absolute poverty—however defined and with whatever country-to-country variations included in that definition—is generally viewed as a strategy to be implemented in *all* developing countries with the proper variations and not limited solely to the so-called Fourth World countries. It should be made a part of a *global* development strategy and should be dealt with according to the specific profile of the poverty problem in each country.

(5) Finally, it is recognized (and implicit in point four above) that this approach raises two intimately related issues of extreme delicacy at the present stage of international relations. The first is the "domestic elite" problem. No program to eliminate absolute poverty can be constructed and implemented without the necessary degree of commitment of a country's governing elite groups and political system. No amount of foreign resources can overcome domestic resistance or indifference to the achievement of this goal. The other side of the coin is the international "intervention" problem. If such an approach is to be internationally sanctioned and supported, what "oversight" mechanisms should be included, and with what implications for national sovereignty? Even if the approach is limited to bilateral relationships, will the issue of interventionism kill the prospects for progress? If no mutually satisfactory agreement can be reached at the international level, what, if any, is the likely impact of such an outcome upon both international and domestic reforms which will significantly determine the course of North-South relations?

This brief exposition of the major perspectives on North-South relations within the OECD countries indicates that in this area as in many others, Mr. President, the reading of existing evidence, the differing order of personal values, and the resulting spectrum of policy suggestions likely to be presented to you for consideration will and *should* be extraordinarily broad and complex, reflecting the true nature of the subject.

Differences will inevitably arise, reflecting differing perceptions of the "problem." Is the real issue captured in terms of traditional statecraft? Is the problem therefore a (Southern) revisionist challenge to (Northern) status quo powers? If seen in this light, policy responses will be developed in accordance with the following modes: resistance, co-option, and compromise. If the "challenge" from the South can be easily turned back, *resist*. If it cannot be easily beaten, try to *co-opt* the most powerful Southern states (e.g., ask them to join the OECD). If the challenge is viewed as even more serious, then formulate *compromise* policies which give just enough to save the major elements of the status quo structure.

Is the real problem captured in terms of the necessity to achieve a North-South *modus vivendi* in order to focus more effective attention on "global agenda" problems? If this viewpoint prevails, then solutions should be sought to present North-South conflicts that will hopefully create a more cooperative relationship between Northern and Southern governments—so that multilateral diplomacy can produce collective action on such problems as pollution, nuclear proliferation, population growth, and food production. Such "solutions," of course, may be very imperfect when measured against other goals—for example the goals of economic growth, *intrastate* equity, and basic human needs.

Is the real problem economic growth in the developing countries? If so, then policies should in most instances be designed to achieve the highest possible rates of economic growth in the South. This approach might involve the removal of market imperfections at both the international and national levels, an increase in North-South resource transfers, and a host of other changes in the present system which are demonstrably effective in increasing the pace of development.

Is equity the real issue? If so, how is it defined? Are we more concerned with equality of *opportunity* or equality of *results*? And are we concerned primarily with equality between states, or with equality between persons? Finally, when we talk of equality in the intrasocietal, interpersonal sense, are we really thinking of moving toward equalized incomes or toward a basic human needs strategy? And is this last dichotomy viewed as a continuum, in the sense that the fulfillment of basic human needs will automatically produce greater earning power among the bottom deciles of the population in any country?

Thus the current discussion of "equity" and "fairness revolutions" often clouds at least two crucial distinctions: the first between states and individuals, the second between equality of opportunity and equality of results. It is crucial to bear the distinctions in mind, because each of the four possible goals suggests the need for its own set of policies; often the policies called for will be radically different.

Obviously, Mr. President, the answer to this series of questions about the real nature of the problem is that it is a bit of all of them. There is a serious problem captured by the historically tried and tested realpolitik perspective. There is another, and far more novel, problem captured in the "interdependence" and "global agenda" arguments. Likewise, there are fundamental problems captured by the concerns (prudential as well as normative) over the issues of economic growth within the South and all four just-mentioned facets of the "equity" question.

A Real World of Overlapping Objectives

Under present conditions, Mr. President, you face a serious dilemma. Your problems would be difficult enough if your Administration could keep the major issues disaggregated and attack them individually. You might be better able to follow that old economists' dictum, "one policy instrument for each policy goal"—though you would still be faced with the potentially enormous constraints of domestic political feasibility and international acceptability. But in today's world, few foreign policy issues can be resolved independently of others. Over the past decade, and especially over the past three years, all nations have learned that present degrees of global interdependence allow individual states and groups of states to manipulate that interdependence through the process of issue linkage. The latest example before you: the explicit Saudi Arabian linkage of oil prices, a Middle East settlement, and progress on North-South relations at the Paris CIEC talks. Thus even if the United States desired to approach these North-South problems one by one with the best of intentions, it is most unlikely that the developing countries would accede to such a process.

On this optimistic note I turn to an examination of what I consider to be the three general options most likely to be brought to your attention. As the concluding pages of this letter will suggest, these three "options" are not "tight" and mutually exclusive; various combinations of all three are possible. They are initially presented separately and distinctly simply in order to facilitate analysis. Furthermore, I should emphasize that I am focusing attention on those major options which I would expect to be forthcoming from the spectrum of advisers you have chosen. The options explored here in this sense cover only the relevant "middle" of the possible spectrum.

Option 1: Continuation of Present Policies with Marginal Changes

Economic and Political Components of the Option

As the title suggests, the major elements in this option would represent a continuation of present U.S. policies (and recent policy proposals) which are perceived as major ingredients in the North-South arena. The option does allow room for better implementation of recently stated policies and for marginal changes—particularly as part of tactical responses to Southern demands and pressures. For shorthand purposes I will often refer to it as the "marginal change" option.

Economic Policies

1. *Trade Policy.* The United States would continue to follow the policy of general trade liberalization which has marked this country's trade policy since the mid-1930s. In the present Tokyo Round of trade negotiations under the General Agreement on Tariffs and Trade (GATT), it would bargain for a reciprocal lowering of tariff and nontariff barriers to trade in accordance with the authority granted in the Trade Act of 1974. In keeping with its more recent trade policy toward the *developing* countries, the United States would continue to urge, but not insist upon, reciprocal tariff and nontariff concessions from these countries. Additionally, it would continue to extend its own version of the Generalized System of Preferences (GSP) to the developing countries, again in accordance with the provisions approved by Congress in the Trade Act of 1974.

On the issue of commodity trade, the United States would continue to insist that the discussion and possible negotiation on international commodity schemes be held on a case-by-case basis, reserving judgment on whether or not to become a party to each scheme until a decision could be made on the feasibility of the final proposal. As part of its policy regarding commodities, the United States would support the establishment of a "common fund" to finance individual buffer stocks only on a case-by-case basis, holding open the possibility that the common funding for certain commodity stocks might be linked *if* such a proposal met the tests of economic feasibility. Finally, the United States would continue to view the purpose of such schemes to be the *stabilization* of commodity prices around long-term market trend lines, and not the *raising* and/or *indexing* of commodity prices.

2. *Aid.* In this field the United States would generally continue to follow past policies, but with slightly more emphasis on recent trends in aid policy that have led to a gradual reversal of the downward trend of aid flows. The Administration would request from Congress modest increases in aid funds for economic assistance that would keep it from falling below the present level (0.26 per cent of U.S. GNP) and that might advance it in small increments toward the considerably higher average disbursements (0.5 per cent) of other OECD countries.

In addition, the Administration would, in accordance with the spirit (as well as the legalities) of recent congressional legislation, use rising proportions of aid funds to support development programs which a) aided the world's poorest countries, and b) supported programs most likely to increase the living standards and life chances for the poorest people within all countries receiving U.S. economic aid funds. In accordance with these priorities, disbursements would be concentrated on program areas such as rural development, technology, and infrastructure investment designed to increase developing-country food-production capacity, and rural health, nutrition, and education programs. Finally, since Congress has shown increasing interest in the possibility of splitting economic aid from military and "supporting" assistance, the Administration might closely weigh the advantages and disadvantages of introducing such a split in the requests it sends to Congress. This is clearly an instance in which trade-offs will have to be carefully assessed. But if the Administration's commitment to a slowly increasing economic aid package is strong, the arguments for splitting the two forms of "aid" will become increasingly compelling.

At the multilateral level, the Administration would continue to ask Congress to support modest real increases in commitments to the World Bank, the International Development Association (IDA), and regional development banks.

3. *Responses to Developing-Country Foreign Exchange Shortages.* Even if the reasons for such shortages in developing countries form a continuum, it is still helpful to think of them as representing two rather different types of problems: some are short-term in nature, others long-term. Cyclical fluctuations in demand for developing-country exports; natural disasters (which do major damage to domestic food supplies and crops grown for export); and sudden, major increases in the cost of highly price-inelastic imports (e.g., oil) are perhaps the best examples of uncontrollable events which can cause major short-term foreign exchange shortages. With regard to this type of problem, the United States would continue to focus its efforts on improving the capacity of the International Monetary Fund to respond to these situations. Recent changes in the IMF—increases in quotas and thus drawing rights, increased access to the Compensatory Finance Facility as well as increased funds at its disposal, and the establishment of the Trust Fund from the profits made on IMF gold sales—have all enhanced the IMF's capacity to respond to such short-term needs. In addition, the United States might consider some measures to ease this type of problem similar to those discussed by Secretary of State Kissinger in his proposal of a "development security facility" to stabilize overall export earnings; this concept was first publicly presented in the Secretary's speech to the Seventh Special Session of the U.N. General Assembly in September 1975.

U.S. policy concerning the longer-term foreign exchange shortage problems of the developing countries would hold to one long-standing principle while considering two other possibilities. The long-standing principle would be that the United States would oppose any schemes for *generalized* debt rescheduling, thereby naturally excluding any consideration of a generalized moratorium or of a generalized debt cancellation. The two newer themes which might be closely examined include 1) some form of generalized debt relief for those poorest countries "most seriously affected" by price and demand fluctuations and present global stagflation, and 2) further consideration of the proper use of "automatic" resource transfers to developing countries through such instruments as the (potential) deep seabed regime being discussed at the Law of the Sea Conference. Under this "marginal change" option, the United States would not stress an *active search* for sources of "automatic resource transfers" but would simply consider such transfers and their optimal use when and if they appeared as elements of negotiations which the United States had entered to serve *other purposes* (as in the case of LOS III).

4. *Other Economic Issues.* This "marginal change" option would not include much more than a defense of other U.S. international economic positions and policies currently under attack in a plethora of international and regional institutions. It would continue to resist demands for a code of conduct for multinational firms along the lines of those proposed by most developing countries; it would resist any movement toward "global planning" of the allocation of industrial production; and it would resist codes on technology transfer which interfered with present "proprietary rights," although it would continue to support developing-country research institutions working to identify and develop technology "appropriate" for national development strategies.

Political Policies

It is becoming increasingly difficult to disentangle economic, political, and security problems and policies, particularly in the North-South context. With a bow toward the definitional problem, a brief look should be taken at the elements of the "marginal change" option in the *non*economic, or broadly "political," area.

1. The United States would continue to work both overtly and covertly to undermine the fragile yet resilient unity of the developing countries, the alliance of OPEC and other developing countries, and Southern bloc tactics as applied in the United Nations, UNCTAD, CIEC, LOS III, and in every other major international forum since the early 1970s. The reasons will include both "high politics" traditional statecraft (such as undermining the position of an "actor" whose international policies range from marginal annoyance to a serious threat to various U.S. global policy goals) and "low politics" technocratic assumptions (such as the view that Southern bloc politics leads to *very* suboptimal policy choices for development and makes "rational" approaches to other global agenda items impossible).

2. The United States would continue to emphasize the importance of bilateral relations with "key" developing countries (e.g., Brazil, Saudi Arabia, Iran) for a host of political-security reasons ranging from maintenance of the mildest form of "influence" at one end of the spectrum to an all-out "devolution of power" strategy on the other.

3. The United States would continue to view the price of (and assured access to) oil as the only truly *salient* North-South policy problem and would therefore put overwhelming emphasis on this issue (and, of course, on the Arab-Israeli conflict as a crucial ingredient in this issue). The United States would continue to register concern over nuclear proliferation involving developing countries and the need for a settlement of Southern African conflicts short of war, but neither of these issues would be viewed as much through a North-South policy lens as through a more straightforward "national interest-national security" lens.

Support for Option One

I suspect, Mr. President, that a sizable number—probably the majority—of your advisers would offer support for the general approach to North-South issues sketched out above. The arguments in favor of such an approach can be outlined as follows, again employing the obviously oversimplified economic-political dichotomy.

Economic Perspectives

The main economic arguments that tend to support the above option cluster along three highly interrelated lines:

(1) The present international economic system is not the source of the economic problems of the developing countries.

(2) Development is 90 per cent a domestic affair. Countries which have the appropriate socio-political and "human resource" infrastructures can overcome the obstacles to economic development; those that do not are not likely to be assisted in the process by the receipt of major foreign assistance, whether in the form of "free" resource flows or greater developing-country access to Northern commodity markets, technology, and international credit mechanisms.

(3) Many of the specific developing-country proposals which have been on the North-South agenda for the last several years are, when closely analyzed, not even in their aggregate long-term interest. In the cases of some of these proposals, this criticism is taken to apply to *all* developing countries. With respect to others, the point is made that while they may benefit one group of developing countries, they may also prove harmful to a great many others.

Each of these three arguments can easily be defended at the right level of generalization. With regard to the *first*, the most obvious and commonly cited points run as follows. During the 1960s, the aggregate growth rate of the developing countries was well over 5 per cent per year—and thus higher than the First U.N. Development Decade target (which represented what was thought to be the maximum feasible target in light of historical experience)—and produced annual per capita growth rates in excess of 2 per cent. These rates *increased* during the late 1960s and the early 1970s. Moreover, many Third World countries have developed so successfully that they are now being compared (by some observers, at least) to Japan in the 1950s. The comparison is meant to suggest that these countries have reached that point in the development process where they are now ready to fully utilize the potential role of international markets and comparative advantage in order to grow at even *more rapid* rates than those of the past decade. (For over twenty years Japan grew at better than 10 per cent per year.) For those developing countries whose socio-political and economic infrastructural "act" is considered to be sufficiently "together," the international economic system is viewed as *ripe for the picking, not as a barrier to growth.* Finally, to the extent that the international economic system has presented barriers to development in certain economies, slow but steady marginal changes in both the international political and economic systems have gradually diminished those barriers and will continue to do so. One example cited in support of this point is that growing competition among multinational corporations from many different countries has gradually increased the bargaining power of the developing countries, improving the terms of their access to technology, capital, markets, and commodities. Thus many of the worst market imperfections which the multinational corporations once represented are rapidly diminishing, particularly as knowledge of their operations and of their technologies becomes "common property" among the developing countries. Another example is that the growth of the Eurodollar market has increased developing-country access to an international capital market, a market which is also free from political pressures that have often been associated with national capital markets. It is also pointed out that recently improved access to larger amounts of foreign exchange through the IMF's Compensatory Finance Facility has provided a major increase in the capacity of developing countries to finance the short-term, cyclical, foreign exchange shortfalls that the global economy often inflicts upon them. For these and other reasons, it is concluded, major reforms of existing international systems are not necessary; many of the market imperfections they might attempt to redress are already disappearing quite rapidly.

The *second* line of argument relies on the still overwhelming consensus among non-Marxist Northern economists that developmental problems are to a very great extent a reflection of domestic, not international, systems, and that they therefore should receive priority attention *domestically* rather than *internationally*. Surely, this argument maintains, greater access to foreign exchange might ease certain developmental bottlenecks; therefore more aid, trade, technology, and access to international capital could help at various stages of the development process. But, it is argued, there is a great deal of substitutability between international and domestic measures. Proper domestic development strategies remain the crucial ingredient in the development process; and this implies the capacity to implement such strategies. *Without that capacity,* no amount of international economic reform can produce development—if what is meant by development is the institutionalization of the growth process itself.

The *third* and final economic argument asserts that the current set of developing-country reform proposals is shot full of analytical contradictions and by no means represents the most effective approaches to assisting development. Integrated commodity schemes, for example, are likely to have very perverse distributional effects *within* the South; the rich will get richer, the poor, poorer. The call for a debt moratorium could well pull the plug on the growing capacity of many Southern states to borrow on international capital markets; hence the split between developing countries on this issue clearly evidenced at the Colombo meeting of the Non-Aligned Countries in the summer of 1976 and again at the Manila meeting of the World Bank Group of governors in the fall of 1976. The demand for nonreciprocity and generalized preferences in trade negotiations in effect allows many developing countries the unaffordable luxury of avoiding needed domestic reforms that would make their products competitive in world markets. The list could be lengthened far beyond these few illustrations.

Political Perspectives

Two major political-strategic sets of arguments are likely to be resorted to by advisers favoring the marginal change option:

(1) To compromise is simply to invite ever increasing demands; and
(2) The Southern "bloc" can be fragmented by policies of resistance, co-option, and/or a combination of the two.

Building upon earlier discussion and analysis, both arguments can be presented very briefly. The *first* argument emerges from one of the most fundamental elements of any dynamic model of interstate behavior: the assumption that, other things being equal, states will seek to maximize their security/status/power positions in the international system. Of course, major objections have always been raised against this oversimplification of state behavior, increasingly so in recent years. But after all the objections are analyzed, the following observations would seem to remain valid, *particularly* in terms of North-South relations. As a "first cut" at explaining state behavior, this characterization tells us more than any other single statement on the subject. And while the pattern of state behavior suggested by this characterization may be weakening considerably as applied to developed-country relations, the same cannot be said when it is applied to the developing countries. The model may no longer be adequate to predict the policies of industrialized states that are increasingly busy and perplexed in their efforts to satisfy the welfare wants of their citizens and increasingly forced into modes of interstate coordination and cooperation in their efforts to satisfy those wants. For these states, it can be argued, more and more conflict is over *modes of cooperation* and not over the presumably timeless goals of "power, glory, and idea."

With regard to most developing countries, however, the old model still appears to have a great deal of validity. They have yet to taste either the sweet or the bitter fruits of "power, glory, and idea." Never (in recent centuries) having possessed power and status and having instead suffered the humiliation of their subordination to Western civilization, they retain the goals of pre-"welfare-state" Western nations. Furthermore, at their present levels of development, they do not face the same types of domestic pressures for welfare performance currently experienced in the Western countries. For all of these reasons and more, it can be rather persuasively argued that the NIEO smacks as much of politics as of economics; that *a* if not *the* major goal of most developing countries is a significant increase in their status and power in the international system; and that if this is the case, each Northern attempt to "accommodate" Southern demands will simply be met by new ones.

The *second* major "political" argument advanced in support of the "marginal change" option is that one effective, low-cost strategy is available for overcoming the present stalemate: a combination of resistance and co-option, with perhaps a dash or two of compromise. Proponents of such a strategy consider that it could bring an end to both Southern solidarity and the problems for U.S. foreign policies in the North-South and other arenas which that solidarity has caused. Since the potential weaknesses of such groups as the Non-Aligned Countries and the Group of 77 were analyzed earlier, they need not be repeated here. Suffice it to say that proponents of this option would point out that the combined effect of the economic weaknesses of most developing countries (particularly at the present stage of the global business cycle); the prospects for continuing oil-price increases; the rapidly growing differentiation in economic structure and economic needs of the OPEC countries, the Third World, and the Fourth World; and the varying political and security interests of individual Southern states and groups of states all suggest a Northern capacity to achieve a fragmentation of the Southern bloc *if* such a policy goal is embraced and the appropriate policies are pursued with a modicum of skill.

Finally, one should note the *normative congruence* between the economic and political reasons for supporting this option. It is all too easy to portray the proponents of the marginal change option as selfish, self-interested, and status-quo-oriented pragmatists. In fact, however, it is quite humane and reasonable to support this option from a normative standpoint if one believes in the strength of the economic analysis which underlies it. For if Southern solidarity is responsible for economic demands which are *not* particularly responsive to their developmental problems—viewed from either the growth *or* the equity perspective—then it can logically follow that only a political strategy of resistance and co-option to break the coalition will allow real progress to be made on those crucial issues.

Personally, Mr. President, I do not find myself particularly comfortable with this option from either a normative or a prudential point of view. But I recognize that some supporters of it as a general model are motivated by deep and honorable conviction. To impugn the motives of all who hold this position not only is ethically reprehensible but also serves to undermine the entire debate over the proper policies for the United States vis-à-vis the developing world.

Opposition to Option 1

Economic Perspectives

Three highly interrelated arguments are suggestive of the potential weaknesses of this option from an economic perspective. They concern the following issues:

(1) The number and degree of market imperfections present in today's international economic system;

(2) The potential in at least some Southern ideas for major benefits to the development process in particular, as well as to the international economic system in general; and

(3) The potential gains to the *developed* countries which might flow from a greater willingness to examine more fundamental reforms in the present system.

In the case of the *first* issue, the argument boils down to some very erudite and highly technical questions concerning the degree to which the present international economic system is free of major market imperfections. If it *is* relatively free of them, and if those that do exist are generally beneficial to the development process (for example, the explicit and implicit current international norm that developing countries are given wide latitude to use policies to promote infant industries and subsidize entry into export markets), then the economic arguments in favor of this option are strengthened. However, to the degree that market imperfections do prevail, especially those which would a priori be suspected of impeding development efforts, the economic case for this option weakens. The greater the market imperfections, the weaker the *economic* arguments for "a continuation of present Northern policies with marginal change."

This is not the proper place to begin to tackle this difficult and highly technical set of issues. Any attempt to do so would be repetitive of the excellent work of many who are far more capable of performing this task than I; and even if reproduced, the arguments would not be overwhelming in one direction or the other. Let me attempt the briefest possible summary.

There is little disagreement that the present international economic system contains many market imperfections, and in that sense alone is far from optimal. It is also agreed that once major market imperfections are admitted, the case for free market orthodoxy is out the window. In economic jargon, we are then into the "theory of the second-best" world, and into a policy maze that produces doctoral dissertations which, however brilliant technically, are likely to be incomprehensible to generalists.

The real debate concerning this first option is not whether we are operating in an international economic system free from market imperfections but whether or not those imperfections that do exist are *major*, whether or not they are *biased* in the aggregate against the developing countries, and whether more optimal alternatives require minor reforms or major surgery.

Among the more obvious market imperfections are the following: very little international labor mobility; only slightly more capital mobility (considered globally); and many impediments, both tariff and nontariff, to the free flow of commodities. These are considerations at the most aggregate level. They do not begin to examine imperfections in *individual* markets for specific commodities and specific technologies.

Is there a bias against the developing countries? The answer would seem to be yes. Again speaking in aggregate terms, typical developing-country exports face higher tariff and nontariff barriers than do products of developed countries; capital market imperfections (institutional, legal, and other) have weighed more heavily on developing-country borrowers than on those from developed countries; and it surely would be difficult to argue that the restrictions on immigration into high-wage countries from the developing countries have been offset by capital flows from North to South or by Northern liberal trade policies which might have eased problems caused by the general international immobility of labor.

If the present system does contain significant biases against developing countries, how can these best be overcome? Here we arrive at the *second* major economic rationale for questioning the approach suggested in this first, "marginal change" option for handling North-South relations. Since the international economic system is not free of major imperfections and pro-Northern biases, shouldn't U.S. policy makers take a much closer look at developing-country economic proposals; and if those proposals are found wanting, shouldn't the United States make counterproposals which it considers to hold more potential? In the trade field for example, is the United States prepared to make significant counteroffers which would become the legitimate focus of developing-country attention, thereby ridding North-South discussions of many of the inadequate proposals that now appear in relation to major joint commodity funding schemes and to the generalized system of preferences? With regard to commodities, is the United States prepared to recognize the fact that "free markets" have always played a very limited role in this arena—and to examine commodity issues without bias for or against the policy implications of fresh and (hopefully) convincing econometric studies? In the case of a global food regime, is the United States prepared once again to consider major changes rather than incremental ones if serious research supports the former approach?

This type of question leads to the *third* and final economic argument against the marginal change option. Whether analyzing such issues as food production and distribution, energy production and consumption, or environmental decay, it is clear that it may often pay significant dividends to *Northern* as well as Southern countries to *at least begin to examine* the pros and cons of a more global approach to the organization of some sectors of economic activity. In the field of fisheries, for example, we are already doing so as we learn more about "maximum sustainable yields." In the course of such examination, some begin to think of the most optimal way to make such global arrangements work, and some see in such international approaches a potential source of revenue—collected, in the case of our example, in a manner which optimizes global fish harvests—which can then be used to aid the South in the process of development. One of your most highly respected economic advisers is at the forefront of this particular innovative approach.

This is *not* to argue that one morning soon we will awaken in a global community in which all the talk of optimal use of resources, positive-sum games, and the making of collective choices representative of universally recognized superordinate norms suddenly assumes a relevance for state behavior heretofore sadly lacking. The point made by those opposing this marginal change option for *both* economic *and* political reasons is much more modest. It is that one's frame of reference often restricts one's range of options. If one examines North-South issues *without ever asking* if there are any areas in which major innovative reforms can benefit all parties, one can be assured that none will be found. Once the question is asked—once we are caught with our standard parameters down—we can no longer be assured that all major reforms are out of the question.

Political Perspectives

Again, and not surprisingly, there is a logical fit between the political and economic critiques of this option. Those who argue against it on political grounds do so for two major reasons:

(1) They see no reason to believe that well-designed reforms in the economic (and global institutional) realm will of necessity lead to greater demands from the developing countries.
(2) They generally are seriously concerned about what we have labeled "global management" issues or "global agenda" issues, and they feel that the degree of global collective action necessary to achieve progress in these arenas will be forthcoming only if efforts to ease present levels of North-South tensions and problems are attempted and are successful.

Many of those who oppose this option can be *relatively* optimistic on both points because they *do* see room for some more-than-modest reforms in the international economic realm which would be responsive to developing-country demands as they interpret them. Others may not share the view that the economic arguments rehearsed above are all that persuasive, but they still may feel that the proper diplomatic gestures and the occasional major reforms, even if suboptimal in global efficiency, developmental, or equity terms, are well worth the price if they purchase needed collective action in other realms of international politics—action on both the "hard" issues (e.g., security and nuclear proliferation) and the "soft" ones (e.g., fisheries agreements and environmental programs).

Thus some opponents of the "marginal change" approach of Option 1 think a strategy laden with reform and compromise would have *economic costs*, but they argue that the *political benefits* defined in terms of lessening North-South friction and increased capacity for collective action on other global issues would *exceed the costs*. Others contend that a strategy of reform and compromise would produce *both* economic and political gains. The major *difference* between the two views lies in a judgment concerning global economic reforms; some see potential costs where others see potential benefits. The major *similarity* between them is the belief that their preferred strategy will produce political benefits in terms of increased North-South collaboration on a broad range of "global agenda" items. On this latter point, Mr. President, their view is diametrically opposed to the view of those who support Option 1 for political reasons. The greatest concern of this group of Option 1 proponents is that "accommodation" will breed further North-South conflict, not convergence. Perhaps those best trained to offer an expert opinion on this question are historians. However, to the degree that the international system is in a period of change—e.g., increasing types and levels of interdependence, a diminished degree of hierarchy in the system accompanying the diminished utility of force in controlling the outcome of events, the globalization of the system, and the institutionalization of the Southern bloc—even the observations of the most well-trained historians may be irrelevant to the problems you must wrestle with and the decisions you must make.

Option 2: A Policy of Accelerated Reform

Economic and Political Components of the Option

In contrast to the "marginal change" approach of Option 1, Mr. President, Option 2 would emphasize the *active search* for, *consideration* of, and *potential acceptance* of a broader and more significant range of reforms of existing international economic and political systems—reforms which would be responsive to Southern desires for change in the present international status quo as well as to some of the needs of Northern economies and societies in coming decades.

Economic Policies

In the economic arena, Mr. President, a number of major innovations have been discussed in recent years which, it is alleged, could greatly help to meet the development needs of a large number of Southern countries. Many such innovations are catalogued in the official resolutions on the New International Economic Order; others have been surfaced by institutions and individuals with no link to the set of proposals which emerged from the Sixth Special Session of the U.N. General Assembly. Under this "accelerated reform" option, many of these proposals as well as proposals originating within the OECD countries would be examined. Those which (with more or less reshaping) appeared beneficial to the development process *as well as* to the international economy as a whole would form a central element of U.S. negotiating proposals. A second category of proposals to receive serious attention would include those which would plausibly benefit the developing countries *at some cost* to the North, but at a cost considered to be legitimate on either moral or prudential grounds. The following discussion, in no way exhaustive, is offered merely to suggest some major areas in which a search for such reforms would take place.

1. *Trade Policy.* This is one area in which supporters of the accelerated reform option see major potential benefits to the North as well as to the South in acceding to many developing-country demands. Despite the existence of the market imperfections noted earlier, most economists would still argue strongly that a significantly greater degree of trade liberalization on the part of the OECD countries would be to *their own aggregate advantage*; simultaneously, it would greatly benefit many developing countries. The number of the latter countries that benefited substantially would depend upon the profile of trade liberalization in the North (i.e., which tariffs and which nontariff barriers were lowered and by what degrees) as well as upon the supply capabilities within developing countries.

The World Bank has estimated that the elimination of all Northern tariff and nontariff barriers could lead to an increase in developing-country export earnings of over $30 billion (in constant dollar terms) within ten years. Even if these calculations are best used merely to suggest orders of magnitude, they do indicate the potential gains to the South implicit in a set of Northern policies that under most conditions can only be viewed as beneficial to the developed countries as well.

In response to developing-country interest in a host of international commodity arrangements and a common fund to support them through a system of buffer stocks, supporters of this "accelerated reform" option would, in contrast to advocates of the "marginal change" option, call for a less guarded U.S. response—one which examined commodity problems, though most likely still on a case-by-case basis, to see which commodities made sensible candidates and which might be considered for common funding. Again the goals would be of the joint-gain nature: where can such schemes limit unnecessary price fluctuations and assure *global* access to needed supplies?

2. *"Global Regime" Policies Which Are of Particular Benefit to the South.* Supporters of the accelerated reform option would argue that the United States should examine the potential in various approaches to "global agenda" problems which might be of particular economic benefit to the South, but which in many cases might also entail significant benefits for the North. Global regimes for food, fisheries, and energy can serve as proxies for many others. Can a global food system be constructed which addresses a) emergency shortage problems, b) the major price fluctuation problem (including its cyclical inflationary pressures), and c) the longer-term problem of increasing the capacity of the developing countries to feed themselves through increased domestic production? Can the newly created International Fund for Agricultural Development (IFAD)—financed almost equally by the OPEC and the OECD countries and constituted on a tripartite basis by the OECD, OPEC, and other developing countries—play a significant role in developing the mechanisms to successfully address these problems? If it can play such a catalytic role, a major step will have been taken toward resolving one of the most serious "global agenda" problems —perhaps benefiting the developing countries the most, but at the same time offering significant benefits to the North and doing so (potentially) at a very low cost to those states which are funding the regime.

The idea that the IFAD and concomitant efforts can evolve into a successful "global food system" is still but a gleam in the eye of optimistic global humanists. Proponents of the accelerated reform otion would merely point out that ideas, money, and international machinery in this functional area are beginning to come together; that this approach, if nurtured, might prove to be the least costly and most beneficial way to move toward the resolution of the food problem; and that one cannot rule out the possibility of similar "global breakthroughs" in other functional areas such as energy and fisheries *before* they are analyzed and discussed from a global perspective. Analytically, the problem areas mentioned may have little in common. For example, economists may view the fisheries issue as an "externalities" problem—but not so the global food and energy problems. From a broader political economy point of view, however, all of these areas do have one important similarity. Other things being equal, the lower the supply, the higher the price; the higher the price, the less developing-country importers can rely on international markets to provide even their minimum food and energy needs.

Thus for supporters of this option, the "private marketplace" parameters are dropped when the arenas of *essential needs* are examined and potential shortages are discovered. If and when it appears that, given plausible supply and demand projections, any number of countries may simply be priced out of the marketplace; and if it also appears that these same countries face limited, short- to medium-term domestic substitution possibilities, the question becomes: Is there a plausible global response to this problem which is better than a series of ad hoc, bilateral responses? The short-term answer may well be "no," but the proponents of this option would argue that the question should be posed and studied before an answer is given.

3. *Automatic Resource Transfers.* Many developing countries of the Third and Fourth Worlds rather consistently face "foreign exchange bottlenecks." Simply put, they do not seem able to acquire enough foreign exchange (through export earnings, foreign borrowings, or restraints on "nonessential" imports) to purchase the imports needed by any rapidly developing economy. Under the accelerated reform option, alternative methods of increasing the flow of foreign exchange to these countries would be explored which were *automatic* (i.e., not dependent upon the political decisions of individual Northern countries or even of the developed countries as a group).

Sources of revenue for such automatic transfers have been discussed and analyzed for years, although no concrete results (in terms of actual flows) have been achieved. Taxes on international trade, the allocation of Special Drawing Rights, the proceeds from an international deep seabed regime, and tax proceeds from a global fisheries regime have all received considerable attention as potential sources of automatic resouce-transfer mechanisms. Each scheme would involve a different type of "cost" and a different method of allocating the proceeds. In some instances, the cost might be measured in terms of Northern abstention from claims to an as yet unappropriated *source* of wealth (e.g., a deep seabed regime); in others, the North might be expected to tax itself to provide the source (e.g., a tax on international trade). In still other cases, such as an ocean fisheries regime, the revenues might flow from taxes set to optimize global levels of fish harvests. Proponents of the accelerated reform option would favor a serious look at the "automatic resource-transfer" issue, suggesting that there is far greater potential for such transfers than the more or less conventional analysis of the 1960s revealed.

4. *Greater Developing-Country Access to IMF Resources.* Over the past two years, some significant changes have taken place within the International Monetary Fund which affect its capacity to assist developing countries facing foreign exchange bottlenecks. Country drawing rights have increased substantially (chiefly due to expanded quotas), access to the Compensatory Finance Facility has been considerably broadened, and gold sales have provided the Trust Fund with a source of revenue for lending to the poorest countries on very easy repayment terms. Five years ago, the IMF was not in the "development" business; it still is not. But recent reforms suggest the possibility that the IMF can assist developing countries more than conventional wisdom once assumed. A very valid question to ask is: How far can this recent trend be pushed without raising problems for the international financial management role which the IMF was initially

constituted to play? This is one of the boundaries which the accelerated reform option would explore with analytical rigor but with a minimum of ideological preconceptions.

5. *Aid.* A final major ingredient of this option concerns U.S. efforts to increase aid levels and funding to international institutions that lend to developing countries. To the extent that the concentration is on aid for *economic development*, and not on other forms of assistance, the aid arena presents less of a joint-gain situation than many of the others discussed under the four previous headings. Furthermore, arguments based on self-interest will be hard-pressed to be convincing. Most supporters of this option view the necessity for the Administration to attempt to win congressional approval for increased amounts of aid, higher contributions to IDA, and an increased capitalization of the World Bank and regional financial institutions through a strictly normative lens. The United States presently contributes a smaller percentage of its GNP to official development assistance (ODA) than do eleven of the seventeen countries that are members of the Development Assistance Committee of the OECD; it concentrates that aid on a few countries where its security interests are salient; and it has recently played a leading role in opposing an attempt to increase the capitalization—and thus the lending power—of the World Bank.

Supporters of the accelerated reform option generally propose serious efforts to reverse the aid priorities reflected in these figures and their present pattern of concentration. Many of them view an annual level of U.S. aid disbursements of 0.5 per cent of GNP—a level comparable to that sustained during the 1960s—as the minimum goal to be achieved by the early 1980s. While they may argue from a national-interest point of view, their arguments in most cases reflect the persuasion that it is reprehensible for the United States to be so delinquent in the performance of its "moral" duty.

Political Policies

The "political" policies advocated under the "marginal change" option have a clarity and conciseness, Mr. President, that is necessarily lacking under this second, "accelerated reform" option. Under the marginal change option, the three salient policies were to 1) "break" the Southern bloc, 2) emphasize security-related bilateral relations, 3) and devote all energies to the resolution of the OPEC-Middle East problem. Supporters of the accelerated reform option are unlikely to display the same degree of political consensus. This point can be illustrated by examining the likely *reaction* of Option 2 supporters to these three broad policy goals of Option 1.

1. Many supporters of the accelerated reform option would be inclined to see a good deal of merit in some Option 1 arguments against Southern unity. Pointing to the Law of the Sea Conference, they observe that Southern "bloc" politics has been very costly to potential outcomes that would have been of great benefit to the development process as well as to the more general needs of the international system as a whole. Noting the

record of UNCTAD IV and the ongoing GATT trade negotiations in Geneva, they would observe that the Group of 77 has locked itself into many negotiating positions that represent fourth- and fifth-best solutions to problems which have much better—and in their judgment achievable—solutions. And they acknowledge that the carry-over of Southern bloc politics into the U.N. General Assembly and UNESCO, leading the developing countries to vote en masse for resolutions such as that which equated Zionism with racism and which effectively removed Israel from UNESCO's European chapter, make it very difficult to carry the day for the Option 2 approach within the United States. Therefore many Option 2 advocates desire an end to "strident" Southern solidarity.

Other Option 2 supporters, however, feel that in an altered psychological setting—one marked by somewhat more trust and somewhat less conflict—the same solidarity that now creates major problems might well produce an effective and constructive bargaining mechanism. Such a change might make more manageable the problem of "too many actors," which is much more prominent today than in previous eras of major "global" negotiation. They recognize, furthermore, that any overt attempts to crack the degree of Southern solidarity that now exists run the risk of limiting most possibilities for successful North-South negotiations on many of the economic issues discussed in this option. More broadly, they consider that serious "global agenda" issues of a political-security nature would suffer from any U.S. attempts to undermine a unity so long in the making and so suspiciously guarded precisely because it *is* so fragile. On balance, therefore, Option 2 *might* benefit from a slow disintegration of present degrees of Southern unity, but supporters of the option both a) perceive the risks of advocating any active U.S. role in such a process and b) sense the potential benefits which might arise from Southern cohesion if North-South bargaining were to achieve a better balance between conflict and accommodation.

2. The same supporters of "accelerated reform" would be at least as hesitant to embrace fully the bilateralism which is an integral part of Option 1 as they would be to subscribe to a "break Southern unity" approach. They recognize the natural short-term advantages that certain bilateral relationships may entail, but they are likewise aware of the potential costs involved. Can strategies of strong bilateral ties and regional devolution of power be mixed with some of the potentially global approaches that attract the supporter of the accelerated change option? Can the United States defend close ties with Brazil, major support for IBRD loans to Chile, and major arms sales to Iran on the one hand, while strongly supporting the concept of human rights on the other? For some, the answer is yes; for others, no. For most supporters of the accelerated reform option, the answer probably lies—somewhat uncomfortably—between the two.

3. Finally, while supporters of the accelerated reform option may be deeply concerned about the oil problem and access to energy supplies, it is clearly not their sole concern in North-South relations; they see other salient

international issues at stake. While they perceive some potential advantage in a break between OPEC and the rest of the South, they also see some merit in exploring the implications of the IFAD model for other international problem areas. Are there additional areas in which OPEC money can be combined with OECD funds and technology in efforts to break development bottlenecks in the developing countries? A long shot, certainly; but worth exploring?

In short, the proponents of the accelerated reform option, like so many professional international relations analysts, find themselves caught between two worlds. Their hunch is that the world of realpolitik is slowly ebbing away; they would like to believe that the prospective world of increasing interdependence (North-South as well as intra-Northern) need not be one marked by increasing disorder and the manipulation of asymmetrical interdependencies; but they recognize that their preferred option calls for sailing in uncharted waters.

My second editorial, Mr. President: Beware the self-assured supporter of this option. His or her optimism may prove to be correct, but it is grounded in personality, not in empirical or analytical evidence. On the other hand, have a degree of sympathy with the uncertain articulator of the option, for he is groping and is sensible enough to know it. Therefore *he can neither be as assured nor as assertive in his convictions and presentations as the proponent of the marginal change option.* The latter's model of the world is a simpler one. The crucial issue is whether or not it is the more accurate one.

Support for Option 2

Since the accelerated reform option contains more novelty than the marginal reform option, its economic and "political" components were necessarily spelled out in some detail. Having been implicit in much of the preceding discussion, the perspectives in support of Option 2 therefore can be presented quite briefly. Three major strands of thinking—the normative, the prudential, and the technical economic—converge in support of this option. These strands are extremely difficult to delineate sharply, but a brief examination of each should, at least indirectly, encompass the major arguments in favor of the "accelerated reform" economic policy package.

Economic Perspectives

1. *The Normative Argument.* The normative support for Option 2 grows directly out of one aspect of the "equity" issue discussed earlier and indirectly out of a second. In the first case, supporters of the option simply feel that the present per capita income differentials between Northern and non-OPEC Southern states are ethically unacceptable. If they saw the income "gap" between developed and developing states narrowing, they might support the marginal change approach and let time solve the problem.

But they see the reverse. The relative per capita income gap *may* be narrowing slightly; the *absolute* income gap continues to widen and will probably do so for decades to come.

Those supporters of the "accelerated reform" Option 2 approach who are less concerned with interstate equity issues than with interpersonal equity issues and "basic human needs" concerns see the economic contents of the option as a *necessarily* indirect route to the resolution of their own normative concerns. They might well prefer to attack the income distribution question much more directly, but they feel that there is no way to bypass the nation-state in the near- to medium-term future. Therefore they support Option 2 types of proposals in the hope that economic development in general will *eventually* have a favorable impact upon income distribution and the problems of the poorest people in the developing countries. While "accelerated reform" supporters of this persuasion might try to slant many of the Option 2 reforms in the direction of *intra*national equity goals, they are willing to accept a good deal of "leakage" in the implementation of "poverty-oriented" reforms on the assumptions a) that Southern states will tolerate very little international or bilateral "intervention," and b) that deviations from strict implementation will simply reflect the power realities in the socio-political systems of specific developing countries.

2. *The Prudential Argument.* Those who support Option 2 from the point of view of prudent statesmanship make two assumptions. First, in their view, the developing countries *are* interested in economic development issues—increasingly so as unemployment and its accompanying tensions grow—even if, like all nations, they are also interested in status, power, and security. Therefore they feel that the Southern economic demands should be considered as serious economic issues rather than as simple proxies for greater "status" in the international system.

Second, they believe that Northern treatment of Southern economic demands as serious and negotiable issues will produce positive gains for multilateral diplomacy in general by easing the confrontational aspects of North-South relations. They argue that only this option's broad examination of international economic issues—with a bias toward the hope that *mutually* satisfactory responses to Southern demands *can* be found—will provide for that minimum degree of North-South amity needed to begin constructive work on the broad array of "global agenda" items which the United States will face in the coming decade.

Those who generally support the prudential argument also point to the fact that when the United States switched positions between the Sixth and Seventh Special Sessions of the U.N. General Assembly and pronounced itself ready to enter a period of serious examination of issues and negotiation, the "moderates" within the Southern bloc were able to resume leadership of that coalition and to begin a process of dialogue at a far lower decibel level and in a far more businesslike manner—a process that has now lasted for well over a year. These supporters of the accelerated reform option also note the progress which the Organization of African Unity made in moderating resolutions at the fall 1976 UNESCO conference on issues ranging from Israel to the treatment of the Northern press in developing countries. And the conclusion they draw from such disparate events, Mr. President, is that Northern unwillingness to even *examine* the economic issues relevant to the Option 2 approach is as much responsible for the current impasse in North-South relations as Southern "stridency."

3. *The Technical Economic Argument.* Finally, there is an element of support for the accelerated reform option's economic content that has *nothing* to do with normative choice and little to do with the age-old "statecraft" type of prudence discussed immediately above. Support of this type comes from those analysts of the economic issues raised by the recent NIEO debate and by the performance of the international economy since the early 1970s who are convinced that, if cast in the proper analytical framework, the examination of at least several major international economic issues can produce proposals for reforms that would prove to be of the "positive-sum" variety. That is, such reforms would benefit the developing countries at *no cost* to the developed countries and might in fact contain major *benefits* for the North as well. Since several examples already have been noted in discussing the contents of the option, they will not be repeated here. But one example might be cited that has not been mentioned: the potential inherent in several possible reforms for helping to control inflationary pressures in developed countries. Presume the development of a set of commodity schemes (not at all necessarily resembling the present UNCTAD package) which did moderate price fluctuations and did assure increased investment and access to supplies. Presume the development of a global food regime which smoothed price fluctuations and increased developing-country capacity for self-sufficiency in basic foodstuffs. And presume a trade negotiation which permitted increased access of competitive developing-country products into the markets of the OECD countries. Each of these measures, other things being equal, should have an anti-inflationary impact both globally and within the OECD countries.

None of the analysts supporting an "accelerated reform" approach is unaware of the slips which can and often do take place between an optimal economic blueprint and an internationally negotiated and implemented agreement. They are simply saying that the *potential* is there, if political systems can bring such blueprints to fruition.

Political Perspectives

Even less discussion of the "pros" is necessary here. Suffice it to say that each of the strands in the supportive arguments from the economic perspective presented above—the normative, the prudential, and the technical economic —has its political counterpart. Those supporters of Option 2 who argue the normative case feel that there is a morally reprehensible "political" gap as well as an economic one. They maintain that the developing countries deserve higher status and effective influence in the international system. They tend to focus their attention on existing decision-making patterns in international organizations and to suggest that the South be given far greater influence than it now has in these organizations. Some look at the tripartite OECD/OPEC/developing-country organization of the International Fund for Agricultural Development as a model applicable elsewhere. Others suggest considerable reforms in the existing weighted-voting arrangements, such as those of the IMF and the IBRD—reforms which might leave the OECD countries with only a slim majority. The result, of course, would be to increase the propensity of the OECD countries to consider developing-country proposals, since any split in OECD-country votes might deliver the developing countries a winning coalition.

The prudential strand is also obviously represented in the political perspective which supports Option 2. Again, it is based on the dual view that a) Southern cooperation is needed on many global issues which can only be managed optimally through multilateral diplomacy; and b) that the developing countries will respond on these issues with more of an eye to global needs if some progress is made on the narrower North-South front.

Finally, many of those who support the "accelerated reform" option on the basis of economic analysis rationales pay little attention to broader political questions. But to the extent that they do, many of them argue that the growing degrees of cooperation achieved in the economic arena will have a constructive impact on most other realms of North-South interaction.

Opposition to Option 2

Economic Perspectives

The two major arguments against the accelerated reform option from an economic perspective are captured in the following assertions:

(1) Economic reforms of the magnitude considered under this option are unnecessary, and
(2) Reforms of this type would undoubtedly prove to be harmful—certainly to developed countries, and most probably to developing countries as well.

Regarding the *first* point, most opponents of this option are likely to believe that the present international economic system is marked by a limited number of imperfections; that recent years have seen considerable progress in removing them (or, at least, in removing their aggregate bias against developing countries); and that continued progress of the "incremental reform" nature considered in Option 1 is more than sufficient to produce outcomes that meet both "developmental" needs and global economic needs. Proponents of this argument are likely to see the 1976 reforms of the IMF as an example of such a successful "global-developmental" mix.

The *second* assertion—that this option's economic ingredients would inevitably produce harmful outcomes—draws its support from three different sets of conjectures.

First, Option 2 opponents argue that the types of reforms contemplated would inevitably call forth an increasingly bureaucratized and politicized international economic system. An international deep seabed regime, a global fisheries regime, commodity agreements, and an international system of food reserves all require managers, no matter how much decentralization is built into such schemes. And no matter how deftly codes are written in order to limit interference with "free-market forces," there will be an inevitable tendency for the growing international bureaucracies (regional, domestic) that form a part of the new network to impinge upon these limitations as they seek to expand their tasks and to improve their bureaucratic performance.

Second, opponents assert that the very aims of most of the states entering such schemes—i.e., most if not all of the developing countries—will be in conflict with the aims of any regimes to which the OECD countries would become a part. Thus there would a built-in conflict from the outset that would guarantee either *failure* of the reforms themselves or a *misuse* of them by the developing countries. An obvious example of this danger can be discerned in the commodity agreements issue. Governmental leaders from most developing countries already have declared that one of the major purposes of such agreements is to *increase the price* of raw materials covered by such agreements with no reference to longer-term, market-trend forces. Developed countries for the most part have insisted that the role of commodity agreements should be limited to stabilizing prices around long-term market trends. Opponents of the accelerated reform option are concerned that such fundamental conflicts would tend to be papered over during the course of negotiations in which the North is searching for "constructive compromise" but would reappear after such arrangements had been constructed. At that point, they fear, the North would be faced with two alternatives, both unpalatable: 1) a failure and breakup of the agreements, or 2) further Northern compromises which eventually legitimize the "price-raising" goals of the developing countries. Either outcome would be likely to have serious adverse consequences: the first for North-South political relations; the second for the international economy.

Third, opponents of "accelerated reform" argue that the very step of beginning discussions on major reforms with a "bias toward hope" would place the United States at a severe bargaining disadvantage (thereby also jeopardizing reasonably optimal international economic reforms). The rationale is simple: not only would the United States face a remarkably "solid" South less interested in globally optimal reforms than in reforms which guarantee major gains for the South without regard for efficiency criteria; it would also face a divided OECD delegation unwilling (or unable) to bargain as a unit for the most sensible reform packages. Many European members of the OECD seem far more willing than the United States to accept reforms of dubious value to the global economy *or* to development progress in all countries simply because they are being demanded by the South. Hence the fear that Northern—not Southern—unity would crack during such negotiations, and perhaps at a considerable economic cost when measured against optimal reform schemes.

Political Perspectives

Not surprisingly, two of the three major arguments against the "accelerated reform" approach are mirror images of the arguments in favor of the "marginal change" option. The third is of an entirely different nature. The first argument stems from the fear that all attempts to "accommodate" Southern demands will simply produce a step-by-step escalation of Southern expectations. To the extent that these demands are as much a reflection of psychic needs and traditional desires for power and status as they are demands for economic reforms, this argument is difficult to refute in the aggregate.

The second argument in opposition to the accelerated reform approach reflects the fear that serious Northern consideration of developing-country demands will serve to legitimize the very Southern "bloc" tactics that have produced them. In other words, a serious negotiating response to the Group of 77 demands may be perceived as proof that when the developing countries act as a bloc, they significantly increase their capacity to influence the course of international events. Those who feel that these same bloc tactics have produced bottleneck after bottleneck in major "global agenda" negotiations —as well as a set of seriously suboptimal economic reform demands—argue that any constructive U.S. policy response that can be perceived as a direct result of such bloc demands would invite an escalation of "misdirected" Southern bloc activity.

Finally, a third and quite different argument against Option 2 notes the concern that the packages of reforms considered under the accelerated reform option are highly unlikely to be successfully negotiated and, even if negotiated, unlikely to be successfully implemented. The North will be looking for "mutual-benefit" (or "positive-sum") negotiating outcomes. The South may not object, as long as it gleans most of the "mutual" benefits produced by the reforms. More important, the South is much more likely to be looking for immediate gains, which are less likely to be found in "positive-sum" outcomes than in "zero-sum" outcomes. For example, the developing countries are likely to look for immediate resource transfers in the form of higher commodity prices, the issuance of Special Drawing Rights (SDRs) with an aid-SDR link, and debt moratoria.

Moreover, even if the negotiations are successful, implementation could prove to be very difficult within developed countries. Here the critics will describe in great detail the formidable *domestic constraints* facing the accelerated reform approach—particularly those posed by important elements of organized labor and industry. First, such agreements may fail to achieve legislative approval in the forms negotiated. Well-known precedents for such a prediction abound in the fields of trade and aid—in the form of domestic constraints on trade liberalization and on increased aid appropriations. Second, loopholes added to such reforms may cause serious Southern disappointments and exacerbated North-South conflict if they are used in ways that deprive developing countries of expected benefits.

Two types of examples might be cited to illustrate this problem. Developing-country access to the markets of the OECD countries is constantly in jeopardy of being limited through the use of domestic "escape clauses" within these countries. This is particularly true for those products which enter Northern markets under the Generalized System of Preferences (GSP). Thus the advantages of trade liberalization can be severely undermined as a result of political pressures *within* developed countries which governments may be unwilling or unable to overcome. The degree of importance given to this argument is related to assessments of the present strength of most Northern governments and their capacity to defeat such pressures.

The second type of implementation problem concerns "linkage politics" and "extraneous" events. In the past several years, Congress has tried increasingly to place "forgotten 40 per cent" and "human rights performance" strings on U.S. foreign aid programs. It has also barred the OPEC countries from access to trade preferences granted under the GSP program. There is little reason to think that such activities on the part of Congress will not continue.

Given these problems of negotiation and implementation, the opponents of Option 2 fear that an attempt as encompassing as that presented in an "accelerated reform" approach inevitably will result in major disappointments, further exacerbating rather than soothing North-South relations.

In summary, Mr. President, it is clear that the Option 2 "accelerated reform" approach is far more ambitious in scope and potential (for better or worse?) than the Option 1 "marginal change" approach. In a major sense, the former option suggests using the present North-South debate as an *opportunity* not only to examine and hopefully to resolve some conflict-ridden North-South issues but also to begin to assess the opportunities for establishing new global mechanisms that are perceived as needed on their own merits. For this reason alone the approach will win the interest—and perhaps support—of those analysts who agree with Stanley Hoffmann that the United States should seize the present opportunity to make "world order politics" the chief priority of U.S. foreign policy, arguing that a) there is no more important goal, b) there is no alternative, and c) it is a good moment. A not insignificant segment of the members of your own Administration probably will agree both with these sentiments, Mr. President, and with some major elements of the accelerated reform approach. I personally would hope that their views will be tempered by some of the insights coming from the proponents of the marginal change option and enriched by some of the normative concerns explicit and implicit in the third approach identified in this letter.

Option 3: U.S. Support of a "Basic Human Needs" Strategy of Economic Development

This option could be devised and implemented in a manner that made it a logically consistent adjunct to either of the first two options discussed; it could also contain a set of policies that made any such combination inconsistent. The determining factor would be the definitional content of the term "basic human needs" and the policies adopted to achieve the goals set forth in the option itself.

The basic human needs option discussed here will be one which will appear very conservative by comparison with some now in circulation (such as the already-mentioned Dag Hammarskjöld Foundation report or the Aspen Institute proposal for a "planetary bargain"). But the purpose of this letter is to focus attention on varying approaches to the problems of North-South relations that will be germane to the policy maker over the next eight years. Hence the option scrutinized in this section is one which is, in my view, defensible on both technical economic and normative grounds. It is also not so far beyond the realm of the feasible as to preclude consideration as a policy goal during the coming decade.

Option 3 focuses upon the problem of the most basic needs of the roughly one billion persons thought to be living in "absolute" poverty. Its immediate object is to analyze and propose various strategies to eradicate the global problem of extreme poverty, and its longer-term objective is to see that such a goal is achieved in a manner that gives the phrase "equality of opportunity" a substantive content that, while inevitably diluting the phrase itself, nevertheless lifts it far above the level of empty rhetoric. For purposes of brevity, the option will often be referred to simply as the "basic human needs" option.

What U.S. policies would constitute such an option? Perhaps they can best be delineated through a brief analysis of the problem they would be attempting to overcome.

Changing Dimensions of the Poverty Problem

Some 0.7-1.2 billion people in the world are presently subsisting in extreme poverty, caught in a vicious circle in which their levels of food consumption and its nutritional value lead to high levels of disease and infant mortality and to low levels of life expectancy. (The frequently cited 0.7 billion figure estimates the number of people in the developing countries who are "destitute"; it is also recognized, however, that another 0.5 billion people are surviving not much above this level. Given the short- to medium-term insurmountability of the definitional problems involved—conceptual as well as statistical—both the 0.7 billion and the 1.2 billion figures represent at best rough orders of magnitude.)

Contributing to the syndrome of extreme poverty are inadequate infrastructures for appropriate health, sanitation, and education programs. The end result in most cases is early death or, for those who survive, insufficient job opportunities to break out of this absolute poverty cycle. The most obvious symptoms of the problem would seem to be limitations on food and nutrition, health care systems, and educational opportunities. Of course, the list of symptoms can be expanded, together with the definition, to include, for example, shelter, clothing, and drinking water. Yet even this lengthier list is limited to minimum *physical* needs and does not begin to examine the broader issue of psychological needs.

The one essential need itemized that clearly is more than "physical" is basic education. It is generally included in the basic human needs approach because it is seen as a critical element in breaking the absolute poverty cycle. The assumption is that a minimum level of literacy will generally be required to enable individuals to take advantage of the employment opportunities that much also be presented if the problem of extreme poverty is to be overcome.

These employment opportunities must be produced—or at the least be *allowed*—by the development strategy chosen in each developing country. While the international system can and often does have a significant impact upon both prospects for and the relative success of differing development strategies, let us focus initially on the most fundamental link—that between domestic development strategy and opportunities for those who are living in extreme poverty.

In an effort to capsule approximately ten years of academic controversy in a few paragraphs, the following generalizations are offered without further apology for their monumental lack of nuance.

The general development strategies of the 1950s and 1960s placed their bets—and therefore their incentives—on limiting consumption, raising savings and investment rates as rapidly as possible, investing heavily in the protected "modern" sector of the economy, and concentrating government expenditures on "economic" rather than "social" overhead projects such as education, health, housing, and sanitation. They did so on the assumption that this strategy would ensure rapid economic growth, the benefits of which would in turn "trickle down" to the entire population in the form of growing per capita income. The costs to the poorest 40 per cent of the population in many countries that followed this "trickle-down" strategy have now become clear. Not only have the *relative* incomes and standards of living of this group decreased, sometimes markedly; considerable evidence even suggests that the *absolute* incomes of the bottom 10-20 per cent may have fallen.

The reason that the "trickle-down" strategy has produced such distributional results even in cases where it has also achieved commendable aggregate growth rates—for example in Mexico, where the average annual growth rate has exceeded 6 per cent in real terms for over thirty years—can be understood when one identifies the constituents of the "forgotten 40 per cent." The overwhelming majority of this large poverty group is rural in origin, composed of landless rural labor or of subsistence farm families. In the developing world as a whole, these rural groups constitute over 70 per cent of the poverty population. Obviously, a strategy of economic development that concentrates tax structures, commercial policies, and public expenditures on the development of a modern, capital-intensive, industrial sector does nothing of a direct nature to increase the development prospects for the rural poor. "Trickle-down" policies will affect such groups only as increased employment in the modern sector absorbs surplus labor (thus creating a situation in which rural wages may be expected to rise) and increases the urban demand for agricultural production. (The latter may also have the effect of raising rural wages, *unless* capital-intensive modes of agricultural production limit the use of rural labor and increase the concentration of landholding to the detriment of the country's smallest agricultural producers.) Much evidence suggests that, in developing countries following the "trickle-down" strategy, agriculture has become both more "extensive" *and* more capital-intensive, contributing directly to the falling relative incomes of the rural poverty groups.

The impact of the standard "trickle-down" strategy has produced similarly equivocal, if not detrimental, results for urban poverty groups—the unemployed, the underemployed, and the self-employed in the service sector and in the traditional manufacturing sector. The concentrated rewards to both capital and labor in the protected modern sector—resulting from limited competition, skewed prices of the factors of production favoring capital-intensive modes of production (despite average unemployment and underemployment rates of more than 30 per cent) and the development of a "labor aristocracy" within modern industries—have prevented the anticipated rapid absorption of the urban unemployed and the drawing down of excess labor reserves in the rural areas. These outcomes have thus severely limited the capacity of the modern sector to perform the function required for "trickle-down" to benefit an entire population.

To summarize, the "standard" development strategy of the past two decades emphasized rapidly increased investment and employment in the *modern* sector of industry financed by the savings from that sector's newly generated income. It generally limited its agricultural concerns to the production of commercial crops to feed urban populations and earn foreign exchange. The explicit or implicit premise of this development strategy was that it would produce significantly higher rates of savings and investment than alternative strategies, and that the growth of the modern manufacturing sector would eventually ease whatever unemployment problems were developing in rural areas and traditional urban sectors as a result of the concentration of incentives in the modern sector.

Even in countries where this policy approach has succeeded in *aggregate growth terms*, it has generally failed by all *equity* measures for several reasons. First, and in many ways foremost, with only a few exceptions, rates of growth in employment in the modern sector have been very disappointing. In some countries, such as Mexico, they have exceeded population growth rates, but not by enough to limit rising rates of urban and rural unemployment. In many other countries, labor absorption in the modern sector has hardly done more than keep pace with population growth.

A second reason, intimately related to the first, is that living conditions in rural areas have often deteriorated for landless laborers and subsistence farmers. A policy which concentrated rewards almost exclusively in the *modern* sector (and, to a degree, in commercial agriculture), without producing high rates of labor absorption in that sector, inevitably contributed to a steady deterioration of living standards for these two rural groups. Only a comprehensive strategy of rural development, including family planning, could have produced different results. Without such a strategy, conditions for the poorest segments in rural areas were bound to deteriorate, if only because rural population growth rates in the developing countries have averaged close to 2.5 per cent annually.

A third indicator of failure is that the urban poor—the unemployed and major segments of the service and traditional manufacturing sectors —have benefited little from the "trickle-down" approach. In simplified terms, the major reason has been that while output per worker has grown faster in the modern than in the traditional sector, the modern sector has not grown significantly as a proportion of the total labor force. Contributing to this phenomenon have been the emerging political power of unionized labor in the modern sector, the resort within it to capital-intensive technology, and inappropriate governmental policies which encouraged such development (e.g., subsidized credit, overvalued exchange rates for capital-goods imports, and high degrees of protection). Thus the traditional manufacturing and service sectors have also paid a price in terms of relative deprivation for the standard "trickle-down" strategy.

The Emergence of a Basic Human Needs Strategy

The overall results of the "trickle-down" growth strategy have, as already noted, led a growing number of governments, economists, and aid practitioners to examine alternative approaches to the problems of economic development in the past several years. While it would certainly be an exaggeration to suggest that anything approaching unanimity exists concerning all the major ingredients of a new approach, it would not be misleading to suggest that a general consensus does seem to be emerging on

63

several conceptual issues that might well provide the major impetus for significant changes in development strategies.

One can conceptualize the newly emerging approach—which attempts to maximize *employment* as well as growth—as having four major ingredients: 1) a strategy for rural development, 2) a strategy for urban development, 3) a strategy for the training and education of both men and women, and 4) a strategy for population stabilization.

A strategy for rural development designed to meet the goals of increased employment, fewer cases of extreme poverty, and greater equity in income distribution would ideally entail significant changes in: a) land tenure, b) access to agricultural production inputs in addition to land, c) increased expenditures on rural public works projects, and d) increasing rural access to health and educational facilities. In many countries, land reform is both the key to the success of the rural strategy and its most formidable political obstacle.

Like its rural counterpart, the new strategy for urban development would attempt to achieve two related goals: to overcome some of the past deficiencies of over-rewarding growth in the modern sector, and to undertake a new set of policies to increase employment in the traditional urban sectors and gradually transfer some assets to the poor in order to improve their longer-term life chances. It now seems generally agreed that in all but the most exceptional developing countries, continued reliance on a capital-intensive expansion of the modern sector to solve the urban poverty problem will produce disappointing results. Skepticism concerning the capacity of the modern sector to absorb the already excessive urban labor force is based on present rates of urbanization (often in excess of 4 per cent per year), the small share of the modern sector in total urban employment, and the generally low opportunities for job creation through modern-sector growth.

A good deal of thinking is now being devoted to the general question of human resource development. The emphasis is on the provision of adequate levels of education (formal, informal, on-the-job training, etc.), nutrition, and health to enable entire populations—both men and women—to contribute to economic development within a policy framework that is geared to provide increasing job opportunities. The rural and urban strategies noted previously are essentially designed to expand employment opportunities; both strategies imply increased access by the poor in all areas of the country to primary-education and health facilities, with greater emphasis on preventive medicine, postnatal care, and nutrition. The provision of such facilities not only creates jobs in the initial construction phase; the completed facilities themselves are part of the asset-transfer process whereby the poor develop an enhanced capacity to increase their standard of living by *their own efforts* and rise above extreme poverty levels. It is worth underscoring this point by noting the conclusion of a recent World Bank study:

The design of a poverty-oriented strategy requires the selection of a mix of policy instruments that can reach the target groups that have been identified. While we advocate maximum use of instruments that operate through factor and product markets, often they will not be sufficient for this purpose. We have therefore given particular attention to a range of direct measures, such as land reform, the distribution of education, and other public services, and measures to redistribute assets toward the poverty groups. Without such a redistribution of at least the increments of capital formation, other distributive measures are not likely to have a lasting impact on the poverty problem.

The reason for including a strategy for population stabilization in the new development perspective goes well beyond the demonstrated demand for birth control facilities. Some proponents are primarily concerned about the ecological capacity of the globe to absorb population increases which at present rates double the world's population every thirty-five years (or, more dramatically stated, lead to a sevenfold increase over a century). Others are more specifically concerned with the effect of high population growth rates on the poorest strata of the population in the developing world; they reason that a labor force growing faster than employment opportunities in most developing countries leads to lower wages, increasing unemployment, greater fragmentation of miniscule agricultural landholdings, increasing numbers of landless rural laborers, and fewer social infrastructure expenditures to give the poor access to basic health and educational facilities.

Finally, there are those proponents of population control policies who emphasize a more subtle argument—that high birth rates in developing countries are a *reflection* of poverty and exaggerated income inequality and that birth rates will fall as a consequence of the successful implementation of the other development strategies sketched above.

Thus the four major elements of this alternative strategy of economic development close the circle. Its proponents start with the hypothesis that a new mix of policy priorities can achieve much greater productive employment and a much more equitable pattern of income distribution than was achieved in the 1950s and 1960s—but with little sacrifice in rates of economic growth. From this base flow logical policy prescriptions for coping with the problems of rural and urban poverty and unemployment. Inherent in such prescriptions are efforts to slowly redistribute incremental assets to the poorest strata of society, providing them with access to long-term benefits from continued economic growth. Among such proposed asset transfers are health and educational infrastructure expenditures to bring to the poor those forms of health and nutritional care, family planning services, and education most relevant to their needs; in most cases these are the least expensive forms—for example, preventive medicine via paramedics, and primary rather than secondary and college education. Finally, the creation of more jobs, rising levels of literacy, and health standards which lower infant mortality rates are perceived to lead to changing views on optimal family size and to gradually lowering fertility rates within the target groups of the new strategy.

U.S. Policies

Against this background, Option 3 would place primary emphasis upon the development and implementation of a set of U.S. policies that would give maximum assistance to those developing countries attempting to eliminate the most debilitating aspects of poverty problems along the general lines suggested by the above analysis. These policies would pay particular attention to a) the short-term problems of food supply and nutrition, health, and education; and b) the longer-term problem of ensuring that the so-called "asset-transfer" mechanism would gradually provide the "forgotten 40 per cent" with enough owned resources and assets to enable them to acquire their basic needs *through their own enhanced capabilities.*

If the longer-term solution were to fail, Mr. President, "equality of opportunity" would indeed prove to be a cynical, empty phrase. If it succeeded, "equality of opportunity" would still face all the conceptual and empirical problems of definition and fulfillment that it does in Northern states; but only a fool or an idealogue of the most committed sort could then deny that major progress in alleviating the worst forms of physical poverty had been made.

The number of policy arenas and the actual substance of each component of this "basic human needs" policy would to a large extent be determined by the choice of U.S. approach: unilateral action, joint OECD action, or "global" action.

The United States might choose to implement such an option unilaterally, in which case its efforts on behalf of the "basic human needs" approach probably would be limited to the field of foreign aid. The problems encountered in any other arena through this unilateral approach would be monumental; even the potential room for unilateral action in the field of tariff preferences has already been limited by their *general* nature. To start advancing and withholding them on the basis of a developing country's commitment to a basic human needs strategy probably would have a net negative effect on the very goals of the option itself.

Hence, if approached unilaterally, the basic human needs option would consist of developing aid policy packages that would be available to governments interested in them. The major "strings" would simply be performance criteria tied to the acceptance of U.S. funding for such programs (e.g., in the areas of rural development, health, and education). Countries which were prepared to invest in such programs would be eligible for U.S. economic aid funds; those which were not prepared to do so would not receive them. No valid charge of internal "intervention" could be raised, since only countries requesting funds on their own initiative would have to measure up to performance criteria.

If the policy were launched jointly with other OECD countries, this would more than double the potential magnitude of funds available for its implementation. The trade-off for the United States would be some loss of "authority" over its own official development assistance transfers in return for a greater source of funds (and potential leverage) for the Option 3 approach *and* a lower degree of visibility vis-à-vis individual developing countries that would be requesting such funds not from any individual Northern state, but from the OECD countries as a group.

Finally, the United States might attempt to achieve an even broader consensus for major elements in such an approach by sounding out the possibilities for a *joint* North-South acceptance of the basic human needs approach. Any such attempt would have to surmount two major hurdles, to say nothing of a host of minor ones. The two major hurdles consist of 1) the bill the North would be asked to pick up if such a program were to be accepted with *any promise of success* within developing countries, and 2) the easy-to-predict insistence of the middle-income developing countries that any consideration of the basic human needs approach be linked directly to Northern acceptance of an expansive (and potentially expensive) "accelerated reform" option responsive to the demands of the Third World countries.

Concerning the price tag on the "basic human needs" option, one sentence will be allowed for numbers, since the present state of research in the topic merits no more. Let it simply be stated that two estimates resulting from different approaches and methodologies suggest that absolute poverty could be virtually ended within ten to fifteen years at a cost of $125 billion (in 1973 dollars); and that an asset-transfer policy to assure the "forgotten 40 per cent" of a firm floor above that level in the future might cost approximately $250 billion. Now to the important political issue: Who pays the piper—the developing countries themselves, the Northern countries concerned with the problem (if only normatively), or some combination of the two? *If* there were an absolute minimum of "leakage," and *if* the available estimates are at all meaningful, we are talking about an annual cost of $10-$13 billion per year (in constant dollars) for the next fifteen to twenty-five years, depending on the thoroughness of the job. A glance at the latest figure of $13.6 billion for the annual flow of official development assistance (ODA) from the member states of the OECD's Development Assistance Committee shows that ODA alone could *more than cover* the cost of implementing this option's "basic human needs" approach if the great portion of it were devoted to its objectives and if the above conditions were met. This is a very big "if," considering that over 50 per cent of ODA is presently being allocated to middle-income countries and for programs unrelated to the goals of the basic human needs option.

It is also obvious that the same achievements theoretically *could* be financed from within the developing countries without *any* North-South transfer whatsoever. The World Bank has estimated that a 2 per cent annual transfer from the upper classes to the bottom 40 per cent of the populations of the developing countries could successfully finance both the short-term and the long-term goals of the strategy over a twenty-five year period.

Two per cent of annual developing-country GNP today approximates $10 billion. Stated this way, the annual transfer sounds manageable. It sounds less manageable when one considers that 2 per cent of GNP is equal to 10-20 per cent of total government revenues in most developing countries. In order to transfer that 2 per cent to the poor via new investment programs, either taxes (or other forms of government revenue) would have to be significantly raised, or major cutbacks would have to be made in present government programs. The adoption of either course would guarantee dissent of varying proportion from those domestic groups currently favored by tax profiles and government expenditure programs.

The *domestic* asset-transfer strategy seems even less practicable in the case of the poorest countries. In these countries, where per capita incomes average about $150 (at official exchange-rate terms, which do produce misleadingly low dollar figures), the changes in tax and expenditure programs needed to eliminate absolute poverty within twenty-five years would be far greater than those implied in the preceding discussion of aggregate developing-country averages.

Thus the "basic human needs" option inevitably arrives at the political constraint that confronts any ambitious "attack on poverty" program. In this context, it is worth quoting the reaction of Pranab K. Bardhan to the World Bank's proposed strategy mix:

> The problems of poverty in India remain intractable, not because redistribution objectives were inadequately considered in the planning models, nor because the general policies of the kind prescribed in this volume were not attempted . . . the major constraint is rooted in the power realities of a political system dominated by a complex constellation of forces representing rich farmers, big business, and the so-called petite bourgeoisie, including the unionized workers of the organized sector. In such a context, it is touchingly naive not to anticipate the failures of asset distribution policies or the appropriation by the rich of a disproportionate share of the benefits of public investment.

One rather obvious conclusion following from the above considerations is that the likelihood of a major movement within a large number of developing countries toward the comprehensive development strategy outlined earlier may depend *very significantly* upon the degree to which the world's developed countries share the costs, thereby easing the political constraints on such an approach. Is it realistic to expect such cost-sharing to be forthcoming in the foreseeable future?

The second major problem concerns the *inevitable* Southern linkage of a basic human needs option with *their own version* of an Option 2 approach—for obvious reasons. First, it is basically the Fourth World (particularly the Asian subcontinent) which would benefit from Option 3 in any intercountry comparative sense. The Third World, with smaller populations in the absolute poverty range, has *comparatively* less to gain from such a strategy; indeed, some could be net losers if other forms of aid which they had formerly received were dropped in the transition to the new approach. Second, comparative benefits aside, *any* Northern proposals along the lines of Option 3 would be met by the insistence of the more advanced developing countries on major reforms along the NIEO lines as a quid pro quo. This is simply to be expected as an everyday part of the present system of North-South linkage politics.

A final observation should be made on the potential connection between the "accelerated reform" option and the "basic human needs" option: the linkage concept is reversible. If the developed countries were to agree upon some form of an Option 2 position, *they* could also demand a linkage, in this case to the goals of a basic human needs policy as presented in Option 3.

But what if that link ended up costing the North an additional $7-$10 billion more per year than present ODA transfers? Three responses would be made by supporters of Option 3. In the first place, that additional amount would already be available if the OECD countries alone were achieving the 0.7 per cent ODA figure accepted by most of them as part of the international strategy for the Second U.N. Development Decade (quite apart from the contributions already and potentially available from the OPEC countries). Second, in the view of Option 3 supporters, the global acceptance of this strategy would in effect be a *major step* toward the consolidation of a positive, new international norm in an era which could sorely use one. It would involve a commitment to virtually eliminate absolute poverty *globally* within a generation; assigning this objective *first claim* on all international aid funds; and *global* negotiation of and agreement to this goal. Finally, they would argue that an additional $7-$10 billion a year split among all the OECD countries is a small sum if it can come close to achieving its major purpose: the elimination of absolute poverty and the rehabilitation of the notion that "equality of opportunity" is not an empty promise after all.

In the above discussion of the elements of a basic human needs option, the always-strained distinction between economic and political policies has been dropped, as it will be in the discussion of pros and cons below. In both instances the reason is the same. Without fuller exploration of the option, it is unclear, beyond the most general level, what the *economic* policy content would be; and without negotiations actually under way it is difficult to discern the *specific* political goals as well. The overwhelming reason is that this option, unlike the first two, is less concerned with interstate issues of either an economic or a political nature. For better or worse, its focus is on people, and its support comes not from reasons of economic efficiency, interstate equity, or realpolitik but rather—again for better or worse—from an expression of individual value preferences generally freed from such considerations.

Support for Option 3

The briefs in favor of the basic human needs option are all likely to be filled with economic, political, and prudential supportive arguments that are all somewhat unconvincing. Typical of the economic arguments is the often repeated claim that the development strategy implicit in this option need not cost anything in terms of foregone growth. All one can say about this argument at present is that much more empirical work is needed for the claim to be convincingly substantiated, although the lesser point—that many economists have probably greatly exaggerated the potential GNP growth costs of such a strategy—is well taken and should send committed "trickle-down" proponents back to the drawing boards.

A typical supportive argument in the political category maintains that more and more people throughout the North and the South agree that a basic human needs strategy is appropriate and that its success would be likely if only the United States were prepared to support it. This argument displays the passionate advocacy of the strategy by a small elite group (90 per cent Northern in composition) committed to the principles of greater global equity with an emphasis on the interpersonal equity theme; it does *not* capture an emerging view among the vast majority of Southern *or* Northern elite groups. Indeed, as argued below, it is the outright opposition to the implementation of such a strategy by Southern elites that poses one of the *major* obstacles to the strategy as propounded essentially in the North.

Finally, a typical prudential argument in favor of the strategy suggests that it is the only way to make substantial progress in slowing population growth rates in the near future. This argument exemplifies the willingness of this strategy's proponents to generalize from a slim data base. They may well be right in suggesting a causal relationship between a significant increase in minimum standards of living and the coming of a "demographic transition" to lower population growth rates. But the evidence is partial, the theoretical framework incomplete, and the proclaimed relationship still controversial.

Leaving aside such supporting political and economic arguments, the "basic human needs" approach would seem to stand or fall on three normative notions. First, raising the living standards of the world's poorest billion persons from their present abysmal levels is a goal worthy enough not to need the support of further economic, political, or prudential reasoning. Second, if this goal is achieved through a strategy that does produce a partial redistribution of assets—of even a minimal nature—to these billion people, *permanent economic opportunities* will be opend up to them and their children that clearly distinguish this basic human needs approach from a "dole"—domestic or international. At the end of a twenty-five year period, what will have been achieved is a *structural change* in developing countries that has the effect of establishing a *permanently rising floor* under basic human needs. And third, the present opportunity to solidify this potential global norm conceptually, to negotiate it internationally, and to implement it institutionally is one which combines a high probability of low-risk failure with a low probability of success—but one that contains an extremely high payoff for the United States, for North-South relations, and for all "global agenda" issues if success is achieved.

Opposition to Option 3

Why must the "basic human needs" option be given a high probability of failure? While endless reasons might be cited, briefly focusing on five of them should serve to exemplify the hurdles which such a strategy would have to clear in order to have any chance of success.

Feasibility: The Southern Elite Problem

Will a set of policies which, in the medium-to-long term are bound to reduce the socio-economic status, political power, and relative economic position of most developing-country elite groups—even if these reductions are slow and incremental—ever be accepted and implemented by most developing countries? Many strongly doubt the possibility. The entire "dependencia" school of analysis would deny the possibility, as would many Northern and Southern observers of different persuasions. Let me quote one distinguished "Southerner," Mahbub ul Haq, who makes the point quite strongly:

> Fundamental institutional reforms are, in fact, the essence of new development strategies. At the heart of these reforms is a change in the existing control over the means of production and access to key services. Normally, the rich exercise enormous economic power within these systems because they control most of the means of production in the society, such as land and capital. That is why land reforms and public ownership of major industries have become the key elements in any institutional reforms. But these reforms can easily become a whitewash, and have, in many societies. Unless there is the necessary political will, it is impossible to change the established relationship between the owners of the means of production and those who have been perpetually denied these resources. What normally happens in many societies is that the governments nationalize a number of industries, banks, and some key services, like education and health, and they place these industries and public services in the hands of the

bureaucrats or the same interest groups as before. It is not surprising, therefore, that these reforms amount to mere tokenism and not any real restructuring of society. This is really what has happened in a good part of South Asia, where the bureaucracy or the landlords or the industrialists have readily and enthusiastically embraced all the symbols and slogans of socialism.

Haq adds the obvious point that it may take entirely new political alliances to implement basic human needs strategies in these countries, and ends by noting that the restructuring of economic and political power needed to implement the policy at the local level "cannot happen without a mass movement or a popular revolution." Even if Haq's analysis of the requirements may be overstated—for example, if the income transfers to finance the new programs consist largely of Northern official development assistance—the problem he poses cannot be underplayed without inviting a global charade at the expense of the poorest people in the South and the taxpayers in the North as well as growing domestic and international cynicism about the "egalitarian" content of all economic assistance programs negotiated by governing elites, North *and* South (shades of the Alliance of Progress).

Feasibility: The Northern Elite Problem

As Haq's remarks suggest, a basic human needs strategy could not succeed without major changes in development strategies; such changes would almost inevitably shake elite structures in developing countries, and one result of the attempt might be "mass movements" and "popular revolution." While I personally think this characterization exaggerates the "revolutionary" possibilities, it is obvious that the probability of sudden and uncontrolled political changes—mostly likely with a large degree of political mobilization in rural areas—would be increased if and as major changes were made in development strategies.

What would be the reaction of Northern governing groups and business elites to such forms of change? Opponents of Option 3 would focus much criticism on the potential political instability presumably introduced by it, arguing that, for both tactical and strategic reasons, other U.S. foreign policy goals would be ill-served by what they are likely to characterize as a risk-prone strategy. Many members of the U.S. business community would be likely to oppose this option on two grounds. First, they might fear that it could produce a degree of instability in developing countries "incompatible" with good business conditions. Second, they might perceive the strategy to be at least marginally less lucrative for many multinational corporations as they presently operate in highly protected developing-country markets. The issue of more "appropriate" factor pricing might call into question a large number of production processes applied by such companies, and the combined impact of fiscal, monetary, and balance-of-payments policies associated with the new development strategies might limit established developing-country markets for many products of multinational corporations.

Thus opposition to serious support for Option 3 can be expected from elements within both governmental and business circles.

The "Intervention" Issue

Critics of the "basic human needs" approach will be quick to argue that, for one of two reasons, the option will fail to achieve its purposes. First, if such a program—whether unilateral, OECD, or global—is *not administered* in a way which *ensures* that the target populations of this strategy do receive the benefits promised, the program (like many domestic "poverty" programs) will fail. Most of the financial assistance will be skimmed off by those (ranging from major political figures to petty local landlords) who control the political, economic, and social points of leverage in developing countries. On the other hand, *if* an administrative scheme or organization is devised which is truly capable of monitoring program performance, most developing countries will refuse to allow the degree of "intervention" in domestic affairs necessary to carry out the monitoring function.

Either way, opponents of Option 3 will argue, the program would fail. Without some serious form of bilateral or international monitoring of a basic human needs program, "leakage effects" would be enormous. Even if enough were to get through to the target populations to give them a bit more food and a few more health clinics, the outcome would be the worst of all possible solutions—a global "welfare program" which did absolutely nothing to achieve any *permanent structural change* or anything approaching "equality of opportunity." Conversely, if a serious monitoring system were devised and access to developing countries to measure performance were made a *sine qua non* of access to the program's resources, very few developing countries would join. To make matters worse, protests against "neocolonial interventionism" would once again echo through the corridors of every North-South meeting place, limiting the amount of "serious business" which might otherwise be accomplished.

The "Global Agenda" Perspective

As implied above, some critics of Option 3 will suggest that the raising of the extremely sensitive domestic issues which are inevitably part of the "basic human needs" approach—income distribution, choices among development strategies, and the potential impact of discussions of these issues on domestic political structures and coalitions within developing countries—are far more likely to exacerbate North-South tensions than to relieve them. If this is the case, it could become increasingly difficult to get on with what present jargon (thus far euphemistically) refers to as "the management of interdependence." Like it or not, governing elites in the South control the degree of progress in this management exercise, as do their Northern counterparts.

Pushing very hard for Option 3 would be likely to prove counterproductive from the "global agenda" perspective.

The Human Rights Issue

The more sophisticated critics will point out that the problem potentially most difficult to deal with in the approach has not yet been raised in this discussion. This problem is the often implicit, and sometimes explicit, linkage between the "basic human needs" approach and the issue of "human rights." From a *Northern* point of view, such a linkage seems hardly surprising. After all, Option 3 is nothing if not a reflection of norms and value preferences which are generally compatible with Western culture. And when those informed by Western cultural influences focus on *individuals*, as they do when they think of a basic human needs strategy, they reflexively turn their attention to the broader issue of human rights as delineated in the historical evolution of Western culture. Therefore it is no surprise to hear the Northern authors of the most far-reaching set of Option 2 and Option 3 proposals—for example, the authors of the Dag Hammarskjöld Foundation's report cited earlier—add that *no country* which does not observe (undefined) basic human rights should be eligible for the benefits of the international economic and political reforms they advocate.

If *Southern* cultures were congruent with their Western counterpart on the definition and the ordering of human rights as a value in the hierarchy of cultural values, adding human rights to the baggage carried under Option 3 would be of little policy consequence. But as anyone who follows these issues knows, and as *all* the critics of Option 3 will note, the present North-South split on the "human rights issue," however defined (and the *lack* of a common definition is the heart of the problem), threatens to become an abyss. Therefore, the critics will observe, if the first four reasons for opposing Option 3 haven't done it in, this fifth argument should complete the case against a serious effort to implement the "basic human needs" option. To spotlight human rights problems and to potentially constrain policy options on *all other foreign policy issues* involving the United States on the one hand, and one or more developing countries on the other, is a price which, regardless of the commitment to human rights in principle, the United States *cannot* afford.

The arguments against a basic human needs strategy are quite compelling, Mr. President. They suggest that, if taken seriously, the option will definitely run into major domestic and international hurdles. At best, these opposing arguments would seem to leave open a "mini-option" in which the United States postured in favor of the approach by adopting the *absolute minimum* within the option—by allocating most U.S. official development assistance to countries which claimed to have programs reaching those target populations which it pronounced itself to be interested in assisting.

I dislike the thought that a presentation of Option 3 along the above lines will be all that you receive, Mr. President, but that is a distinct possibility. As you have perhaps already discovered, every time you personally speak of "the increasing effort to preserve human rights," some critic or other—even one as gifted with insight into American foreign policy and the present state of international relations as Stanley Hoffmann—will sadly warn you that, "alas, there are many reasons why a crusade for democracy and basic rights is neither feasible nor desirable." And thus runs the very best of conventional wisdom.

This being the case, Mr. President, let me turn to a conclusion which is either unwise, or unconventional, or both. And from here on, the "options paper" conventions are dropped; for better or worse, it's all editorial.

A U.S. Policy for North-South Relations

Let me first outline as simply as possible a set of policy proposals, and then, in closing, attempt a short defense against the most obvious criticisms that can be raised against such a seemingly ambitious package.

The Proposed Policy Package

1. Give immediate consideration to those incremental economic and institutional reforms which are in keeping with the "marginal change" approach of Option 1 (without precluding Options 2 and 3) and which can be offered as signs of constructive intent during the first several months of your Administration. Should there be a CIEC ministerial meeting in the spring of 1977, it will undoubtedly prove to be too early to have given adequate consideration to a broader range of economic responses to Southern demands and the potential political implications of those responses.

2. Begin as promptly as possible the analytical and policy analysis suggested by the contents of the "accelerated reform" approach of Option 2—maintaining close contact with our OECD partners as this process of analysis is under way in order to produce the broadest degree of agreement on the theoretical and policy merits of all potential reforms. Try to rank-order the reforms under consideration in the following manner:

(a) Reforms with a high probability of producing "positive-sum" results for the global economy (e.g., a global food regime, a global fisheries regime);
(b) Reforms which may *not* actually benefit the developed countries in a tangible economic sense over the short-to-medium term, but which seem to have a high potential for assisting the development process (e.g., reforms to encourage the development of processing industries, agricultural production, and relevant technology research and development in the South);

(c) Reforms of either the (a) or (b) nature which contain the greatest potential for assisting the poorest people, particularly in the Fourth World (e.g., schemes to obtain additional financing for the World Bank's soft-loan window and the IFAD).

3. At the same time, begin a similar analytical and policy exercise examining the broadest and most comprehensive set of policies imaginable under the *limited approach* to the "basic human needs" problem outlined under Option 3. As soon as it is deemed feasible, consider the possibility of conducting this particular effort in conjunction with our OECD associates in an attempt to determine a) the potential degree of Northern commitment to such a goal; b) estimates of funding which the OECD might provide for such a program; and c) estimates of the domestic feasibility limitations on such OECD support. How much money could Northern legislatures and parliaments be expected to provide for such a program? On what kinds of oversight mechanisms might governments reach agreement? How willing would various OECD governments be to pledge support for a program facing many serious pitfalls?

4. Unless the discussions with other OECD countries concerning Option 3 measures reveal serious limitations on Northern cohesion, approach the developing countries with the following proposals:

(1) The OECD countries are prepared to undertake serious North-South negotiations on those areas of international economic reform capable of producing joint gains.

(2) With the exception of such areas, the OECD countries are not prepared to negotiate seriously on other "accelerated reform" proposals *unless* the developing countries as a group are prepared to begin simultaneous negotiations on the issues and policy proposals encompassed by the "basic human needs" option.

Rationale

The proposal may seem to disregard some of the most compelling arguments offered in support of the "marginal change" approach of Option 1. However, those arguments *can be accommodated* if the Option 2 approach of "accelerated reform" is accepted and implemented in the appropriate manner. First, only those reforms which are capable of producing mutual gains should be negotiated without further conditions. If the analytical and policy "homework" is good, the results should withstand sharp scrutiny from all relevant perspectives: economic, political, normative, and prudential. Second, if other reforms which are not "balanced" are to be negotiated, they will require a different sort of quid pro quo from the developing countries: namely, a simultaneous negotiation on the basic human needs "basket."

While the insistence on hard bargaining based on the best possible analytical preparation may slightly ease the concerns of the Option 1 supporters, it is likely to be a cause of concern to the strong advocates of Option 2, especially those who display signs of the "all good things go together" syndrome. The latter undoubtedly will pose two serious questions, in ascending order of importance:

(1) Why limit the probabilities of a successful adoption of Option 2 by failing to embrace it without constraints?
(2) Why link it in its broader form to progress on the basic human needs issues, which will greatly complicate an already difficult set of negotiations?

The *first question* is more easily answered than the second. To embrace the accelerated reform option without constraints is to magnify the risks that critics see in it from the start, e.g., that one set of demands will follow another ad infinitum. Rhetorically, this will be the case however Option 2 issues are handled. But beneath the rhetoric, there is much to be gained by establishing a mutual awareness that there are *distinct limits* to what developing countries can expect of North-South negotiations. Perhaps the most important is that, "joint gain" reforms aside, the developing countries must be prepared to pay a price for each benefit received. Sometimes the price may be very modest and demanded so that Northern negotiators can present a package to their legislators which smacks of interest-group "symmetry": one Northern interest group paid a price, another Northern group benefited. Sometimes the price will relate to the scope of a negotiation—that is, to a coverage of both Northern and Southern concerns with regard to a particular issue area. An example of this sort might be the old "access to supply" and "access to markets" linkage. If the developing countries refuse to recognize the legitimacy of such Northern bargaining goals, then it is just as well that the "accelerated reform" option fail—and fail early, before many irreversible trends have been set in motion. But there is no preponderance of evidence to make us think that Option 2 *need* fail. The developing countries are most often represented by experienced negotiators who understand the need for various forms of symmetry and for "balanced packages."

The *second question*, and the one so very difficult to deal with in a few pages, concerns the proposed linkage of Option 2 and Option 3. Why tie the basic human needs (and inevitably the human rights) albatross to an otherwise potentially viable accelerated reform approach, which would seem to merit at least an intense scrutiny over the next several years?

The answers are three. First, if assessed in an eight-year time frame, the aggregate impact of the five major obstacles to the "basic human needs" approach identified in the discussion of Option 3 above may well prove to be exaggerated. Second, this may be one of those few areas of international relations where a negotiation, even in the *process* of failing, could produce more benefits than costs. And finally, the cost of not making the attempt might be greater than the cost of failure.

Are the Obstacles Insurmountable?

The first obstacle noted—the *Southern elite issue*—offers an interesting example of the kind of exaggeration that may be taking place. Those who emphasize this obstacle argue that economic and political elites in the South would never support a basic human needs strategy, essentially because it would tend to undermine their present position in developing-country status and power hierarchies. Yet one suspects that with each passing year the case for a basic human needs strategy *gains* adherents among segments of Southern elites. With birth rates in excess of 2 per cent, with open and disguised unemployment rates running from 25 per cent upward, with increasing international constraints (debt, export demand) on domestic economic growth, and with governing institutions exhibiting serious weaknesses within many developing countries, one begins to wonder how governing elites in many developing countries would respond during the course of a "closed door" North-South negotiation in which the following "bottom line" proposition were tabled:

> The OECD countries intend to put 75 per cent of their official development assistance into "basic human needs" programs within four years. They will also raise ODA levels to 0.5 per cent of GNP for the OECD countries as a whole. Thus the funds for this new set of programs will total $25 billion (in current dollar terms) by 1980. This money will be administered by an Agency over whose policies *no single member country* will have a veto power. Developing countries that wish to have access to these funds will have to meet standardized performance criteria to be negotiated between the Agency and all recipient countries.

How would an "average" developing country respond to such a challenge? Fourth World governments, unless they had chosen the extreme "self-reliance" route, could not help being interested in the prospects of access to a *very significant increase* in a) desperately needed foreign exchange, and b) resources on a scale well above what political constraints would permit them to achieve through domestic tax reforms. Unless the performance criteria and the degree of intervention tied to the use of these funds were so ethnocentrically and ostentatiously Northern as to be unbearable, negotiations might begin rather quickly.

As for Third World countries, consider the following case. An elite group has presided over forty years of growth at better than 6 per cent per year in a country which, among developing countries, is highly industrialized. The elite group's politics are highly institutionalized and it faces no serious organized political opposition. Yet the same set of international economic constraints noted above has hurt it rather severely. Despite the country's growth performance, the "forgotten 40 per cent" of its population is relatively, if not absolutely, worse off than four decades ago. Birth rates are close to 3 per cent; unemployment exceeds 25 per cent, and for the first time in decades, the political "system" shows signs of fragility. What would the governing elite of this developing country think about a potentially significant new source of foreign exchange to help finance programs it has been promising to its constituents and gradually attempting to implement?

The point is simple. If elites are in firm control and unconcerned about potential socio-political disruptions from the bottom deciles of their society, then the "basic human needs" option faces a Southern elite problem. But what if the elite (itself increasingly disparate due to the very process of development) is feeling less and less certain of its position, and sees that a restructuring of some significant government spending programs and fiscal incentives might provide access to fairly substantial international funding —and, not incidentally, an extended lease on its privileged position? Will the implication that, fifteen to twenty years hence, their socio-economic and political status will have been somewhat undercut produce a "let them eat cake" response, or an interest in a serious negotiation? The proposal's linkage of the acceptance of the basic human needs strategy to the accelerated reform approach of Option 2 should increase their interest.

My personal opinion is that, if the OECD countries *were* to act as a group, and *were* to pledge a figure anywhere near $20 billion per year by 1980 to a basic human needs program, one could anticipate the beginnings of a serious negotiation. All the analytical, definitional, and "performance" problems would remain to be resolved, as would such matters as the nature of the international agency chosen to disburse the funds and measure performance. But a *serious negotiation* would have begun—and with it, hopefully, a *joint effort* to resolve the delicate balance between domestic sovereignty and international oversight.

I see the same room for progress on the *Northern elite issue*. There already is a strong movement within many Northern legislative bodies toward limiting ODA to programs focusing on basic human needs. The two major problems here would be Northern provision of *guaranteed amounts* of ODA (without which the option would *not* get off the ground) and *executive branch commitment* to spend the specified percentage of funds on basic human needs targets. Should most U.S. aid continue to flow to diplomatic trouble spots around the world *despite* the rhetorical commitment, again the program would be "dead."

The resolution of the *"intervention" issue* most probably will necessitate the disbursement of funds and "performance" monitoring by some (new?) international institution, perhaps with linkages to the technical and administrative capabilities of the World Bank and major regional institutions such as the Asian and Inter-American Development Banks. If a North-

South negotiation on all the other quid pro quos were to succeed, the need for a highly qualified, specialized and "neutral" agency still would seem essential to the bargain. Its psychological importance can hardly be overestimated. For if the developing countries were to allow some of their "sovereignty" to be diluted by international monitoring procedures, it would be important for the North to make the same type of concession by giving up the right to make the *allocation decisions*. Could this Northern concession of sovereignty be achieved? During the course of several years of planning and negotiation, I certainly do not find the idea beyond the realm of the possible. The issue would, quite probably, be decided by the tenor and outcome of an entire set of North-South negotiations rather than on the basis of the proclaimed merits of the basic human needs issue alone.

Personally I find the fourth problem—the *potential damage to "global agenda" issues*—the least troublesome. We are making very little progress at the moment on "global agenda" issues where North-South cooperation is required. Discussion and negotiation of the type suggested here might not help a great deal; yet in the short term there is little of substance that it could hurt. Those who argue this point most probably have already concluded that the "basic human needs" issue is an idea ahead of its time (or not worth the time); they may be right, but their presentation appears to prejudge the issue without much thought.

Finally, we are left with the fifth and potentially the biggest hurdle of all, *the prospect that the discussion and negotiation of Option 3 cannot avoid introducing the human rights issue*. As noted earlier, opponents of the "basic human needs" approach generally assume that the two will be linked (I think they are right); that the apparently fundamental lack of agreement between North and South on this issue and Southern sensitivity to the present Northern perspective on it will kill all prospects for an agreement on any basic human needs approach (I think they are right unless they are willing to negotiate on the very content of the term "human rights"); and that the fallout from this conflict over human rights could do considerable damage to whatever potential now exists for improving North-South relations (I think they are wrong).

Many treat the human rights issue as the greatest hurdle to the Option 3 approach. I do not disagree with this assessment, but at the same time I *also* see the human rights issue as the one which has the greatest long-term potential for bridging much of the present perceptual gap and value gap between North and South.

Potential Gains from the Negotiation Process

At the present moment most developing countries are united against Northern "interference" or "intervention" on the issue of human rights. In the first place, they fear that the problem will be used as just another Northern pressure point from which to "dictate" developing-country policies. In the second place, there exists a serious definitional problem.

Precisely what do "human rights" comprise? For most Northerners, "human rights" means the classical civil liberties and political rights enshrined, among other places, in the *first* half of the Universal Declaration of Human Rights. These rights include concepts such as freedom of expression, information, association, religious beliefs and practices; equality before the law and government; and a judicial process to protect individual rights.

For most Southerners, the above concepts have far less value than do those which are emphasized in the *second* half of the Universal Declaration of Human Rights. It is in the second section that one finds the following types of concepts: the right to a standard of living adequate for the health and well-being of individuals and families, including food, clothing, housing, and medical care; the right to security in the event of unemployment, sickness, or disability; and access to economic, social, and cultural rights indispensable for dignity and the free development of personality.

The perceptual and value gap between the concepts embodied in the first and second halves of the Declaration has not been bridged since the document was written three decades ago. The concepts in the first half, still supported by all Western·nations, reflect the cultural values and norms of Western civilization. Those of the second, given far greater emphasis by developing countries, reflect the desires of societies and ethnic groups at far lower standards of living to raise those standards.

Unless a serious debate is joined on this amalgam of issues, it is highly probable that North and South will continue to drift even further apart on human rights issues and that the price, measured simply in terms of impact on other joint endeavors, will mount yearly. Several events of recent years are suggestive of this trend, including congressional insistence that governments allowing flagrant violations of "human rights" as defined by Western civilization be made ineligible for U.S. foreign aid other than that clearly earmarked for the poor. Even more recently and dramatically, the World Bank experienced two split votes on loan proposals—two of the very few in its entire history—over the issue of human rights. In both cases, the recipient country was Chile, and highest among the reasons noted by those countries voting against the loan proposals was "the Chilean government's position on human rights." And in both cases almost all European nations voted *against* the loans or abstained—while the United States and almost all developing countries supported the loans.

Given this growing conflict on the human rights issue, given developing-country demands for Northern assistance in reforms to enhance economic development, and given all the concerns and problems captured in the phrase "global management," one wonders whether a new and serious attempt at a joint North-South exploration of the human rights issue is not a better course of action than an attempt to avoid the issue in order to minimize "sensitive" questions of "intervention." Have we not reached that point in international relations when "intervention" of this type *cannot* be avoided; when the real issue is the legitimization of the *forms* and *procedures* of "intervention"; and when an issue like human rights must be examined in this new light? (Lest there be any misunderstanding, the use of the word "intervention" in this letter *never* refers to military intervention.)

If this point is reached in North-South relations—and it most probably will be reached between North and South sooner than between East and West because economic, political, and even cultural linkages between Northern and Southern states are greater than they are between Eastern and Western states—then the interstate "agenda" can no longer be "managed" in a way which avoids "value" issues foreign to traditional statecraft. Foreign aid legislation and World Bank votes already attest to this observation.

If this is the case, it further emphasizes the need for progress on both the basic human needs option and the linked issue of human rights (as defined in Western cultural terms). As the global absolute poverty problem becomes increasingly *visible*, it will trigger two reactions on the part of many Northerners: 1) a humanitarian instinct to ease the problem in one manner or another, and 2) a tendency to criticize developing-country governments for "failing" to meet the basic needs of their own populations. And that criticism, combined with criticism of "human rights" violations, will inevitably be reflected in legislation which will further politicize these issues and exacerbate North-South relations. The net result: it may finally be *too late* for the North to conclude that global absolute poverty is a problem for Southern governments alone to resolve. This would seem to be inevitable. *Western values* again make it *impossible* for many OECD country peoples, legislatures, and executive branches to "leave the problem alone." For those values and norms will eventually be reflected in U.S. and other OECD-country *policies* toward developing countries. If this is the case, and if U.S. policy makers conclude that North and South must be able to work together in some minimal degree of cooperation for all the "global agenda" reasons reviewed in this letter, then the problems which the "basic human needs" option addresses are "our" problems as well as "theirs." *Our own value system makes the problems ours.*

Thus a joint examination of the basic human needs and the human rights issues, complex as it may be, seems unavoidable *unless* Northern countries are prepared to exercise far more restraint on their cultural values and norms than they have yet shown the capacity to exercise. And is not such an examination all the more appropriate *if* the North is at the same time prepared to cooperate in a serious way in the financing of a basic human needs strategy? For the first time since the Universal Declaration of Human Rights was written, the North would—through actions, not simply rhetoric—be *implicitly* recognizing the legitimacy of the concepts in the second half of the Declaration which the developing countries have always pointed to as encompassing "their" fundamental conception of first order human rights (sometimes relabeled human *needs*), namely the right to an economic standard of living without which all other forms of human rights are of secondary importance.

If the North, in supporting an Option 3 type of approach, were to move deliberately toward the acceptance of the human *needs* notion, could a fruitful dialogue with the South then begin over the *proper mix* and the rank-ordering of human "rights" and "needs" that might produce the seed of a new *negotiated* international norm on this most controversial subject? I have to admit that the probabilities for near-term success are not high. I suspect that the developing countries in the aggregate are headed for at least a decade of increasing authoritarianism; and the link between all but the most stable authoritarian regimes and violation of what Westerners generally define as human rights seems to be fairly high. Therefore, trends in developing countries do not allow one to adopt a very sanguine outlook on this issue.

On the other hand, what would be lost in making the effort, even if it failed to produce much by way of agreement? Very little, I suspect. Indeed, each party to the discussions/negotiations might come away with a far better understanding of the concerns of others, the complexities of the issue, and the inherent weaknesses of ethnocentric approaches by *either* side to the establishment of superordinate norms and concepts around which to organize structures to manage global relationships. That is, the effort might fail—probably *would* fail in the short run—to establish a universal norm of human rights/needs around which to develop legitimate forms of "intervention" and "nonintervention." But it still might lead to a greater *understanding*—both Northern and Southern—about the profound complexity of the issues which separate them. And this, in my judgment, would represent *progress*, not failure.

Having emphasized the degree to which success as it is normally interpreted in international negotiations may not be achieved, let me suggest that considerable progress on the human rights issue nevertheless might be made. Success should be measured in the North-South arena not by the signing of a peace treaty but by the changing norms of bargaining and accommodation. Neither side would have to formally accept the other's "definition," or the spelling out of an agreed compromise text on human rights. Success would more properly be judged in terms of *trends* in Southern "abuses" and *trends* in Northern responsiveness to the Southern human rights perspective. Progress in these terms might be considerable over time.

Having reviewed the most compelling arguments *against* serious consideration of the Option 3 proposals, Mr. President, I still feel that on balance an effort by the OECD countries to negotiate and implement agreements in this area with the developing countries *is worth the risks entailed*. The potential benefits are overwhelmingly obvious to Fourth World countries; its link to Option 2 would make it of considerable interest to Third World countries; and its potential for helping to bridge the present North-South "values gap" emphasizes the major contribution it could make to general U.S. foreign policy goals congruent with our own cultural heritage.

Potential Costs of Not Making the Attempt

If one has strong normative desires to attempt to alleviate the conditions under which the world's poorest billion are now living, the costs of not acting become in large part a function of what one thinks would be done in the basic human needs area without any OECD-country push on Option 3. Since I fear that little would otherwise be attempted, let alone accomplished, in the absence of a Northern linkage of policies found in Options 2 and 3, the normative costs of not making the attempt seem very high in my view.

They also seem high in a second sense. In not making the attempt, would we not be selling ourselves short—Northerners and Southerners alike? Statecraft exhibits a well-tested capacity to derive grotesque results from "normative" goals and policies. Stanley Hoffmann is undoubtedly correct in arguing that "a crusade for democracy and basic rights" could turn present aspects of the North-South "values gap" into an abyss. But so could a refusal to make key elements of that gap—particularly human rights and human needs—the subject of North-South discussions and negotiations. In fact, the argument here is that such a discussion—tied to an ongoing set of negotiations so that it would be taken seriously by both sides—should do more than any other approach to *ease* fears such as Stanley Hoffmann's apparent concern that issues such as basic human needs and human rights may be turned into "absolutes" by the United States. I suspect that any such tendency would be *diminished* rather than enhanced by the Option 3 approach for several reasons. First, absolutes would be tempered by discussion and bargaining with other OECD countries undertaken in order to achieve a common negotiating position. Second, they would be tempered by the presentation of sharply differing perspectives from developing countries. And third, they would be tempered by the realization that moderation in the pursuit of such value goals was inevitably necessitated by a set of trade-offs across the entire spectrum of North-South relations. In the course of unending North-South discussions and negotiations in a wide variety of forums over the coming eight years, normative goals will be so compromised by the claims of economic, political, security, and prudential foreign policy goals that a spirited pursuit of normative absolutes is probably the least of our legitimate concerns.

In conclusion, Mr. President, my conviction is that the cost of *not* attempting to link the "accelerated reform" option with the "basic human needs" option during the course of your presidency would be greater than any failure which the attempt might produce. If the choice is ultimately grounded in value preferences, I think that it can also stand the test by which other perspectives (economic/efficiency, political/security, prudential/man-agerial) will judge it. While there is much to be said for the view that shared *procedural values* must be accorded priority in order to handle "global agenda" problems in an interdependent world, I would hesitate far more than many observers to count on the emergence of shared procedural values in the North-South context before we are much more familiar with each other's *substantive values.* Only then can "bargains be struck" and "interdependence managed" with any confidence that today's bargain will be here tomorrow; and that if it is, either party to the bargain will be using it as more than a bargaining chip in the next move on its own hidden agenda. If that is the way the game is going to be played, Mr. President, let us go all the way back to Option 1 and allow the more traditional statecraft approaches to control all of our policies affecting developing countries. But let us not settle for Option 1 until we are certain that the United States, the North, and the South cannot do much better.

CHAPTER III

Recommendations for U.S. Policy: Agenda 1977

A new Administration is assuming leadership in the United States at an open moment in history, when one economic and political world order is passing and another beginning. In this period of transition, a more comprehensive and targeted set of U.S. policies is required if a steady worsening of North-South relations is to be avoided, if the international order is to be reshaped to better meet the needs of both the developed and the developing countries, and if the most debilitating aspects of global poverty are to be eliminated in this century.

The recommendations set out in this chapter for U.S. policy on North-South relations call for the rapid implementation of several different types of measures. Some recommendations propose actions that should be taken in the immediate future to signal constructive intent by the United States to reshape its policies toward the developing countries. Some call for actions over the next two to four years. Still others identify critical areas on which further studies and discussions among both developed and developing countries should be launched now to permit early decisions on a range of accelerated reforms of various global systems and on the international address of the problem of meeting basic human needs. In their totality, these recommendations attempt to elaborate the beginning of the reform and restructuring of existing economic and political systems and the initiation of programs to meet the needs of the world's poorest billion people.

In considering the recommendations for policies on specific problems, it is important to keep in mind the fact that the issues are to a considerable degree interlinked. Thus the question of financing development programs in the developing world necessarily also involves decisions on issues in the areas of trade, commodities, debt, financing, and aid transfer. In effect, a policy "package" must be considered in its totality and not disaggregated into entirely separate policy decisions.

Furthermore, to attract the support necessary for its adoption, the sum of proposals in any specific issue area probably needs to include some major benefits for each of the three principal groups of countries: the *high-income* market economies, the *middle-income* countries, and the *low-income* countries. The priority concerns of these three groups—and their perception of the international actions most needed—may vary considerably. Thus proposals on the debt issue must take account of the needs of the *high-income* countries to protect the financial integrity of their major private banks and to assure the maintenance of substantial flows of their exports to the developing countries. Debt proposals must also include some combination of measures—such as expanded resource transfers at commercial rates from international financial institutions, trade liberalization, and commodity agreements—which enable the *middle-income* countries to resume the development momentum that had existed prior to the global recession of the 1970s. And they must likewise include measures that take cognizance of the long-term nature of the debt problem of the *low-income* countries, through, for example, significantly increased multilateral and bilateral assistance on concessional terms, and in some cases possibly debt forgiveness.

Finally, it is essential to recognize that one of the most important measures that the industrial countries can take for the benefit of all countries is to restore their own economic growth. Without continued growth in the industrialized economies, the developing countries cannot hope to expand their exports of both raw materials and semiprocessed and manufactured goods to earn the foreign exchange for purchasing imports essential to their development. Therefore the measures taken by the OECD countries to ensure a return to growth rates closer to those of the 1960s is of prime importance to the developing world as well as to the industrialized countries.

Trade in Manufactures

The exporters of manufactured products are about to enter the intensive stage of negotiating another major round of tariff cuts—similar to that undertaken during the "Kennedy Round" of trade negotiations in the 1960s. The participants in this "Tokyo Round" of trade negotiations also will attempt to devise codes regulating the use of nontariff barriers. For the developing countries, participation in these negotiations provides the opportunity to press for measures which will help them to increase the level of their export earnings—a matter of crucial importance to achieving their development goals. The current round of multilateral trade negotiations (MTN) was launched in 1973 and began in earnest after passage of the U.S. Trade Act of 1974. Much preparatory work already has taken place in Geneva, and serious negotiations are expected in 1977.

Successive rounds of trade liberalization in the post-World War II period have created an international environment in which many developing countries have been able to greatly expand their exports of manufactured goods. During the period 1965–1973, for example, their exports of manufactures grew at an average annual rate of over 25 per cent. Much of this trade was accounted for by some dozen countries that have relied on intensive programs of industrial diversification, aggressive marketing of their products, and foreign investment by multinational firms. But during the 1970s, developing-country exporters also benefited from tariff preferences, which (although subject to serious restrictions) have provided duty-free entry into developed-country markets for many manufactures and semimanufactures.

The developing countries at present obtain over 80 per cent of their foreign exchange from their export earnings, and nearly 40 per cent of their non-oil export earnings now comes from manufactured exports.[1] Increasing the ability of the developing countries to purchase U.S. goods and services and to provide lower-priced imports that help ease inflationary pressures is clearly in the overall economic interest of the United States and other developed nations. The United States, for example, currently sells 27 per cent of its exports to the (non-OPEC) developing countries, and 23 per cent of U.S. imports now come from the (non-OPEC) developing countries.[2]

But the rapid growth of manufactured exports from developing countries has not been achieved without certain costs to the economies of the developed countries, including the United States. While the lower prices of developing-country imports have benefited developed-country consumers, workers and firms have in some cases suffered significant losses of business and employment as a result of the foreign competition. This has prompted important segments of the labor movement and the industrial sector in developed countries to oppose further trade liberalization.

This is true despite the fact that the U.S. program of adjustment assistance for workers and firms has expanded very significantly since the passage of the Trade Act of 1974. Expenditures for this program have grown from a total of $76 million provided to 27,000 workers between 1969 and March 1975, to a total of $168 million provided to more than 105,000 workers in the first eighteen months that the current Trade Act was in effect. Assistance to companies claiming injury from import competition also has increased. Much of the labor movement nevertheless continues to oppose trade liberalization. Although benefits have increased, the program remains hampered by restrictive criteria for determining worker eligibility and by cumbersome administrative procedures and delays; and only minimal use has been made of its training, relocation, and job-search benefits. The problems

---

[1]Tables C-1, C-2, and C-3 in Annex C of this volume show the composition of both exports and imports (by categories of products) of developed market economies, developing market economies, and centrally planned economies.

[2]See Annex C, Table C-7.

faced by workers affected by imports are further complicated by high levels of overall unemployment resulting from the recession and the lack of an adequate national employment policy. The adjustment assistance program needs significant improvement if it is to win increased domestic support for further trade liberalization. Without such improvement, the tendency of labor and firms to seek restrictions on imports will only be strengthened—to the detriment of both U.S. consumers and exporters in developing countries. *

A forthcoming Brookings Institution study indicates that if the industrialized countries cut tariffs in the present round of negotiations by 60 per cent, this could have the effect of raising developing-country export earnings by more than $2 billion over their 1974 level.[3] Important as these increased earnings would be, however, they would still fall far short of what would be possible—political obstacles aside—if *all* tariff and nontariff barriers on manufactures were eliminated. World Bank estimates indicate that if this were done, the annual export earnings of the developing countries by 1985 could increase by as much as $24 billion—$21 billion of which would accrue to the middle-income countries and $3 billion to the countries with per capita incomes under $200.

The further expansion of their export capability is particularly important for the developing countries if they are to achieve their goal (set forth in the "Lima" Declaration of 1974) of increasing their share of world industrial production from the present 7-8 per cent to 25 per cent by the year 2000. This goal implies a level of exports by the developing countries at the end of the century some 10-20 times higher than in 1973. Whether the lower figure would be sufficient to achieve the 25 per cent goal would depend on the extent to which the developing countries were successful in more effectively developing their own *internal* markets, through greater reliance on labor-intensive development and "basic human needs" strategies. If the 25 per cent target at first sight appears unrealistic, it is noteworthy that even the upper estimate—an end-of-century export level 20 times higher than that of 1973—could be achieved *at rates of trade expansion no greater than those of the recent past*. The attainment of the 25 per cent goal would of course require extensive changes in the world economy—changes based on efforts by individual and groups of developing countries to increase exports on the one hand, and changes by developed countries to lower their trade barriers on the other. A scenario of what will occur even over the next ten years if such special measures are not taken by both groups of countries is provided by a recent World Bank estimate: the manufactured exports of the middle-income countries in that case would be likely to grow by only 10 to 11 per

---

*See Charles R. Frank, *Adjustment Assistance: American Jobs and Trade with the Developing Countries*, Development Paper No. 13 (Washington, D.C.: Overseas Development Council, 1973).

[3]William R. Cline, Noboru Kawanabe, T.O.M. Kronsjo, and Thomas Williams, *Trade, Welfare, and Employment Effects of Multilateral Trade Negotiations in the Tokyo Round.* Brookings Institution, Washington, D.C., forthcoming.

cent a year in the next decade, compared to 18 per cent in the previous one.

The developing and developed countries are currently emphasizing different (but not mutually exclusive) solutions to the problems of increasing developing-country earnings from manufactured exports. The developing countries want not only a reduction in nontariff barriers (which are particularly restrictive in the case of their labor-intensive manufactures) but also acceptance of the principle that their relative underdevelopment justifies special or "differential" treatment in any new trade agreements. The U.S. government accepted the concept of differential treatment for developing countries in 1975, but there may be opposition within Congress and domestic industry to provisions in trade codes which appear to give advantages to foreign competitors—particularly multinational firms with activities in developing nations. The developing countries also seek the extension and improvement of the Generalized System of Preferences (GSP). Although the Generalized System of Preferences is technically outside the scope of the multilateral trade negotiations, the improvement or erosion of the GSP as a result of tariff concessions is very closely linked to the question of trade liberalization. The developing countries want to ensure that the margin of preference (between the reduced-duty or duty-free treatment they receive under the GSP and the tariff applied to all other nations) is not eroded by new tariff cuts negotiated on an across-the-board basis. Indeed, they would like to see the current preferences extended.

In contrast, policy makers in the United States and other developed countries—influenced by the gains that have been made from successive rounds of trade liberalization since World War II—tend to put a premium on multilateral trade negotiations leading to lower tariffs on a "most-favored-nation" basis and agreement on codes or guidelines for use of nontariff barriers. U.S. representatives to the negotiations buttress their arguments for general tariff cuts and codes to govern the use of nontariff barriers by pointing out that the exports of manufactured goods from the developing countries have been the most rapidly growing component of their trade and that trade liberalization therefore should result in greater gains than those likely under various preferential schemes. They likewise argue that tariff cuts have the added advantage of being permanent, whereas preferential schemes—which are viewed by many in the developed countries as an act of charity on their part—are subject to change at any time.

It is true that relatively modest reductions in tariffs would contribute to the opportunities available to developing-country traders to ship their goods to the markets of the industrial world—particularly if the cuts were applied to those goods which at present do not receive preferential treatment or to those which are in effect denied preferential access by the additional application of other restrictions (as in the cases of the goods of the more successful developing-country exporters). But developed-country negotiators should recognize that if the negotiations produce only small reductions in the most-favored-nation tariff rate or in the extent to which nontariff barriers are applied—or if numerous products are exempted from the general tariff-cutting formula—developing-country exporters will make stronger demands for continued preferential treatment. This is so because the higher the most-favored-nation rate remains, the larger the margin of preferences that will be available to the developing countries.

Moreover, completely forgoing preferences and relying *only* on "most-favored-nation" treatment for manufactured goods and on reduction of nontariff barriers to resolve the trade problems of the developing countries would pose a number of additional problems. First, the gains would be concentrated among the few more advanced developing countries that now produce the majority of the developing world's manufactured goods. This approach would not give much assistance to those other countries which depend mainly on the export of primary products; and the poorest countries (which account for only 1 per cent of the total developing-country manufactured exports) would receive even less assistance than they do under the GSP. Second, since negotiated tariff reductions will take place over a five- to ten-year period, the gains to the developing countries would only be achieved in the medium to long term, unless accelerated tariff cuts were instituted. Finally, trade preferences are one of the long-standing demands of the developing countries and are already in effect throughout the industrialized world (even Eastern Europe and the Soviet Union). Thus preferences are a "bird in hand." U.S. implementation in 1976 of its scheme, for example, already has brought trade gains to many developing countries.

Therefore new policies are needed to encompass not only negotiated tariff reductions but also continued preferential schemes and action on commodity issues. One possible compromise that might reconcile the immediate developing-country interest in preferences and the long-term interest of both groups of countries in an open world trading system would involve a) developing-country acceptance of the principle that preferences will erode as tariff and nontariff barriers are reduced and b) developed-country commitment to the extension of preferential schemes for those items on which duties will remain high, paying particular attention to the trade needs of the low-income countries. Moreover (even though the negotiations on trade in manufactures and the negotiations on most commodity issues are taking place in separate forums), the relationship between trade measures and commodity policies must be kept in mind by those concerned with increasing the earnings of the developing countries.*

While pressing forward vigorously with the presently authorized negotiations, the U.S. government (and those of other developed countries) must at the same time begin the groundwork for further rounds of trade liberalization by anticipating the obstacles to continued progress toward a more open world economy that can be expected to come from within the developed countries. Priority attention must be given to thorough advance

---

*See Guy F. Erb, "Trade Negotiations on Two Fronts: Manufactures and Commodities." Overseas Development Council, forthcoming.

analysis of the domestic implications of changes in patterns of international trade and of the governmental and private policies called for by these changes. The objective should be to obtain the data that will permit decisions on further elimination of barriers to trade by identifying the potential benefits—in the form of increased foreign exchange earnings for the developing countries and increased efficiency for the industrial economies—that would result from such action.

Finally, more attention needs to be given to means for increasing trade in manufactures among developing countries, which may hold potential benefits for both developed and developing countries—including the possible easing of the impact of developing-country exports on developed-country economies. Most developing countries find it easier to sell their goods in the large markets of industrial nations than in developing-country markets. Factors responsible for this concentration include the developed countries' far more liberal extension of trade credits for both exports and imports (as well as their greater capacity for quality analysis of other than "brand name" products). Developing countries—unable to offer each other comparable trade credits—use less of each others' products than price and quality alone would dictate.

Recommendations

1. Given the medium- and long-term interest of developing and developed countries alike in the reduction of both tariff and nontariff barriers to trade, the U.S. government should press vigorously under existing legislative authorities to increase the pace of the multilateral trade negotiations in Geneva, seek the largest possible average tariff reductions, and keep to a minimum the list of items it proposes to exclude from overall tariff cuts. Taking particular account of the interests of developing countries, it should make specific proposals for the reduction and/or surveillance of barriers in each of the areas of the negotiations (for example, tropical products; tariff escalation; and subsidies, countervailing duties, and other nontariff measures).

2. The U.S. scheme of generalized preferences should undergo continuing improvement during the course of the multilateral trade negotiations. Such improvements may be related to U.S. requests for developing-country concessions in the negotiations or to other U.S. trade objectives. The developing countries, for their part, need to recognize that their long-run trading interests will not be harmed by the erosion of tariff preferences as a result of the most-favored-nation procedure of trade liberalization. Consequently, their own efforts to improve the GSP should not be carried to lengths which jeopardize their potential long-term trading gains from general trade concessions.

3. The United States and the other industrial countries can make a real contribution to the welfare of the developing countries by maintaining a "standstill" on raising existing trade barriers—even as corrective measures to balance-of-payments crises.

4. *The U.S. government needs to respond adequately to the needs of U.S. workers and firms affected negatively by the trade liberalization measures. A forthcoming U.S. policy in the trade negotiations cannot be sustained without greatly improved programs to assist the adjustment of domestic interests to changes in international trade and to growing U.S. imports. The government should work with organized labor to seek solutions—including legislation if necessary—to problems such as restrictive interpretations of which workers are eligible for assistance, serious lags in the processing of workers' petitions, and questions about the adequacy of the assistance offered.*

5. *The United States must prepare its own economy for the substantial changes in world trade that will result from the continued growth and economic diversification of developing countries and that are required for the continued efficiency of the U.S. economy, particularly with respect to coping with inflation while reducing unemployment. A major domestic effort should be undertaken both to identify measures to support the long-run participation of the United States in the world economy and to determine the costs and benefits of dismantling the remaining trade barriers imposed by the industrial countries on the exports of the developing countries. An analysis of international and particularly North-South trade and investment—a study comparable to that undertaken in the early 1970s by the Commission on International Trade and Investment Policy (the "Williams Commission")—should be launched in 1977, so that when the current round of negotiations is completed, the longer-run task of reforming and adapting the world's trade system may be expected to continue.*

6. *The United States should encourage analyses of the potential for greater trade in manufactures among developing countries and of the financial and other measures required to encourage significantly increased trade among these countries.*

Commodity Issues

The outcome of the commodity negotiations that begin in Geneva in March 1977 under the auspices of the U.N. Conference on Trade and Development (UNCTAD) could greatly influence future relations between the developed and the developing countries. The earnings that the developing countries receive from their exports of raw materials other than oil still account for more than 50 per cent of their total non-oil export earnings, and commodity policies have been a key item in their demands for a New International Economic Order. At the same time, there has been increasing concern in the industrialized world about reliable access to supplies and the need for investment in the extraction and processing of raw materials in the developing countries. These fears have in some cases led private firms to resort to costly stockpiling of minerals—thereby drawing down funds available for more productive investments. Despite their concern about supply scarcity in recent years, the industrial countries continue to give much higher priority to the liberalization of trade in manufactures than to commodity negotiations, which they traditionally view as at best moderately useful to their economies. Yet properly managed commodity agreements that stabilized prices could make important contributions to the anti-inflationary efforts of the commodity-importing developed countries by limiting extreme upward price fluctuations. In addition, by participating in such agreements, commodity-importing developed countries could assure themselves of greater security of supplies within specified price ranges.

The differing concerns of the developed and developing countries on commodity issues are reflected in the specific commodity proposals made by each side. The developing countries, wanting stable (and preferably higher) prices for their raw materials, support the comprehensive "integrated commodity program" elaborated by the UNCTAD secretariat. This proposal includes buffer stocks to stabilize prices, an internationally financed "common fund" to support buffer stock operations, improved compensation for unexpected shortfalls in export earnings, and measures for increasing the processing of raw materials in the developing countries. The general support of the developing countries on two major components of the integrated commodity program—the financing and operation of commodity agreements and an internationally financed fund—has not yet been tested in negotiations. The United States, which has traditionally assumed a guarded, case-by-case approach to commodity agreements, has opposed a common fund for buffer stocks but has supported expanded efforts to compensate developing countries for shortfalls in export earnings. Its primary interest recently has been the maintenance of access to raw-material supplies. Thus at the fourth session of UNCTAD in May 1976, it proposed an International Resources Bank to encourage raw-material production in the developing countries.

Both the developed and the developing nations are now committed to negotiating new arrangements in the commodity field. The question still to be decided is what *kinds* of arrangements can be designed to meet the needs of both groups of countries.[4] Both developed and developing countries must be willing to begin the process of compromise and adaptation that is necessary for the success of any serious negotiation on commodity policy. Developing countries have long made international acceptance of the integrated commodity program, and in particular of the proposed common fund, a necessary element of the commodity discussions. If they show willingness to compromise on specific details of the common fund and of individual commodity arrangements, the United States and other developed countries should match it with willingness to set aside ideology and begin discussion of the many complex practical points that will inevitably arise in

---

[4]For an analysis of this issue, see Jere R. Behrman, "International Commodity Agreements." Overseas Development Council, forthcoming.

the consideration of commodity agreements and a common fund for their financing.

Measures to stabilize commodity prices within a certain range can be expected to benefit both *producers* (by giving them a more secure and stable flow of income from their exports) and *consumers* (by assuring them of continuing supply and by helping to prevent the wild fluctuations of prices of raw materials that have marked the last several years). Price stability will be particularly important to the industrialized countries in the next several years if the pace of recovery in their economies generates increased demand for raw materials.

However, developing-country exporters of raw materials are seeking more than price stability. Their goal in negotiating commodity agreements is to obtain a higher level of export earnings from their raw materials through a) higher prices and b) increased processing prior to export—so that they, too, can benefit from the value added through processing. Higher prices are the most controversial of the developing-country proposals, but some agreements in which the United States has participated (particularly the International Coffee Agreement in the 1960s) have transferred some resources to the producing countries. In the case of the coffee agreement, this outcome was evidently acceptable to the consuming countries that participated in the agreement because of their overall relations with the coffee-producing countries and their desire to maintain order in world coffee markets. A U.S. voice in the management of individual agreements can help it ensure that price provisions do not result in excessive and untenable price ranges. Since increased raw-material prices also would mean higher costs for raw-material-importing *developing* countries—many of which have been severely affected by the higher oil prices and inflation of the past three years—these countries may well give support to moderate price objectives. Finally, producers entering commodity negotiations need to keep in mind that price increases that exceed limits acceptable to consuming countries are not likely to endure and may well, in the long run, encourage substitution and jeopardize existing and potential markets for exporters.

Participants in the commodity negotiations—like those in the trade negotiations that focus on manufactures—must be sensitive to the fact that the trade objectives on their respective agendas are related, especially in the longer run. The World Bank has estimated that the elimination of trade barriers to commodities could increase the annual export earnings of the middle-income developing countries by $8 billion and of the low-income countries by $1 billion by 1985. Particularly important in this connection is the removal or reduction of trade barriers that inhibit the processing of raw materials in the developing countries. In most industrial countries, tariffs are escalated according to the degree of processing of commodity imports. Serious attention needs to be given to enabling developing countries to substantially increase their exports of semiprocessed and processed raw materials.

Recommendations

1. The United States should make an unequivocal commitment to participate in negotiations on a common fund for buffer stocks and on individual commodity agreements—even while making clear that this does not commit it either to participating in any particular commodity scheme or to funding any buffer stocks prior to the completion of negotiations on a common fund (or on individual agreements which envisage stockpiling activities). Such a commitment would give the United States substantial influence in the establishment of guidelines for the negotiations and would ensure that international commodity agreements took U.S. interests into account.

2. A strong commitment to the negotiations by the United States and other developed countries should be combined with their continued support for improvements in compensatory financing systems—particularly that of the International Monetary Fund. Compensatory financing of this type would complement rather than be a substitute for other commodity policies. In the context of a general review of buffer stock operations—in particular those of specific commodity agreements—improvements in the Buffer Stock Facility of the IMF should also be examined.

3. Developed and developing countries should actively explore changes in trade and investment policies relating to the production and increased processing of raw materials in the developing countries—both to increase existing supplies and to help the developing countries diversify their economies. The U.S. proposal for an International Resources Bank should be studied, as should the development of alternative methods to facilitate investment in raw materials, such as a broadening of the capacity of the World Bank and International Finance Corporation to guarantee or finance raw material development.

4. Studies should be made of each major commodity exported by the developing countries to determine the additional export-earnings potential implicit in its increased processing in the country of origin (or in other developing countries). Measures that are consistent with international economic efficiency and could be used to encourage increased processing in developing countries include the reduction of tariffs and other barriers to developing-country exports of processed goods. At the same time, studies should be conducted to identify a) groups of workers, industries, and commodities in developed countries which might be adversely affected by such measures to increase international economic efficiency, as well as b) appropriate adjustment measures.

The Debt of the Developing Countries

One of the issues high on the agenda of the developing countries, and a cause of considerable and growing concern in the industrial countries, is the growing debt burden of developing countries. This problem, however, is

97

only one aspect of the great expansion of public and private debt owed by both developed and developing countries that in the years ahead will increasingly claim the attention of those concerned with the preservation of the integrity of the existing international financial system and with the development prospects of the oil-importing nations, particularly those in the developing world.

Two points are important to keep in mind when considering the debt problems of the developing countries. The first is that what is sometimes referred to as "the world debt problem" is actually a series of individual debt problems which must be examined on a country-by-country basis. Aggregating the problems of individual countries is primarily useful to gain some sense of the magnitude of the problem and to identify some of the linkage consequences that might result from problems in any single country. The second point is that growing debt in itself is not necessarily a dangerous trend. Indeed, many developing nations *should* be borrowing in international capital markets and from international agencies to finance badly needed development programs. Debt becomes a problem when repayments begin to absorb resources needed for development or when loans are used to finance current consumption or low-yielding projects.

Until 1973, the non-oil-exporting developing countries ran current account deficits of $8-$12 billion, which were financed by traditional sources of long-term funds such as official development assistance, government credits, and private investment. Between 1974 and 1975, however, due to the drastic increase in the prices of oil and food imports and to growing inflation in the industrialized world, the current account deficit of the non-oil-exporting developing countries rose from $29 billion to $37 billion.[5] (The 1976 deficit of these countries is estimated to be about $32 billion.) To cover these deficits, the developing countries have had to borrow funds from a variety of sources. As a result, the aggregate public debt owed by the non-OPEC countries grew by over 80 per cent between 1972 and 1975, reaching an estimated level of nearly $140 billion by the end of 1975.[6] Private debt not guaranteed by developing-country governments may add another $25 billion, bringing the total debt owed by the non-OPEC developing countries to around $165 billion.

One striking change from the pre-1973 period is the share of outstanding public debt obligations held by *private* banks. Lending by private banks to non-OPEC developing countries increased nearly sevenfold between 1967 and 1974. As a result, the share of these countries' debt held by private banks rose from approximately 6 per cent of the total in 1967 to some 19 per cent of the total in 1974. Their share is even higher at present. American banks

---

[5]See Annex E, Table E-1, for aggregate current account balances of groups of countries.
[6]See Annex E, Table E-2, for recent public debt trend of the non-OPEC developing countries.

carry roughly two thirds of the total private loans to the developing countries. Private lending is of course characterized by higher interest rates and shorter repayment periods than those associated with traditional governmental or international long-term sources of development capital. As a result, debt service on these loans is likely to grow increasingly significant in 1977 and the years ahead. It should be noted, however, that most lending by private banks and other private sources (such as suppliers' credits) is concentrated primarily in a few middle-income countries, mainly in Latin America.

As noted earlier, the debt problems of the non-OPEC middle-income and low-income countries are quite different and therefore call for different responses. Nearly two thirds ($75 billion) of the $114 billion in public debt owed by the non-OPEC developing countries in 1974 was owed by the *middle-income* countries—countries with per capita incomes of over $300 a year. Of this $75 billion, 44 per cent was owed to private sources, and 25 per cent to private banks alone.[7] Recent capital flows have enabled these countries to maintain a strong rate of growth through 1975. Most of these countries have good prospects for generating the continued economic growth that will enable them to meet their obligations—provided that they are helped to get through the next few years, and provided that the world economy regains rates of growth closer to those of the 1950s and 1960s. The increased role of private banks in financing the needs of the middle-income countries through relatively short-term lending (less than seven years maturity) has created increasingly serious problems as the world economy has proved slower in returning to general prosperity than was expected when the loans were made. The scale of the short-term borrowing is leading to a rapid rise in the debt service ratio, with principal and interest payments rising from about $6 billion in 1974 to a projected $22 billion in 1980. The debt situation of the middle-income countries was clearly stated by the President of the World Bank, Robert McNamara, at the annual World Bank-International Monetary Fund meeting in Manila in late 1976:

The dilemma of the middle-income countries can be simply stated. The sharp increase in their current account deficits has not been rolled back. Deficits at high levels are likely to continue for at least the next five to ten years if these countries are to generate the GNP growth rates of 6 to 7%, which are the very foundation for their creditworthiness. But continued heavy reliance on private sources for the financing of such deficits will require very large increases in the outstanding loans held by commercial banks and other financial institutions. To the extent that a large proportion of such debt is short-term, any temporary

---

[7]Annex E, Table E-3, shows a breakdown by income groups of developing-country public debt.

foreign-exchange liquidity problem—or even the prospect of one—can too easily be turned into a crisis, or the appearance of one.

Although the debt ($38.8 billion in 1974) owed by the *low-income* developing countries—those countries with annual per capita incomes below $300—is smaller in amount, it represents a substantially more difficult burden. For both the medium and longer term, the growth prospects and the foreign-exchange outlook of the low-income countries are far worse than in the case of the middle-income countries. Because the capital flows to these countries come mainly from concessional official development assistance, 88 per cent of the public debt owed at the end of 1974 by the low-income developing countries was held by official rather than private sources of external finances.[8]

Developing countries have recently raised a number of demands in international forums concerning their debt burdens. They have called for a) cancellation of the "official" portion of total public debt for the "least developed" countries ($7.4 billion in 1974); b) debt relief for the remainder of the forty-two "most seriously affected" countries not covered by the "least developed" provision (for which the "official" portion of public debt totaled some $26.9 billion in 1974); c) consolidation of all debt from private sources (which may be more than $45 billion for developing countries as a whole, if short-term and a variety of other credits as well as debt not guaranteed by developing-country governments are included); d) rescheduling of payments to private sources over a twenty-five-year period; and e) calling a debtor-creditor conference to establish principles and guidelines for the negotiation of both official and commercial debts. However, there is dissent from these proposals among the more advanced developing countries, which do not want to jeopardize their access to existing credit sources. Moreover, these demands have been resisted to date by developed countries (led by the United States) on the grounds they would jeopardize the existing international credit system. Instead, the United States throughout 1976 emphasized balance-of-payments financing and measures to increase developing-country access to sources of private finance; the latter is becoming increasingly difficult as more and more developing countries reach or come close to their borrowing limits from private sources.

Can the different approaches be resolved?* For the United States, the first step might be a serious examination of the problems caused by the debt of *all* the developing countries and a calculation of the costs to both sides that would result from slower developing-country growth, increasing economic and political instability, and lower levels of exports and imports. The

---

*Paul Watson, "Debt and the Developing Countries: New Problems and New Actors." Overseas Development Council, forthcoming.

[8]See Annex E, Table E-3.

increasing strain on the international financial system that will result from this growing debt burden clearly will be high—even if generalized defaulting such as that which marked the period between the two world wars does not appear to be a likely possibility at the moment.

A central consideration in debt policy should be the maintenance of the international credit system. If that system were to fail, the future access of the developing countries to both private and public sources of development financing would be severely limited. For that reason alone, no overall panacea—such as blanket debt cancellation or rescheduling—is a viable solution for this problem. Thus the "debt problem" in fact translates into several pragmatic considerations:

(1) How to finance the debt generated by past borrowing as loans come due, particularly to private sources, in the next few years;

(2) How to finance new and continuing deficits at levels higher than those of the years preceding 1973—particularly if the OPEC nations continue to run up substantial current account surpluses in the next few years; and

(3) How to increase the transfer of resources so that the developing countries also can achieve an acceptable rate of growth.

The examination of all of these questions must differentiate between the needs of the middle-income and low-income countries.

Developed and developing countries must, as soon as possible, establish general principles which represent a compromise between the extremes of adamant opposition and general cancellation, and which permit the consideration of the near-term debt problems of the developing countries on a constructive and sympathetic case-by-case basis. The main objective of these principles and actions should be to enable the developing countries to surmount the variety of debt problems that presently impede their economic growth.

Both sides should recognize that the longer-term solution to the debt problem of the *middle-income* developing countries lies not in debt measures alone, but in improving the world's trading and commodity systems (including compensatory financing) so that export earnings from trade in manufactures and commodities can be stabilized and so that developing countries can get a larger share of the earnings from increased world trade. The more immediate need, however, is for the international banking community —public and private—to recognize the long-term nature of the financing problem of many developing countries. The predicament of these countries calls for a significant increase in longer-term lending to the developing countries at non-concessional rates. The bulk of this increase must of necessity come from public sources (either international or bilateral) —through longer-term export credits, rescheduling of official debts, and other measures. This need is becoming increasingly apparent just as World

Bank lending is approaching the limits allowed by its present capital. Unless the capital is increased shortly, lending in the near future will begin to fall in terms of constant dollars.

The short- and mid-term solution to the debt problems of the *low-income* developing countries lies in increased official resource transfers from both OECD and OPEC donor countries in a variety of forms, including compensatory financing for export earnings, the transfer of resources under such devices as the IMF's new Trust Fund, and in some cases debt rescheduling and possibly cancellation. However, this strategy will not solve the poorer countries' long-run debt problem, which can only be met through the implementation in these countries of more successful programs for achieving growth and securing increased foreign-exchange earnings, and through concessional aid from international and bilateral sources at considerably higher levels than at present.

Finally, it is worth noting that the continued economic well-being of the OECD nations is of crucial importance to economic and social progress in the developing countries. Therefore certain precautionary measures to preserve their economic well-being may be in order. Cooperative arrangements among the industrialized countries to ensure the availability of financial assistance whenever it is needed would help them pursue a course of adjustment to future contingencies without resorting to restrictions on trade, capital movements, or undue restraints on domestic economic activity. Such arrangements might include special agreements for a) handling sudden major (and potentially destabilizing) capital movements between industrial-country banking systems, and for b) making the necessary funds available in case of liquidity crises in the various world financial markets.

Recommendations

1. Early in 1977, the U.S. government should encourage a country-by-country review by appropriate international bodies of the official debt predicament of the <u>low-income</u> *countries. The first objective of this examination should be the identification and application of measures that emphasize renewing development progress rather than the early resumption or maintenance of debt service. The combination of measures employed to this end might include increased official resource flows and debt rescheduling and cancellation (for the "least developed" countries), with the objective of maintaining levels of debt service over the next several years below a certain level, e.g., possibly as a percentage of projected trade receipts or GNP. Bisque clauses (agreements under which limited portions of debt service can be deferred at the discretion of the debtor) should also be applied liberally.*

2. Timely and increased concessional aid for the <u>low-income</u> *countries should be made available by the United States and other OECD as well as OPEC countries; through timely and expanded action on bilateral and international aid (e.g., early authorization of IDA V); and through the* allocation of the major portion of concessional aid for the low-income countries. Creating *ex post facto* grants can be done by cancellation, by new flows in amounts adequate to allow full payment of outstanding loans, or by very long-term deferrals plus *bisque* clauses (which together would reduce the net present value of loans to a very low figure).

3. For the _middle-income_ developing countries, the United States should indicate its willingness to consider a call for debt relief by any nation whose burden of debt service is a severe impediment to its development programs—after an assessment under international auspices which include its official creditors. Relief on official debt could be made available through a combination of increased long-term financing and debt rescheduling.

4. To substantially increase the availability of external resources to _middle-income_ countries, the United States should support early action on measures such as increasing the resources of international financial institutions—including the capital of the World Bank and regional banks, IMF quotas, and the amounts available for compensatory finance; establishing one or more commodity funds; and reducing trade barriers.

5. Special attention also must be paid to the new element in the debt of the developing countries: the growing role of banks and other private financial institutions. The long-term interests of lenders, borrowers, and the respective governments will best be served if the private banks continue to lend to the developing countries, both for balance-of-payments purposes where necessary and for individual development projects. Indeed, premature and precipitous reduction in private lending—due to either overreaction to developing-country debt problems or to the "crowding out" of developing-country borrowers by economic expansion within the industrial countries —would place a sudden and very serious burden of adjustment on many developing nations (as well as on some developed countries). Therefore what is needed is a willingness on the part of these banks to participate, where necessary, in agreements to reschedule debt owed by private and official borrowers. Such rescheduling of client obligations is in line with customary banking practice. An important element of this approach in the months ahead should be the maintenance of confidence between banks and their respective governments; efforts by both parties will be necessary to accomplish this goal. Such confidence will be particularly important in the United States, where a lack of mutually satisfactory consultations between the banks, Congress, and the Executive Branch could lead to actions disruptive to the vital flow of credit to the developing countries.

6. At the same time, the private banks are responsible for making certain that their individual lending is sound and in line with the international economic situation now faced by the developing countries. In this regard, both the banks and the U.S. government should explore the possibility of further cooperation with the International Monetary Fund, the World Bank, and the regional development banks—both to exchange information and to expand the opportunities for cooperative financing.

Technology Transfer

Another issue of great concern to the developing countries is the transfer of technology. Japan and other nations, notably Taiwan, South Korea, China, and Singapore, have demonstrated the great gains that can be made from knowing how to tap the existing technology of industrialized nations. Most developing countries, however, feel they lack the knowledge and skills necessary to offset what they consider to be the monopoly of multinational corporations in this area. In general, developing countries want the widest possible access to the entire range of existing technologies on terms that favor optimal use of local resources and access to this technology at reasonable costs. Above all, developing countries seek to acquire their own capacity to create and adapt technologies congruent with their own needs—thereby diminishing their existing dependency on suppliers in the industrial world, whose technology exports are often "inappropriate" in their current form to developing-country needs and resources.

Against the background of these needs, the secretariat of the U.N. Conference on Trade and Development (UNCTAD) has proposed detailed programs to improve the overall terms under which technology is "transferred" from industrial to developing nations. Its recommendations concern issues such as the disparate bargaining strength of buyers and sellers of technology; the frequent inappropriateness of technologies to the factor endowments (materials, personnel, and capital) of resource-poor countries; an unfair price structure (traceable to what they consider to be an oligopolistic market favoring sellers of technology); the prevalence of "package deal" sales that make it difficult for purchasers to make optimum use of their own resources; restrictive commercial clauses; patterns of research and development that concentrate most technological innovations in developed countries or in laboratories under their control; and outdated patent systems (based on the Paris Convention of 1883) that take insufficient account of the need to make innovations not only profitable but also socially beneficial. The measures recommended by UNCTAD seek to establish greater reciprocity among partners to technology contracts, to foster better use of technology for developmental purposes (such as the creation of employment, the improvement of skill levels, the reduction of excessive economic dependence, etc.), and to facilitate developing-country access to the whole range of existing and potential technologies on terms consonant with their needs.

The resolution of differences between developed and developing countries in technology transfers is especially difficult because the practices of transnational corporations, which are key "actors" in such transactions, do not fall under the direct control of either home- or host-country governments. This is one reason why the current developing-country demands for codes of conduct to govern the transfer of technology face serious problems. There will be considerable difficulty both in obtaining the agreement of all parties concerned and then in assuring compliance with such codes in the absence of effective sanctions.

Ultimately, the real solution to the technology problem is the development of a much stronger indigenous capacity in the developing countries to absorb and create technology appropriate to national needs. Meanwhile, however, vigorous measures to improve the quality and quantity of technology exchanges must be taken by the developing countries themselves. Yet many poor countries still lack the skilled personnel and policies that would enable them to make the best use of even the extensive amount of technology that is already commercially available. Equally important, they lack the ability and the institutions to adapt that technology to their own needs or to develop their own appropriate technologies. The objective of acquiring these capabilities calls for a commitment to the long-range process of educating and training their own nationals, regulating technological imports, and providing a variety of incentive systems to encourage local consumers of technology to make use of local suppliers.

The developing countries, individually and collectively, must make their own decisions about the kinds of technology they wish to import or adapt if that technology is to be congruent with the basic objectives of their national development strategies and priority value choices. Much can also be done by the developing countries working together. This has been the case among the members of the Andean Pact in Latin America, and among other nations working through the U.N. program for technical cooperation among the developing countries. The United States should participate in the exploration of possible ways in which the industrialized countries might better assist the effort of the developing countries to expand and improve technology transfers among themselves.

Although outsiders can support this effort only in limited ways, they can do so far more effectively than heretofore. Title XII of the U.S. bilateral development assistance legislation—a new law which supports the work of the land-grant universities in promoting agricultural development in the low-income countries—is one useful effort to improve and institutionalize U.S. assistance to the poor countries for strengthening their agricultural research base. The World Food and Nutrition Study being conducted for the President under the auspices of the U.S. National Academy of Sciences and due to be completed in mid-1977 will make additional important recommendations on issues of technology transfer in the food field.

The proposals set forth by the United States at the fourth session of UNCTAD in May 1976 sought to reflect the reality of both the needs of the developing countries and the nature of the international technology system. In brief, the United States proposed an International Industrialization Institute to encourage research and development on technology appropriate to the developing countries as well as a variety of other steps in this particular area. These proposals included the establishment of an International Energy Institute to help meet the energy needs of both rich and poor countries; improvement of the amount and quality of technological information available to the developing countries through various international and national organizations, as well as through the training of specialists within the developing countries; making the process of transferring existing technology more effective and equitable by suggesting a series of voluntary guidelines for transnational corporations and governments to limit restrictive practices and facilitate developing-country access to technology; and finally, undertaking thorough preparations throughout 1977 and 1978 for the U.N.-sponsored world Conference on Science and Technology for Development scheduled to take place in 1979.

The issues that will be taken up at this world meeting of course encompass a far wider range of technology issues than the "transfer" of industrial technology alone. They include the need to identify how basic research in science and technology might more effectively contribute to the elimination of the worst aspects of absolute poverty before the end of this century. This is an important set of issues that requires urgent attention if there is to be adequate development progress during the last quarter of this century.

Recommendations

1. The United States should implement the commitments relating to technology transfer made by its delegation at the 1976 session of UNCTAD.

2. The preparations for the U.N. Conference on Science and Technology for Development—including the major U.S. national conference on this subject due to take place in the fall of 1977—should be used by both public and private groups in this country to focus attention on technology issues, including those of great interest to the developing countries, such as codes of conduct, disclosure rules for transnational corporations, and possible new tax legislation. The preparatory analyses and discussion conducted by these groups should contribute in specific terms to the formulation of proposals taken by the U.S. delegation to the 1979 world conference. Like the earlier U.N. conferences on the environment, population, and food, the 1979 conference on science and technology can do much to arouse worldwide interest in these issues and begin serious international action to ensure that the development of technology—and the manner and terms of its transfer—in practice promote rather than impede economic and social development, particularly in the poor countries.

3. The United States should cooperate in exploring suitable general investment and technology-transfer codes of conduct to govern relations between transnational corporations and governments of developed and developing countries. For such exploratory discussions, preference should be given to international forums that permit the participation of all potentially affected parties.

4. The United States should support efforts to revise international patent laws so as to render them more equitable and responsive to the legitimate needs of the developing countries.

5. The United States needs to give increased support to those aspects of technology development and transfer that can contribute substantially to the elimination of the worst aspects of absolute poverty. Greater priority needs to be given to research projects that aim to reach the disadvantaged majority of the population in the poor countries.

A Global Approach to Energy

The United States has given the energy problem top priority among its international economic concerns in the last three years. The issue has been discussed in a number of different forums but without agreement on how it should be addressed or on whether it should be linked to the resolution of other issues between developed and developing countries. It is noteworthy that the United States has approached the world energy problem very differently from the world food problem. While it has treated the food question as a comprehensive problem requiring a coherent, multifaceted global approach, its international diplomacy in the energy field has tended until recently to focus primarily on lower oil prices. Solutions to the world's energy problem need to take account of the energy requirements of both the developed and the developing world if they are to adequately serve either. In addition, the problem of energy from nuclear fission, with all of its costs and benefits, now demands international attention.

It is important that the energy problem be recognized for what it is: a global problem that will best be solved through an international approach. Such a global approach would have many ingredients, including helping energy-poor developing countries with the immediate problem of paying for essential energy imports; helping them develop under-exploited petroleum, coal, and hydropower resources; working cooperatively to evolve a safe global nuclear energy policy; developing a world network of research and development efforts to concentrate on developing the small-scale renewable sources of energy needed in the poorer as well as in the industrialized countries; and nurturing the intellectual and institutional capacities (within all countries as well as at the international level) to anticipate and plan globally for the human use of energy on this planet. Such an approach would not only support the needs of developing countries but would also increase U.S. energy security by helping to make the international energy trading system more dependable.*

The majority of the people in the poor countries are at present essentially bypassed by the commercial energy market, relying almost entirely on human and animal muscle power, sunshine, and locally gathered

---

*See James W. Howe and William Knowland, "Energy and Development: An International Approach," Communique No. 31 (Washington, D.C.: Overseas Development Council, 1977).

wood or animal wastes for their energy supplies. What the developing countries urgently need is a secure supply of *low-cost* energy to support their development (particularly in the rural areas) and to lower their currently very high expenditures for imported oil and petroleum products. These payments threaten to increase further as the developing countries industrialize and expand their energy use and as the OPEC countries raise the price of oil. Most developing countries (like the oil-importing developed countries) resent the extent of their dependence on the oil-producing states, but they recognize the potential economic and political gains of maintaining their "alliance" with the OPEC states.

Many developing countries believe that their only realistic alternative to dependence on petroleum to meet conventional large-scale energy needs is the rapid development of nuclear power. Moreover, the nuclear option is still being subsidized by developed countries and advocated by international agencies such as the International Atomic Energy Agency (IAEA).

Yet at the same time concern is mounting in many countries about the spread of nuclear power. There are four aspects to this concern: 1) the danger of pollution stemming from either the disposal of spent fuel, or an accident in a reactor, or the transport of radioactive materials; 2) the danger that the access of terrorists or criminal groups to nuclear material will be made easier by the proliferation of nuclear technology; 3) the potential that the spread of nuclear energy plants will enable an increasing number of countries to produce their own nuclear weapons; and 4) a growing concern that emphasizing nuclear power may be giving the developing countries precisely the wrong advice.

American energy policy in recent years has recognized few of these problems. The policy of "energy independence" initiated by former President Nixon was, until recently, still being emphasized (at least rhetorically) without acknowledgment that a) the estimated cost of this policy might be as high as $1 trillion (in 1976 dollars), and b) that even if it were feasible, this approach would leave the rest of the world—including our industrial allies and the developing world—dangerously vulnerable to continued dependence on oil imports.

Meanwhile the United States had by the end of 1976 made no serious effort to curb energy use. Its dependence on imported oil has *increased* substantially since 1973, and its per capita energy consumption is nearly 40 per cent above that of Western European countries with similar standards of living. Nor had the United States made available any significant support to developing a viable alternative to either oil or nuclear power; it was in fact still advocating use of nuclear power for energy. U.S. research in the nuclear field has been heavily supported by the federal government, and exports of reactors produced by American firms have been financed at least partly by the Export-Import Bank. Recently, however, there has been growing concern about providing developing countries with those nuclear energy technologies that can be used to produce material for weapons.

It is now worth considering whether the long-run needs of the United States (and of other industrial countries) as well as of the developing countries cannot be served better by helping the developing countries to gradually transcend their dependence on imported oil and, in the longer run, to develop secure energy sources. Specifically, a global approach to energy would place emphasis on helping the oil-importing poor countries develop their existing underutilized deposits of oil, natural gas, coal, and hydropower. Currently, only one well is drilled in the developing countries for every one hundred drilled on geologically comparable terrain in the continental United States—despite the fact that the U.S. Geological Survey suggests that about half of the major new discoveries of oil are likely to be made in the oil-importing developing countries. In many of these countries, there also are extensive and underutilized deposits of coal and, in some areas, great potential exists for hydropower.

The United States should begin to support much more intensive research—both in its own institutions and in those of the developing countries—on small-scale renewable sources of energy such as wind, methane gas, sunshine, and other nonconventional energy sources. In 1977, only 10 per cent of the federal funds allocated for energy research will be spent on solar sources (although that represents an increase of 150 per cent over 1976), and most of that will go to large-scale applications.

Most energy specialists now consider such sources to be the harbinger of the twenty-first century technology to which every country will have to turn sooner or later. Unlike the industrialized countries, which have already invested enormous capital outlays in existing energy technologies, the developing countries may now have a rare opportunity to bypass fossil fuel and nuclear technology and move to use of renewable sources ahead of the industrialized countries. The United States and other donor countries also should support the efforts of developing countries to extend such small-scale renewable technologies to rural areas.

Increased research on utilizing small-scale energy technologies would not only help the developing countries with their own needs but could also provide a growing market for American suppliers of such equipment. Such research might even develop methods that are also applicable to the use of nonrenewable energy resources in the United States. When both the transistor radio and the pocket calculator were first introduced, they cost several hundred dollars apiece; currently, however, they are well within the reach of most American families and, indeed, of many within the developing world. The same kinds of cost reductions may be possible when mass markets are developed for small-scale energy technologies.

Recommendations

1. The United States should develop a coherent national energy policy that recognizes the energy situation to be a global problem that can best be solved through a global approach.

2. The United States should support consideration of the creation of a World Energy Council to coordinate the collection of global energy facts, maintain an energy balance sheet, and conduct global energy analyses and planning.

3. Federal research and development expenditures on renewable sources of energy—including small-scale sources—should be drastically increased for the benefit of both the developing and developed countries, including the United States.

4. The United States should use its influence to assure serious collective consideration of the nuclear option. It should discontinue subsidies on nuclear exports; cooperate in revising the IAEA mandate to focus on regulating the production and handling of nuclear materials; help developing countries find better alternatives to meeting their energy needs; and seek institutional improvements providing for the representation of developing countries in nuclear discussions.

5. The United States and other developed countries should work together with the developing countries to develop and put to use alternatives to nuclear energy—whether through the exploitation of existing coal, oil, and gas deposits, or through the use of renewable and inexhaustible energy sources.

6. U.S. technical assistance programs should provide advice on safety and security to those countries which do choose to develop nuclear power. The United States also should seek to establish multilateral guarantees for the supply of enriched fuel and for waste disposal in order to avoid the spread of enrichment and reprocessing technology. The United States also should press ahead with consultations with other suppliers of nuclear power plants to institute a moratorium on the export of reprocessing and enrichment technologies.

7. The United States should take the lead in convening a world conference on alternative energy sources to focus global attention on these issues and to encourage a comprehensive global approach to their resolution.

8. In order to enhance its credibility in assuming a leadership role in a global energy strategy, the United States should—at the same time it takes action in the above areas—launch a government-supported program of domestic energy conservation.

Oceans Issues

The final phase of the law of the sea negotiations represents a first opportunity to negotiate a "package" agreement that encompasses many of the issues and proposals for restructuring the international economic system. It therefore provides some insights into other negotiations concerning the common use of international resources that will take place in the future.[9]

The U.N. Law of the Sea Conference has been under way formally since 1974. Two sessions were held during 1976, with the second ending inconclusively in September; the Conference will reconvene in May 1977. The last session produced a great deal of pessimism among both participants and observers. That pessimism, however, tended to mask the fact that some achievements have been made since 1974—despite major departures from the original concept of the oceans as the "common heritage" of mankind. Among the areas of agreement are a territorial sea of 12 miles, a 200-mile zone of coastal state jurisdiction, and unimpeded passage through international straits. Initial agreement also has been reached on measures to preserve the marine environment, and there is a consensus on the desirability of establishing an international regime to govern the exploitation of the resources of the deep ocean floor beyond national jurisdiction.

The major shift away from the "common heritage" concept has been the establishment of the "exclusive economic zone" of 200 miles over which coastal states will have sole jurisdiction. This decision excludes landlocked states from sharing a large portion of the ocean's more easily accessible resources, particularly off-shore oil. On this issue, the differences were not between developed and developing countries, but rather between those states with access to the oceans and those that are landlocked or otherwise geographically disadvantaged. Agreement between these groups of states now is near on the issues of overland access to the sea and sharing of fishing resources within the zone.

The major remaining area of contention between the rich and poor countries concerns the design of an acceptable procedure for the exploitation of (and revenue sharing from) the mineral resources of the deep ocean. Most nations agree that some sort of "dual" system that will permit exploitation by the proposed international authority and by private firms will be acceptable. The issue is complicated by the fact that developed-country firms (particularly U.S. firms) already possess advanced technology for this purpose, while such technology is not available to the developing countries or to the proposed international authority. To break the deadlock on this issue, former Secretary of State Kissinger indicated at the September 1976 session of the Conference that the United States would be willing to help with the financing of the new international authority and its acquisition of technology. This proposal was rejected by many Conference participants, however, partly because it was not clear how the international authority would be able to compete on an equal basis with multinational corporations, or how the United States would meet the commitment to provide the necessary financing and technology.

---

[9]On this point, see also Chapter II, pp. 29-30.

Despite the fact that many of the hopes of those who first proposed the Law of the Sea Conference have not been realized, both rich and poor countries still stand to gain from a new treaty. The United States and many other developed countries want access to the ocean's resources and agreed-upon rules for both commercial and military use of the oceans. New regulations to conserve and manage ocean fisheries and to alleviate and prevent maritime pollution are important for all countries. The developing countries stand to benefit from the revenues they may receive from the mining of the deep ocean and from oil extraction beyond 200 miles. (Current estimates indicate, however, that potential revenues from deep-ocean mining by the year 2000 will not be substantial, and many developing nations feel it will be a long time before the oil deposits that lie beyond 200 miles will be exploited.) In addition, both sides would benefit from the stabilizing influence of formally accepted procedures and an international authority to govern the exploitation of what has been termed humanity's "last frontier." The establishment of such an authority also could set a valuable precedent for international cooperation in other areas in the years ahead.

The United States initially played a leading role at the Law of the Sea Conference in proposing a series of global arrangements for the oceans. But many of the far-sighted proposals first raised at the Conference have since been rejected as countries have grown progressively more concerned about extending their own national control. Nevertheless, in 1977 all parties must make the concessions necessary to get specific agreement on the establishment of the proposed international authority. If a compromise can be reached, the prospects for an oceans agreement will be greatly increased; if not, it may no longer be possible to contain pressures within the United States and other developed countries for beginning to mine the deep ocean floor on a unilateral basis. It is also possible that failure to reach agreement in this area would jeopardize commitments already made in the negotiations.

Recommendations

1. The United States should press for early agreement on a comprehensive law of the sea treaty. The original concept of the oceans as the "common heritage of mankind" has eroded, but some useful agreements still can be reached.

2. The key to the successful conclusion of the negotiations will be agreement on the design of a new international authority to govern the exploitation of the resources of the deep ocean and to administer revenues allocated for development; the United States, together with the developed and developing countries, must find a compromise solution in this area that will guarantee some international control over this process while meeting the needs of the private concerns that already possess the technology to exploit these resources.

Food Insecurity

By early 1977 much of the widespread concern over the world food situation that marked the years 1974 and 1975 had dissipated—partly because of the reports of good harvests in 1975 and 1976, which spread the unfortunate impression that the global food problem had been solved. But medium- and longer-range world food security in fact remained as precarious as in 1973.

The 1975/76 world crop rose by only 2 per cent over the previous year, not quite enough to meet the average annual increase in demand from population growth and increasing affluence.[10] The favorable monsoons in South Asia and the return of the rains in the African Sahel were offset by the major shortfall in the Soviet crop and the subsequent purchase by the U.S.S.R. of more than 25 million metric tons of grain in the world market. As a result, the world's grain "reserve" was still just over one month's consumption;[11] and even that was simply the amount left in commercial hands or on farms at the end of the crop year. The expected 8 per cent increase in the 1976/77 crop year improves the outlook over that of the previous year—better weather being the main differentiating factor.

But world production of cereal grains, which totalled about 1.35 billion metric tons in 1976, needs to expand by about 25 million tons per year just to meet rising demand. Food production in the developing countries increased by 4 per cent in 1975, but the need for food has continued to grow faster than production during the 1970s. The cereals deficit in the developing world is projected to increase from an average of 16 million tons per year (the average annual deficit for the period 1969-1972) to at least 85 million tons per year by 1985 (about half of which will be incurred in the low-income countries). If the shortfall increases at that rate, bad weather in any major producing area could prove to be even more disastrous in the future than it was in 1972 and 1973.

The 1974 Rome World Food Conference identified three priority objectives to make the world's food system more secure: establishing a minimum level of assured food aid for the immediate future; creating a system of grain reserves for at least an interim period; and increasing food production in the developing countries, which it recognized to be the only realistic long-term solution to world food insecurity.

For the immediate future, increased and better-planned food aid is essential to world food security and is an additional stimulus to self-reliant development in the food-deficit countries. In 1977, U.S. Public Law 480—the Food for Peace program—is again due for its periodic review. The law consists of two parts devoted, respectively, to sales and grants. Title I, which governs sales, provides for food to be purchased for developing

---

[10]See Annex B, Table B-1.
[11]See Annex B, Table B-3.

countries through the Commodity Credit Corporation; the purchase price is a loan that must be repaid in dollars. Interest rates are low, and repayment periods run as high as forty years. Under Title II, grants are administered by the U.S. private agencies (for example, CARE, Church World Service, and Catholic Relief Services) and by the U.N. World Food Programme.

The total amount of food provided under the Food for Peace program has diminished drastically since the mid-1960s, when about 15 million tons were shipped each year. By comparison, about 6 million tons were provided last year.[12] In the early 1970s, much of this food went not to the poorest countries but rather to countries in which the United States had an immediate political interest, primarily in Southeast Asia. In 1975, however, Congress specified that 70 per cent of the food being provided on a sales basis had to go to countries identified by the United Nations as "most severely affected" by sharply increased petroleum costs; in 1976, Congress required that 75 per cent of such food had to go to countries with per capita incomes under $300.

Several changes now need to be considered if the Food for Peace program is to meet the immediate needs of the poor countries more effectively than it does at present. First, the United States should urge that the World Food Conference's *minimum* world target of 10 million tons of food aid per year be reviewed and, if necessary, raised to a more realistic figure—in which case the U.S. share should be increased from our current 6 million tons to 7 or 8 million tons if appropriate. Second, priority among recipients should be determined by need; only after needs have been satisfied should other considerations be permitted to enter into allocation decisions. Third, there should be more "forward" planning of food aid. Developing countries, which must plan ahead to use their agricultural commodities wisely, need at least a three-year advance commitment; such a pledge also would be useful to American farmers, who face continuing instability in the market. In this sense, the developing countries would be assured of the same long-term commitment for market access that the United States recently extended to the U.S.S.R. and Japan.

Finally, special consideration must be given to the role of food aid in supporting the new development strategies that attempt to combine growth with the more effective address of basic human needs. Indeed, care must be taken to ensure that food aid does not, as it sometimes has in the past, act as a *disincentive* to food production in the developing countries. In the short run, food aid may be a necessity for those countries which undertake a rural development strategy aimed at increasing the purchasing power of their poorest people. A country adopting such a rural development policy places itself at the mercy of the weather; it is therefore important to guarantee access to supplies on concessional terms in case of crop failure.

---

[12]See Annex B, Table B-5 for a summary of Public Law 480 dollar costs.

Little progress has been gained on the global commitments made at the Rome Conference for needs beyond the immediate future—the commitments to create a grain reserve system and to increase agricultural production in the developing countries. Negotiations on a *grain reserve* have proceeded in a desultory fashion and are currently at a stalemate. Over a year ago, the United States proposed to the International Wheat Council that a 30-million-ton grain reserve be created, but discussions foundered over differences between the United States and the European Communities about how food stocks should be acquired and released. These negotiations urgently need to be resumed. Recent research indicates that a 15-million-ton reserve might satisfy anticipated needs and achieve about the same price stabilization effects as the originally proposed 30-million-ton reserve.[13] Thus the cost of a grain reserve system might be considerably lower than originally estimated.

Both rich and poor countries stand to gain from measures to create a global grain reserve system. For the United States, such a system would mean steadier markets for American agricultural products—a factor which could be of immediate benefit if the forecast of bumper crops for 1977 proves accurate. In addition, reserves would help stabilize the wide swings in prices in the U.S. market, thereby benefiting American consumers. It remains important, however, to work out a grain reserve formula that assures farmers in this country an adequate return for their efforts.

The World Food Conference objective of *increasing food production* in the developing countries would help in the long run to keep consumer prices from rising ever higher in the U.S. market by relieving pressure on the North American "breadbasket." Even the abundant agricultural resources of the United States are not likely to be able to meet projected world demand through the 1980s without major price rises. Moreover, the longer-term benefits for the developed countries of increased production in the developing countries should include lowered inflationary pressures, since the developing countries, unlike the more advanced industrial countries, have a real potential for increasing food production at or near current world price levels.

For the developing countries, increased domestic agricultural production would of course mean strengthened food supply stability and would help to meet the needs of their own malnourished populations—not only by increasing the *supply* of food but also by providing greater employment opportunities, thereby increasing income to purchase available food. In the longer run, increased production in the developing countries would also lessen the extent of their dependence on the food-exporting developed countries[14] and would enable the developing countries to use scarce foreign

---

[13]Lance Taylor with Alexander Sarris and Philip Abbott, "Grain Reserves, Emergency Relief, and Food Aid." Overseas Development Council, forthcoming.

[14]Annex B, Table B-4 indicates world net grain trade.

exchange to pay for other imports necessary for their long-term development.

Although much remains to be done if food production in the developing countries is to be increased, some progress has been made in this area. Official assistance by governments and international financial institutions for agricultural development in the poor countries rose from $3.9 billion in 1974 to $5.5 billion in 1975. The OECD- and OPEC-financed International Fund for Agricultural Development (IFAD), first proposed by the OPEC countries at the 1974 World Food Conference, has finally been established and will begin operations shortly. The World Food Council has identified forty-three "priority countries" to which special attention should be directed to increase agricultural production. Four of these countries have already agreed to work out their national food plans with another unit created on the recommendation of the World Food Conference, the Consultative Group on Food Production and Investment in Developing Countries.

Much of the effort to avoid the food deficits projected for the next decade, as well as to improve the longer-term food prospect, will fall to the developing countries themselves. Many of the poor countries have the capacity to produce more food. (If rice farmers in Bangladesh, for example, were to attain Japanese yield levels, their rice production would more than triple.) But the attainment of increased production in many developing countries still requires, among other things, a strong commitment by the governments of these countries to implement a range of rural development measures—including such politically contentious steps as land reform—a commitment that often has been lacking. In addition, the developed world has an important role to play in the efforts to increase food production in the poorer countries, particularly in providing the resources to support greatly expanded rural development programs; in preventing actions that inhibit genuine rural development; and in cooperating with the developing countries on increased and more effectively targeted research.

This discussion and the recommendations set forth below focus primarily on food insecurity resulting from market demand for food outrunning supply and from crop shortfalls due to weather changes and other natural disasters. A separate hunger issue is presented by the poverty problem itself—a subject which is discussed under the heading "Basic Human Needs" in these recommendations. It is important to remember that even if world food production were to increase very substantially along *present patterns* over the next five years, this increased production alone would not greatly affect existing patterns of malnourishment and hunger—which are the principal reasons why millions die prematurely every year. Over the short run, hunger and malnourishment are less a problem of production and market price than a consequence of the lack of purchasing power among the growing body of underemployed and unemployed in the developing countries. There is even evidence that some patterns for greatly increasing food production—for example, the spread of large mechanized farms in northern Mexico—can aggravate the hunger and poverty problem for a growing body of underemployed landless laborers. An effective attack on the world hunger problem must include a comprehensive strategy to eliminate the worst aspects of the basic underlying problem of pervasive absolute poverty in the poor countries.

Recommendations

1. As the world's largest food exporter, the United States must more effectively exercise its responsibility for ensuring that the world's food system functions. This means, above all, that it must have a responsible food policy. In 1977, Congress is due to re-examine most major U.S. food and agriculture legislation. It is essential that their re-examination treat both the international and the domestic aspects of this issue as parts of a single system which requires a unified policy.

2. Global food production and distribution are areas in which this country should be exercising consistent leadership. The United States should therefore increase its commitments to bilateral and multilateral development assistance programs, giving particular emphasis to programs which support the low-income developing countries in their efforts to increase food production and improve its distribution.

3. The United States should give high priority to resuming negotiations within both the International Wheat Council and the World Food Council aimed at establishing a world food reserve. Without waiting for these negotiations, however, the United States should make available the 450,000 tons of grain still needed to establish the emergency reserve of 500,000 metric tons called for by the Seventh Special Session of the U.N. General Assembly in September 1975.

4. The United States should commit itself to guaranteeing an annual minimum of food aid on the basis of a three-year advance commitment. In both sales and grant programs, first priority should continue to be provided to the countries experiencing the greatest need. New legislation should ensure that the food provided is used to advance, not undercut, development goals. The 1975 provision allowing recipient countries to keep up to 15 per cent of the funds generated from sales if they use these funds for agricultural development purposes should be expanded where experience indicates that this is desirable.

Basic Human Needs

Nearly one billion people are believed to live in absolute poverty around the world in the mid-1970s. It is estimated that absolute poverty characterizes the lives of 750 million people, or nearly two thirds of the population, in the low-income countries; 170 million people in the middle-income countries;

and 20 million in the world's richer countries (those living in relative poverty would, of course, be several times as high).[15]

Recent OECD studies indicate that relative poverty in the industrial countries results mainly from inadequate political will to address the problem seriously. Those countries which have introduced policies to eliminate internal poverty problems (e.g., Germany and the Scandinavian countries) have only some 3 per cent of their populations living in relative poverty and a much smaller proportion living in absolute poverty. The proportion living below the relative poverty line in the United States decreased substantially after sustained attention was devoted to anti-poverty programs in the 1960s, with the number living below the relative poverty line having been more than halved since the mid-1960s.[16]

The changes in the various international economic systems proposed earlier in these "Recommendations for U.S. Policy" should provide the governments of many of the *middle-income* developing countries with the additional income needed to eliminate the worst aspects of absolute poverty in their countries within the next twenty-five years—provided that these countries themselves adopt policies for securing the more effective participation of the majority of their citizens in development programs and for delivering services and benefits to the poor majority. As in the developed countries, the question of meeting the needs of the poorest people within these countries therefore becomes one of the political will of those in power and of the internal distribution of political power among groups.*

However, eliminating the absolute poverty of the one billion people who live mainly within the more than forty *low-income* countries raises a quite different set of questions. Because of their lower gross national product levels, these countries face not only more difficult political problems in redistributing both income and productive assets but also far more intractable *economic* problems than the middle-income countries in attempting to finance health, education, and other services for the "poor majority" of their populations. In many cases it will be virtually impossible for these countries to overcome their problems in the years immediately ahead without substantial outside concessional assistance. The poorest countries are not just last in the world's economic growth race. Their per capita incomes—averaging $150 in 1973—are approximately half those of the United States in 1776, or of Great Britain at the beginning of the Industrial Revolution. They are pervasively poor in a way that was not true of today's rich countries in the early stages of their own development—when Europeans by the millions were free to settle in the vast, lightly populated lands of the Americas, Australia, and Siberia.

---

[15]See Annex A, Table A-7, for data on disparities between groups of countries.

[16]Organisation for Economic Co-operation and Development, *Public Expenditures on Income Maintenance Programmes*, Studies in Resource Allocation No. 3 (Paris: OECD, July 1976), Annex II, pp. 108-9.

*See Mahbub ul Haq, *The Third World and the International Economic Order*, Development Paper No. 22 (Washington, D.C.: Overseas Development Council, 1976).

As noted earlier in this *Agenda*, there is a growing consensus among development specialists in both rich and poor countries concerning the set of development strategies that could be most effective in eliminating the worst aspects of absolute poverty in the developing countries by the end of this century. In this connection, one recent proposal—the Club of Rome report entitled *Reshaping the International Order* (RIO)—suggests that such a common goal for *all* countries might consist of the achievement of the following targets by the year 2000: life expectancy of 65 years or more (compared with 48 years at present in the low-income countries), a literacy rate of at least 75 per cent (compared with the present 33 per cent), an infant mortality rate of 50 or less per thousand births (or less than two fifths of the current average), and a birth rate of 25 or less per thousand (compared with the current 40 per thousand in the low-income countries).[17]

There is increasing agreement that economic growth and a more equitable distribution of its benefits can be achieved simultaneously. The strategies that promote this outcome—by using relatively more labor and less capital and by emphasizing programs aimed directly at meeting minimum human needs for health care, education, nutrition, and housing—are discussed in detail elsewhere in this volume.[18] A neglected aspect of most of the strategies designed to date is the situation of women in developing countries, especially in the rural areas, where the majority of the people live. In many countries, women suffer more than men from poor health, lack of education, and inadequate nutrition, and often carry the most burdensome workload. In many countries, their traditional roles confine them to tasks which, however critical, are not remunerated in cash, and deter their entry into more specialized paid work. These factors reinforce their low status. Traditional development programs may alleviate the physical aspects of the condition of women, but equitable improvement of their status requires far-reaching changes in existing socio-economic structures to provide for their participation in both decisions and benefits on the same basis with men. Development programs that do not make improving the situation of women an integral part of their planning are not likely to succeed. This problem is not primarily a "women's" issue, but rather an important challenge to be met in the design and implementation of any basic human needs strategy of development.[19]

The new basic needs approaches raise serious political problems, as already mentioned, in that they would require most developing-country governing elites to allocate scarce resources differently than they do at present. They would, for instance, require either very significant increases in taxes or a sharp reduction in government services now provided to the

---

[17]*Reshaping the International Order* (RIO), A Report to the Club of Rome, Jan Tinbergen, Coordinator (New York: E. P. Dutton & Co., Inc., 1976), p. 130.

[18]See pp. 61-66 of this volume.

[19]See Irene Tinker, Michèle Bo Bramsen, and Mayra Buvinić, eds., *Women and World Development*, 2 Vols. (Washington, D.C.: Overseas Development Council, 1976).

relatively advantaged groups within these countries, or some combination of both. Therefore the adoption of these new approaches in the near term in many of the developing countries is not likely without increased financial, political, and moral support from the outside.*

Estimates of what it would cost to eliminate the worst aspects of absolute poverty indicate that if programs costing somewhere in the range of an additional $10-$15 billion per year (in 1973 dollars) were to be undertaken to assist the poorest groups within the low income countries, the worst aspects of absolute poverty could be eliminated before the end of this century. The funds generated for this purpose—through internal taxation, assistance from the outside, or, in most cases, a combination of both —would be used for programs designed to provide improved food and nutrition, education, water supply, transport, health, and family planning.

This necessary additional $10-$15 billion appears difficult to achieve when it is recognized that the sum of $10 billion represents about 6-7 per cent of the GNP of the low-income countries; and this percentage of GNP, in turn, roughly equals their total current revenues from taxation. This "fact of life" makes it quite apparent that undertaking the political and economic costs of such programs would call for great political courage—and strength—on the part of political leaders in developing countries. It also makes it amply clear that the action to implement such programs may, in many developing countries, depend *very significantly* on the degree to which the industrial countries are willing to ease the political burdens by sharing the costs during the initial years, with the poor countries themselves providing, over a longer period, a progressively larger share of the total out of their own growth.

With this difficult reality firmly in mind, it certainly should be recognized that the sum of $10-$15 billion appears much more manageable if assessed in comparison to the $13 billion official development assistance provided by the industrial countries in 1975. Of course most of this $13 billion was not targeted to reach the poorest groups within the poorest countries. In fact, most did not even go to the poorest countries.[20] A major portion of U.S. development assistance was provided to a number of relatively higher-income countries—including, among others, Egypt, Syria, Israel, and Jordan—for a variety of political, economic, and military reasons.[21]

A $10 billion increase in aid for the purpose of meeting basic human needs would in fact be feasible a) if the developed countries were to reach or exceed an aid level of at least 0.5 per cent of GNP by 1981; b) if some portion of the aid now going to middle-income countries were redirected to

*James P. Grant, "The World's Poorest Billion People: A New Approach to Basic Needs." Overseas Development Council, forthcoming.

[20]See Annex E, Table E-23.

[21]See Annex E, Table E-18.

120

low-income countries; and c) if these increases were to be earmarked solely for a more effective address of basic human needs for jobs, health, nutrition, education, and other essential services.

Recommendations

1. The United States should significantly increase its financial support to programs in the low-income countries that are designed to address the basic needs of their poor majorities.

2. The United States should support major studies to explore:

(a) What measures would be required in developing countries to eliminate the worst aspects of poverty (among women as well as men) including measures required within developing countries to enable all people to attain, by the year 2000, life expectancy of at least 65 years, literacy rates of 75 or more, infant mortality of less than 50 per thousand births, and a birth rate of less than 25 per thousand; and

(b) The extent and forms of cooperation required from the industrial democracies to make the attainment of these goals possible in both the low-income and middle-income developing countries over the next generation.

These studies should also encompass the exploration of possible mechanisms for such cooperation and the potential degree of Northern commitment to such a program.

3. The United States government should—on all appropriate occasions, including its statements in major international forums and discussions with foreign leaders—emphasize its interest in significantly more supportive cooperation with governments that are prepared to seriously address the basic needs of the "poor majority" of their populations. U.S. policies should be designed to favor such countries in a variety of ways, ranging from increased aid to increased attention from American leaders.

Population

At its present annual rate of growth of just under 2 per cent, the world's population of roughly 4 billion people is expected to near the 6 billion mark at the turn of the century and to double in the second decade of the twenty-first century. This continuing growth constitutes a most serious problem for humanity in a myriad of different ways, including its pressure on limited food supplies, the environment, and on the already precarious situation of the world's poorest people.

The world's population has grown very rapidly in the past twenty-five years, mainly in the developing world, because death rates have until recently declined faster than birth rates. In the past several years, overall population growth rates have been declining. To lower the birth rate as rapidly as possible toward a stable level, the worst aspects of poverty in the poor countries must be relieved by improving health care, nutrition, employment, education, and the status of women. In addition, family planning and related programs need to be substantially expanded and improved through research and other means.

The Agency for International Development (AID) began family planning assistance in 1965. With strong congressional backing, funding rose rapidly to about $100 million in fiscal years 1974-1976 and may reach $150 million in fiscal 1977. Thus over the last ten years about $750 million has been made available for "population" and the same amount for health. The program's emphasis to date on the delivery of family planning supplies and services rather than on research on the factors that motivate couples to have large families has made it controversial in many circles. The support provided by the United States government goes to developing-country governments either directly, or indirectly through the U.N. Fund for Population Activities (UNFPA), to whose total resources of $90 million in 1976 the United States contributed $25 million; and to private associations in developing countries through the International Planned Parenthood Federation (IPPF). Together, AID, UNFPA, IPPF, and some fifty governments (including Germany, Japan, the United Kingdom, and the Scandinavian countries) now provide about $230 million for international population assistance. Additional assistance in this field is needed both to provide substantially increased funds for basic research and to support expanded family planning programs. Indeed, since the World Population Conference in Bucharest in 1974, requests for assistance to initiate or expand family planning programs have doubled, exceeding the resources now available.

The population growth rate is also very much dependent upon the development process. Parental motivation on the size of families is a key factor in the situation. When parents no longer need to have six children to ensure that one or two survive to help support them in old age; when infant mortality has dropped below 50 per thousand; when literacy and employment increase; and when women are provided with economic and social options that make childbearing, too, more of an option, it is highly probable that the birth rate—and with it, the population growth rate—will decline. What differentiates the handful of developing countries which have experienced sharply decreasing birth rates while their per capita income remained low and when they had not yet launched major family planning programs (e.g., Sri Lanka, Taiwan, South Korea, and probably China) is that they have all been far more successful than other low-income countries in addressing the basic human needs of their poor majorities. Those low-income countries which have achieved dramatic reductions in birth rates in recent years have done so through a combination of such developmental approaches with vigorous family planning programs.

One of the best commentaries on the relationship of development and population growth was made by John D. Rockefeller III at the 1974 Bucharest World Population Conference:

> The only viable course is to place population policy solidly within the context of general economic and social development . . . This approach recognizes that rapid population growth is only one among many problems facing most countries, that it is a multiplier and intensifier of other problems rather than the cause of them . . . It recognizes that motivation for family planning is best stimulated by hope that living conditions and opportunities in general will improve.

Recommendations

1. Through its national, bilateral, and multilateral population programs, the United States should significantly increase support for expanding acceptable family planning programs in the developing countries.

2. The United States should greatly increase research efforts to develop more effective and acceptable methods of fertility control and to assess the impact of different kinds of health, nutrition, employment, and other basic needs programs on decisions concerning family size.

Human Rights

For reasons elaborated in Chapter II of this volume, the United States and the developing countries may soon find it necessary to jointly consider the basic questions of human rights—including the difficult and complex relationship between political rights and economic rights.[22] These different aspects of human rights are quite clearly reflected in the two parts of the U.N. Universal Declaration of Human Rights. The first half of that document sets forth a series of political rights; the second, a wide-ranging set of economic and social rights. The former tend to be given higher priority by the industrialized countries and the latter by the developing countries. But there is at present no agreement—and even very little discussion—on how these two aspects of human rights should be related, which should be given priority, and how the United States might seek to advance both types of rights simultaneously.

These issues are highly sensitive to begin with, and their serious discussion at the international level is made extremely difficult by the fact that the governments of a growing majority of the developing countries are—in varying degrees—authoritarian regimes. This is particularly true in the low-income countries, many of which are characterized by the threatening combination of extreme poverty among the majority of their popula-

---

[22]See especially pp. 74-75 and 82-85.

tions, acute stagflation (particularly since the events of 1973), and growing political awareness among their citizens.[23]

The human rights issue has grown increasingly important both because of its intrinsic merit and because it has become an item of contention between Congress and the Executive Branch. Congress has expressed its concern about human rights and has been placing restrictions on both the development assistance program (International Development and Food Assistance Act of 1975) and the security assistance program (International Security Assistance and Arms Export Control Act of 1976). Both statutes specify that assistance is to be cut off (with an exception procedure for development aid) from countries that engage in "a consistent pattern of gross violations" of those rights, "including torture or cruel, inhuman, or degrading treatment or punishment, prolonged detention without charges, and other flagrant denial of the right to life, liberty, and the security of person." Countries which officially discriminate on the basis of race, religion, national origin, or sex or which "grant sanctuary to international terrorists" also fall under this policy. The President is also directed to avoid identifying the United States with governments that deny their citizens these rights. Specific written justification for exceptions in the case of development assistance is required, indicating that "such assistance will directly benefit the needy people in such country."

Congress also has taken specific action on the question of economic and social rights. In 1976, both the House and the Senate passed very similar "Right to Food" resolutions, initiated and supported by a large number of private organizations and individuals concerned about hunger and development issues. The House resolution stated "that every person in this country and throughout the world has the right to food—the right to a nutritionally adequate diet; that this right is henceforth recognized as a cornerstone of U.S. policy; and [that this right should] become a fundamental point of reference in the formation of legislation and administrative decisions in areas such as trade, assistance, monetary reform, military spending, and all other matters that bear on hunger."

---

[23]The Comparative Survey of Freedom conducted annually by Freedom House categorizes all countries under the three headings of "free," "partly free," and "not free." There is considerable dispute about the criteria that this survey employs, but it is noteworthy that its list identifies as "free"—among countries with a population of over 1 million—only one low-income country (Sri Lanka) and only seven middle-income countries (Venezuela, Turkey, Trinidad, Papua-New Guinea, Jamaica, Costa Rica, and Colombia). In population terms, the survey lists only some 100 million of the 3 billion people in the developing countries as being under systems of government which are relatively "free." Countries such as Tanzania, Cuba, and China—which are widely considered to be countries seriously interested in addressing the basic human needs of their poor majorities—are classified as "not free." The populous countries of Bangladesh, Brazil, Egypt, India, Indonesia, Mexico, Nigeria, and Pakistan are listed as "partly free." Sri Lanka is the only one among the poorest countries to rank high under both the political and economic justice headings. See *Freedom at Issue*, No. 39, January-February 1977. Published by Freedom House, New York.

The usual remedy proposed for violations of human political rights that are deemed gross in the congressional initiatives has been to cut off economic and military assistance. But cutting development aid in particular is usually a weak lever to force governments to restore human rights to the people, especially in the absence of other stronger indications of U.S. displeasure with the actions of other governments. In recent years, U.S. development assistance programs, although diminished, have concentrated on programs that reach the poorest people within recipient countries. Cutting off aid to these groups on the grounds that their government is exercising political oppression may have the effect of punishing them further for the very actions which victimize them and over which they have no control. Consequently, any U.S. Administration seriously concerned about human rights violations in other countries must use a variety of other means to express that concern—preferably means which inflict costs primarily on the aggressors and not on their victims. A much more comprehensive and effective approach than the severance of aid would be a response combining statements by the President or the Secretary of State commending governments that honor human rights and condemning those which do not; visits by the President or Secretary of State to countries on that basis; restraint of U.S. private investment and requirements that development aid demonstrably reach needy people in countries where "gross violations" are the practice; the easing of immigration and asylum requirements for victims of such violations; support for recognized international organizations concerned with human rights; and the requirement that development assistance truly benefit the poor majority. Cutting off aid is only a marginal penalty (at best) in most cases, and it may, in addition, prove highly disruptive to other long-range objectives of the United States, such as helping countries to achieve population stabilization and increase food production.

Recommendations

1. The United States should take vigorous action to ensure that the bulk of its development assistance funds is allocated to projects which benefit the poor majority in the poorest countries; assistance to countries which do not share this commitment should be reduced or terminated.

2. The United States should, through appropriate international action, actively seek to establish widely accepted criteria for the assessment of "gross violations" of political human rights—preferably by recognized international organizations such as the United Nations' Human Rights Commission, the Red Cross, the International Commission of Jurists, or Amnesty International. A senior official in the State Department (preferably at the Under-Secretary level) should have responsibility for U.S. actions to further human rights.

3. The U.S. should recongize that merely cutting off aid is unlikely to end gross violations of human rights. Instead, the whole range of U.S.

policies toward countries that engage in such violations should be re-examined to identify internationally acceptable ways of exerting pressure upon such regimes to change their policies.

4. The United States and other democratic countries need to jointly consider what kinds of international policies would effectively promote human rights in the years ahead. This consideration should focus not only on political rights, but also on economic rights—on effective international cooperation to enable the world's one billion people living in extreme poverty to attain their basic human needs.

Development Assistance

The programs that will be among the most beneficial to the development of the low-income countries in the foreseeable future are those which transfer resources to them on a concessional basis. Most of the poorest countries will need "aid" in one form or another for the balance of this century. The United States now provides resources on concessional terms to the developing countries through a variety of development assistance programs. These "official development assistance" programs (ODA) include bilateral development assistance in the form of both grants and loans, and U.S. contributions to multilateral institutions, including the World Bank's International Development Association (IDA) and the U.N. Development Programme (UNDP). In the future, additional resources for development may be available from "automatic" sources, such as an international regime for the oceans or from international taxation.

If this country is to support efforts to alleviate the worst effects of absolute poverty, these programs will be of renewed importance in the years ahead. Development assistance therefore will be a key issue for the United States in 1977. Two of the major bilateral programs—bilateral development assistance and Food for Peace—will be up for reauthorization, and funding for a variety of multilateral programs, including the fifth replenishment of IDA, will also be at issue.[24]

American efforts in the area of development assistance have been conspicuously lagging. Currently the United States contributes less than 0.3 per cent of its GNP as official development assistance, and this percentage is headed downward in budget projections for the next several years.[25] This total contrasts with the target of 0.7 per cent set in 1970 as part of the International Strategy for the Second U.N. Development Decade and agreed to by most developed countries (but not the United States). The 0.3 per cent contribution of the United States is a lower percentage of national

---

[24]For recommendations on food policy, see pp. 113-17.
[25]See Annex E, Tables E-9, E-10, 11, 12, 14, 15, 16, 17, for information on U.S. ODA and that of all other OECD Development Assistance Committee (DAC) countries as well.

wealth than that contributed by twelve of the seventeen other OECD aid donors. (The only countries providing a lower percentage are Switzerland, Italy, Finland, Austria, and Japan). It also is lower than that of a majority of those oil-exporting nations which are providing development assistance.[26] In terms of constant dollars, U.S. ODA has declined by nearly 50 per cent since 1963, from the equivalent of approximately $7.8 billion in 1975 dollars to $4 billion in 1975. During this same period, U.S. GNP has increased by more than 20 per cent, or by over $300 billion in 1975 dollars.

U.S. Official Development Assistance, 1961, 1964-1966 Average, 1970, and 1973-1977
($ millions and percentages)

	Current $	Constant 1961 $	As Percentage of Federal Expenditures	As Percentage of GNP
	(millions)			
1961	2,943	2,943	3.0	.56
1964-1966 Avg.	453	3,203	2.9	.50
1970	3,050	2,540	1.6	.31
1973	2,968	1,789	1.2	.23
1974	3,439	1,682	1.3	.25
1975	4,007	1,797	1.3	.26
1976	4,222	1,789	1.1	.25
1977	4,530	1,819	1.1	.24

SOURCE: Based on Organisation for Economic Co-operation and Development (OECD) and U.S. Office of Management and Budget (OMB) data.

The new Administration should commit itself to an increase in the level of U.S. development assistance, moving gradually toward the 0.7 per cent target. A reasonable interim goal would be to reach by FY 1981 a minimum level of disbursements equal to the 0.5 per cent of GNP that prevailed in the mid-1960s and to maintain thereafter at least the average of the other industrial countries. Indeed, this target was endorsed by President Carter on several occasions during his election campaign. (If all OECD countries had provided 0.5 per cent of GNP for development assistance in 1975, total ODA would have been nearly $19 billion rather than $13.6 billion.) In dollar amounts, a 0.5 per cent target would increase U.S. official development assistance from $4 billion in 1975 to over $9 billion in 1981 (in 1975 dollars).

---

[26]See Annex E, Tables E-8 and E-22, for comparisons of ODA of DAC countries, OPEC countries, and centrally planned economies.

These funds could be transferred through a variety of bilateral and multilateral mechanisms, but they should be focused on programs aimed primarily at the poorest majority living mainly in the poorest countries. In the middle-income countries, where severe poverty persists in certain areas, the U.S. government should provide bilateral assistance in greater partnership with American private and voluntary organizations.

An increase in U.S. development assistance of this magnitude would raise a number of questions concerning the mechanisms for ensuring that these additional funds were spent wisely. A good portion of the increased amount of aid would have to be channeled through international financial institutions. Currently about 25 per cent of U.S. aid—about $1 billion in 1975—is contributed to multilateral financial institutions.[27] Another problem with advocating increased resource flows to the developing countries is the lack of an adequate measure of need. The standard now in use—that each donor nation should provide 0.7 per cent of its gross national product in the form of development assistance—is based neither on the amount that might be required to achieve economic goals (e.g., a certain growth rate in GNP), nor on social goals (e.g., targeted reductions in illiteracy, infant mortality, or malnutrition). Nor is there any comprehensive assessment of what would constitute a "fair share" for aid donors, including the industrialized countries as well as OPEC, Eastern Europe, and the Soviet Union. In effect, the accepted 0.7 per cent target which has been agreed to by most nations is a measure of willingness *to give* but not a measure of *need*.

At the present moment, accelerating the development progress of the world's poorest countries is not a priority goal for most aid donors. When there is general agreement on such a goal, some type of "global development budget" will have to be formulated to assess the needs of the developing countries on an annual basis and to determine the fair share of participation of various aid donors. Such a process should take into account factors other than development assistance—for instance, trade, capital flows, and debt problems—and should be carried out by one or more international institutions with the participation of both developed and developing countries. Some work already has been done in this area both in the International Development Strategy adopted by the United Nations at the beginning of the First Development Decade and within groups such as the U.N. Committee on Development Planning. Similar processes have been carried out on an international basis (as in the case of the consortium of governments and agencies that provides aid to India) and on a regional basis (as in the new consultative arrangements involving both donors and recipients interested in long-range development in the Sahelian region of Africa).

Bilateral Development Cooperation. The American bilateral development aid program has gone through a number of permutations since it was first established in the late 1940s. There was no significant change in the

---

[27]See Annex E, Table E-11.

emphasis of development assistance, however, between 1961 and 1973. In 1973, bilateral development assistance legislation was totally rewritten, largely at congressional initiative. The redirection that took place at that time shifted the emphasis from strategies aimed at maximizing economic growth and industrialization to those focusing on helping the poorest groups within the poorer countries, particularly those in the rural areas. Funds were appropriated according to functional categories: food production and nutrition, health and population, and education. This new objective was summarized in the preamble to the current legislation, which states that American development aid will be used to

> help countries solve development problems in accordance with the strategy that aims to increase substantially the participation of the poor. Accordingly, greatest emphasis should be placed on countries and activities which effectively involve the poor in development by expanding their access to the economy through services and institutions at the local level, increasing labor-intensive production, spreading productive investment services out from major cities to small towns and outlying rural areas, and otherwise providing opportunities for the poor to better their lives through their own effort.

This legislation put the congressional sponsors of the bill clearly on the side of those who favored the "basic human needs" development strategies described elsewhere in this volume. Yet the United States—despite claims that it is making an effort to redirect its aid to the poor countries—still provided 47 per cent of its bilateral ODA to countries with per capita incomes of under $200 in 1975, and only 22 per cent in 1976.

The bilateral aid legislation—the International Development and Food Assistance Act of 1975—requires reauthorization in 1977. This offers Congress a good opportunity to review the record since 1973 and to institute whatever changes are necessary, including increased authorizations, to make the program more congruent with the needs of the developing countries.

Special consideration should be given to programs in countries that have committed themselves to increasing equity within their own societies and to meeting the minimum human needs of the majority of their populations. Equity-oriented countries such as Sri Lanka and Tanzania should receive more U.S. support than they have in the past. The United States also should fulfill its implicit commitment to support the multinational effort now under way to promote long-term development in the desperately poor Sahelian region of Africa; a "fair" U.S. share of this effort could run as high as $1 billion over a period of more than a decade. Unfortunately, American policy often has moved in the opposite direction from supporting equity-oriented countries. This was the case with Chile, where the regime of former President Allende, despite its faults, was committed to meeting the minimum basic needs of the Chilean people; and also with Thailand, where the United

129

States tended to oppose rather than support the democratic regime that came to power in 1974 and was overthrown by right-wing military forces in 1976.

The two-decade-long effort to separate economic and military aid programs should be made final in 1977. Military aid itself will be largely phased out at congressional direction by 1978. But politically oriented economic aid, known as "security supporting assistance," which was originally designed to provide assistance to countries that had to maintain high defense budgets because of a threat from a common enemy (i.e., communism) remains. Currently the great majority of security supporting assistance goes either to the Middle East or to countries where the United States has a particular political interest, such as Portugal, Malta, and Zaire.[28] These programs may well be important for political reasons, but their linkage with assistance for the development of the poor countries leads to confusion in the minds of both Congress and the public. This confusion is enhanced by the fact that supporting assistance is counted within the definition of official development assistance. Funds for political purposes should be more clearly identified as an entity separate from the development assistance program.

Finally, mention needs to be made of U.S. bilateral cooperation with India. Since a majority of the world's poorest people live in India, there cannot be an effective global address of the world's population, poverty, and food problems without effective Indian participation. Yet ever since the revolution in Bangladesh in 1971, the United States has suspended all major non-food aid programs to India. The previous Administration had never evinced much enthusiasm, either before or after 1971, for development cooperation with India. Following the Indian nuclear explosion in 1973 and Prime Minister Indira Gandhi's declaration of the State of Emergency in 1975, which was accompanied by political arrests of thousands and the imposition of censorship, this coolness increased and affected a much larger proportion of the American public. While as much or more political freedom remained in India as in most other developing countries with which the United States had major programs, the retrogressive nature of political developments in India and the circumstances under which they occurred contributed considerably to sapping remaining American support for India's development. With the advent of a new Administration in Washington coincident with what appears to be a significant reversal of political trends in India—notably the release of most political prisoners, significant easing of censorship, and general elections in the spring of 1977—the stage should be set for increased bilateral cooperation on fundamental issues and support of population stabilization programs and addressing basic needs.

Multilateral Development Cooperation. The United States now contributes to a number of multilateral aid programs that provide assistance

---

[28]See Annex E, Table E-18, for major recipients of U.S. economic assistance, including security supporting assistance in FY 1975.

to the developing countries. These include the World Bank and its associated agencies, the Asian Development Bank, the Inter-American Development Bank, and the African Development Fund, as well as the U.N. agencies, including the U.N. Development Programme, the U.N. Fund for Population Activities, and the U.N. Children's Fund. These programs have become increasingly important in the last decade, both in the amount of resources they provide to the developing countries and, particularly in the case of the World Bank, in the intellectual leadership they provide in the international development effort.

The year 1977 is particularly crucial for these institutions. The United States already is in arrears in its contributions to the regional banks and some U.N. agencies, and new authorizations are pending. Replenishment of the International Development Association—the World Bank's "soft-loan" window—and an increase in the capital of the World Bank and of its private-sector affiliate, the International Finance Corporation, also are at issue. The future of IDA is particularly important because its programs focus almost exclusively on the poorest countries. IDA is replenished every three years by pledges from a variety of countries, and its fifth replenishment is now being negotiated. The target figure accepted by most countries for the fifth replenishment is $7.2 billion from the OECD countries, with one third of that amount to be provided by the United States, the remaining two thirds by the other OECD countries, and an additional amount yet to be determined by the OPEC countries. As of early 1977, the United States was in default in appropriating $55 million for the fourth replenishment (to which it had agreed) and a year behind in actual contributions.

If the United States is to make a serious commitment during the coming years to supporting programs aimed at meeting minimum human needs in the developing countries, decisions taken on the next replenishment of the IDA, as well as on increased support for the regional development banks, will be of crucial importance. For that reason, the United States should advocate that IDA be replenished at a level of $9 billion, with at least $8.1 billion coming from the OECD countries. An increase of this amount is advisable for several reasons. First, if the United States is to reach a level of development assistance equal to 0.5 per cent of GNP, a good deal of this increase, as mentioned earlier, should be channeled through multilateral agencies. Increasing the IDA replenishment to a level of $7.2 billion would require only $800 million of U.S. funds a year; an increase to $8.1 billion would mean only $900 million annually from the United States. Second, this level of increase will be necessary just to soften the effect of inevitable inflation. Finally, an increased U.S. contribution to IDA in 1977 would be seen by many people both in the United States and in other countries as a timely indication of America's serious concern about economic and social progress in the developing countries.

The issue of expanding the World Bank's capital resources also must be resolved. There must be an increase in capital beyond the current

131

statutory limit of $33 billion so that the Bank can expand its lending at market rates to the middle-income developing countries. A selective capital increase of $8.9 billion already has been agreed that will allow the Bank to maintain its present rate of lending in current dollars. In the future, the question of further increasing the Bank's capital will need to be faced in order to enable its lending to keep up with growing needs. Several countries, led by the United States, have expressed reservations on this quesiton. Given the expanding potential and needs of the middle-income developing countries, the United States should strongly support an appropriate increase when the question is raised.

Automatic Sources. Over the longer run, it would be desirable to provide the resources necessary to meet the needs of the developing countries through a series of more *automatic* sources of transfers that will ensure a continuing flow of resources without the year-to-year uncertainties that now mark the development cooperation process. In effect, this process would institutionalize much the same principle that has led most developed countries to institute income taxes and a variety of other taxes on economic activity within their own boundaries.

The idea is not as far-fetched as it may seem at first glance. Indeed, the first "automatic" source of development assistance for the developing countries—the International Monetary Fund's Trust Fund—already is in the process of being implemented. The Trust Fund will use a portion of the difference between the price obtained from selling some of the IMF's gold at the official rate ($35 an ounce) and the market value to help developing countries that are having balance-of-payments difficulties. Another "automatic" source may come into existence when the nations of the world come to agreement on a new law of the sea treaty; the international authority to govern exploitation of the minerals of the deep ocean will use some portion of its revenues for the development of the poor countries.

A number of other automatic sources currently are under discussion. One which has received considerable attention is the link between the issuance of Special Drawing Rights, the International Monetary Fund's new reserve asset, and their use for development needs. Other proposals include taxes on a variety of items: exploitation of nonrenewable resources, international pollution, activities of multinational corporations in developing countries, earnings of developing-country citizens working in the developed countries (which would be rebated to their home countries), and revenues from the world's "commons" (including not only the seabed but also areas such as Antarctica and activities such as satellite communications).

One key issue to be resolved, however, concerns the difference between resources which are *generated* "automatically" (as are taxes currently) and those which are *distributed* "automatically." Many developing countries will want the revenues from these sources distributed automatically among countries on the basis of some formula considered to be equitable; the developed countries are much more likely to want to see these funds transferred through some international mechanism for internationally agreed objectives in support of development.

Recommendations

1. New U.S. economic assistance legislation should authorize a substantially increased level of official development assistance expenditures for FY 1978 and FY 1979, including a commitment to meet a disbursement target of 0.5 per cent of GNP by FY 1981 on the conditions that a large share of the funds (at least as high as 75 per cent) will go to countries with per capita incomes below $300 and that there is reasonable assurance that these funds will primarily benefit their poor majorities.

2. The legislation should make it clear that the principal purpose of the bilateral development aid program is to improve the productive capacity and well-being of people through the development of recipient countries. All other benefits for the United States, whether economic (such as the development of markets for American exports) or political (such as greater receptivity to U.S. influence), should be considered as beneficial side-effects and subordinated to the central goal of development.

3. U.S. bilateral development assistance to the low-income countries should be provided on substantially more concessional terms in recognition of the increasingly serious long-term debt problems of the low-income countries.

4. The United States should renew a substantial development cooperation program with India that would be in a form appropriate to current circumstances and would be focused primarily on assisting India with addressing basic human needs, increasing food production, and accelerating rural development in general.

5. The United States should urge an early decision on the level of replenishment (and make a commitment as to its own share) of the World Bank's International Development Association at a level for the OECD countries of $8.1 billion.

6. The agreements to increase the capital of the World Bank should be approved by Congress as soon as possible. The U.S. position on future capital increases for the World Bank should be to support an increase to a level that would allow the Bank to continue its vital role in providing development finance.

7. The United States should eliminate existing arrearages to IDA and the regional development banks as well as to U.N. development agencies.

8. The United States should channel a growing proportion of its development assistance through international financial institutions, and a substantial proportion through the Inter-American, African, and Asian Development Banks.

9. The United States should begin now, in conjunction with both the other industrialized countries and the developing countries, the active exploration of a wide range of "automatic" sources which could provide

133

additional support for the development process in the low-income countries.

10. During 1977, the United States should initiate a comprehensive review, for completion by 1978, of all aspects of development assistance. This should include the amounts required; the forms (such as foreign exchange or food aid) in which it might best be provided; and the various mechanisms (such as multilateral, bilateral, or private channels) through which it might be administered. This clearly needs to be done in association with, and is dependent on, the results of analytical and policy studies both of the objectives the United States seeks in its relations with the developing countries over the balance of the century and the possibilities for securing domestic and international support of these objectives.

Arms Transfers

The "arms transfers" programs that supply military equipment, services, and training (through both aid and sales) to the developing countries have been a major component of U.S. policy toward those countries in the postwar period.[29] In sheer dollar volume, these programs have in recent years overshadowed many other aspects of American foreign policy toward the developing countries. Sales orders from developing countries (including Israel) increased from under $1 billion in 1970 to nearly $8 billion in 1974 and to $6.2 billion in 1975. This trend will continue unless other factors —such as a change in U.S. policy—intervene. The United States is presently the major international supplier of arms. According to the Arms Control and Disarmament Agency, the United States in 1974 provided 45 per cent of military equipment *delivered* worldwide; this compares with 31 per cent supplied by the Soviet Union, 6 per cent supplied by France, and 5 per cent by the United Kingdom.[30]

American arms transfers have been justified on a number of different grounds. Proponents of the various programs under which arms are transferred stress that such programs: 1) directly contribute to our own security; 2) provide the United States with political influence in other countries; 3) enhance the regional security of various parts of the world; 4) help to maintain the capacity of defense industries; 5) provide employment in this country; and 6) contribute favorably (in the case of sales) to our balance-of-payments position.

---

[29]"Arms transfers" as used here include the transfer of military equipment and services—whether lethal or not—from one nation to another. Included are both sales orders (which generally result in future deliveries) and military assistance agreements. Thus the value of arms transfers may include infrastructural support, spare parts, training, and the services of specialists. U.S. transfers take place through several different channels. *Sales* take place under the Defense Department's Foreign Military Sales Program (FMS), which provides credit at market rates for sales to developing countries. *Aid* transfers of arms are funded by the Military Assistance Program (MAP), the Excess Defense Articles Program, and direct Defense Department financing known as Military Assistance—Service Funded (MASF).

[30]See Annex D, Table D-4.

Those who oppose such programs, however, do so for precisely opposite reasons. They hold that rather than contributing to regional stability and American security, providing arms, equipment, and training to developing countries often produces regional instability, thereby indirectly threatening American security. They further claim that the presence of American weapons and specialists increases the risk of U.S. involvement in local conflicts; that the availability of arms encourages the establishment of repressive military regimes and helps to preserve those already in existence; and that growing expenditures for arms burden the development efforts of the low-income countries. Moreover, many consider it morally wrong that the United States has become the world's major supplier of weaponry and military training and services.

Arms transfer programs have changed in three major ways in the decades since the United States first became a major source of supply. In those years, a much greater proportion of transfers took place under *aid* programs rather than as a result of sales agreements, credits, or cash transactions. Today, however, the level of aid is diminishing and the level of sales is increasing rapidly. U.S. sales (i.e., orders placed for future delivery) to all nations increased from a worldwide total of $1.2 billion in 1965 to $9.5 billion only a decade later. Similarly, whereas the military assistance provided in the early years consisted primarily of equipment left over from World War II or the war in Korea, transfers taking place today (through both aid and sales) often include the latest military technology similar to or, in some cases, more advanced than that in the current inventory of the U.S. armed forces. Finally, it is no longer our NATO allies that are the major recipients of U.S. arms transfers but developing-country governments.

Iran, Israel, and Saudi Arabia together placed 86 per cent of all developing-country sales orders of American weapons, equipment, and services during the years 1973-1975. But the volume of arms transfers to the Middle East and Persian Gulf regions should not obscure the fact that arms transfers to other developing countries are increasing. In 1975, the United States provided $771.1 million of equipment, training, and services to developing countries other than OPEC members or countries considered by the government to be of special interest to the United States (Israel, Korea, Taiwan, Cambodia, Laos, and Vietnam). In 1971, U.S. arms transfers to these same countries totalled only $306 million. Sales figures alone show even more dramatic increases in the level of arms supplied to these countries, going from $109.1 million in 1971 to $605.5 million in 1975—a 500 per cent rise in a period of only five years.[31]

The United States of course is not the only supplier of arms to the developing countries. Various European countries (especially France and

---

[31]A summary of U.S. arms transfers (in the form of sales orders and of assistance) for the years 1971-1975 can be found in Roger D. Hansen and the Staff of the Overseas Development Council, *The U.S. and World Development: Agenda for Action, 1976* (New York: Praeger Publishers, 1976), Statistical Annexes, Table D-1, pp. 186-7.

the United Kingdom), the Soviet Union, and China all provide equipment, weapons, and training to these countries—many of which have been spending increasing amounts each year on military purchases in order to meet a variety of legitimate needs. Indeed, *overall* military expenditures (including foreign purchases) by the developing countries have risen more rapidly than those by the developed countries. Even in constant dollar terms, aggregate developing-country military expenditures doubled from 1965 ($24.5 billion) to 1974 ($50.2 billion.)[32]

In recent years, arms transfer programs have been an issue of contention between the Congress and the Executive Branch. The Executive Branch has considered arms transfers to be a key element in its post-Vietnam foreign policy. Congress, on the other hand, perceiving danger in the global proliferation of arms, in 1976 passed major legislation to phase out military assistance programs and to tighten congressional control over sales.

The new Administration has expressed an intent to work toward achieving a lower level of arms transfers. For a number of reasons, however, it is unlikely that the United States could soon eliminate all programs of military aid and sales. In some regions of the world, particular U.S. interests will dictate that we provide at least some military equipment to countries of special concern to us. The U.S. interest in a settlement of the dispute between Israel and its neighbors is a case in point. Similarly, it will be in the U.S. interest to help some countries meet genuine internal or external security needs.

The problem at the moment is that the United States currently does not have a coherent policy governing the transfer of weapons, military equipment, and services to the developing countries. Current policy is partially a reflection of old cold war strategic doctrines and partially a reflection of balance-of-payments considerations. In the future, however, having a clear arms transfer policy—grounded in a foreign policy congruent with the needs of the late 1970s and the 1980s—will be imperative. Without such a policy, arms transfers will continue to be haphazard and the level of such transfers will continue to increase. With such a policy, it will be possible to assess which countries have the special needs, and in which countries the United States has the special interests, that make it desirable for the United States to supply some amount of arms transfers.

The United States—as the world's major supplier of arms—holds considerable international influence. In developing a new arms policy, it should be remembered that U.S. decisions on the supply of arms through aid and sales will inevitably have a major impact on the policies of other countries.[33]

---

[32]See this volume, Annex D, Table D-1.

[33]For a detailed series of policy recommendations on arms issues, see the recent report of the UNA-USA National Policy Panel on Conventional Arms Control, *Controlling the Conventional Arms Race* (New York: United Nations Association of the United States of America, November 1976).

Recommendations

1. The new Administration should undertake, in cooperation with Congress and at an early date, a review of all U.S. programs of arms sales and aid. This review should identify the countries in which the United States has a genuine security interest in order to restrict programs to those countries. The aim of such a review should be to reduce substantially the level of arms transfers within the next five years. In the interim, arms transfers to the developing countries should not exceed the 1975 level.

2. Policy measures such as pledges of "no first supply" to developing countries of a variety of sophisticated weapons should be considered (if other suppliers are willing to make similar commitments).

3. Because a reduction in the level of arms transfers will have an impact on industry and employment in various parts of the United States, new and expanded programs should be instituted to assist industries in converting production lines and workers in retraining.

4. The United States should take the lead in instituting consultations with a) other major arms suppliers with a view to reducing arms transfers and b) the developing countries in order to urge them to begin to discuss regional security measures and to indicate U.S. support for such measures.

Organizing for Interdependence

Two final areas for immediate action relate to organizational structure. The first is the need for better international mechanisms through which to negotiate on North-South and other global issues. The second is the need to reorganize the U.S. government to deal effectively with the multiplicity of political and economic negotiations that will be going on between developed and developing countries, and also to manage a new U.S. commitment to the development of the poorest countries. At present, neither set of issues can be adequately handled by existing governmental structures.

In the immediate future, the resumption of North-South negotiations will be complicated by the lack of effectively working institutions that encompass the broad range of discussions now going on between developed and developing countries. The key element in reaching agreement is, of course, the will of all parties to make concessions. Nevertheless, institutional questions remain important. The industrialized countries tend to feel that universal membership bodies, such as the U.N. General Assembly or the Economic and Social Council, are too unwieldy, while the developing countries consider the U.N. Security Council to be dominated by the major powers and restricted by its mandate to issues of international peace and security rather than to problems of economic and social interdependence. In the economic arena, the General Agreement on Tariffs and Trade, the International Monetary Fund, and the World Bank tend to be regarded as part of the "rich man's club," i.e., dominated by the developed countries. Conversely, the industrialized countries view the U.N. Conference on Trade and Development (UNCTAD) as mainly created by and for the developing countries. The developing countries also argue that they should be given a greater share of the decision-making power within existing institutions. At present, voting rights in the World Bank's International Development Association, for instance, are based on cumulative contributions since IDA was established in 1960. Therefore, even if the members of OPEC were to agree to contribute 50 per cent of IDA's next replenishment, they would obtain only about 10 per cent of the total voting rights. That prospect is not likely to make their increased participation particularly attractive from their standpoint.

Recently there has been an increasing amount of examination of the need to reform old institutions and to establish new patterns for international institutions.[34] In addition, several new institutions have been created that represent departures from previous participation patterns. For instance, the "Group of Ten" nations, which formerly was the de facto decision-making body in the International Monetary Fund, has been superceded by a more formalized committee of 20 nations, 9 of which are developing countries. Similarly, representation on the governing board of the new International Fund for Agricultural Development, which is jointly funded by the OPEC and OECD countries, will be divided equally among the industrialized country donors, OPEC donors, and other developing countries. The World Food Council also was designed to include as members all parties at interest. Seventeen of the thirty-six members are developing countries, and the Soviet Union also participates.

The Conference on International Economic Cooperation (CIEC), which has been meeting in Paris since December 1975, was the major institutional departure of the mid-1970s, and its establishment was proof of the need for major new mechanisms. It was established to link the concerns of the North and the South and to allow discussions to be held among a smaller yet representative group of countries—i.e., a total of 27 countries, including 8 OECD countries, 7 OPEC countries, and 12 other developing countries. It was designed so that all parties with major interests at stake could feel that their legitimate concerns were represented. However, twelve months of experience with CIEC has given rise to considerable dissatisfaction on all sides, not only because of the slow pace of negotiations (which may be more the fault of governments than of the CIEC mechanism) but also because the deliberations have been dominated on both sides by a small group of countries. Among the developed countries, the United States, the European Communities, Japan, and Canada have tended to set the tone for

<hr />

[34]See C. Fred Bergsten, Georges Berthoin, and Kinhide Mushakaji, "Reform of International Institutions," Triangle Paper No. 11 (New York: The Trilateral Commission, 1976); and The Report of the Group of Experts on the Structure of the United Nations System, *A New United Nations Structure for Global Economic Cooperation*, U.N. Document E/AC.62/9, May 28, 1975.

the discussions; among the developing countries, a smaller group—comprised of India, Brazil, Saudi Arabia, and Iran—has played the dominant role. The other countries fear that their interests have not been adequately represented. In addition, there is continuing dissension on the developing-country side among the 19 countries participating in CIEC and the much larger "Group of 77" developing countries. Other countries feel that CIEC derogates from the United Nations system and would rather see the negotiations shifted to the United Nations or to the Development Committee of the World Bank and the International Monetary Fund. Finally, CIEC does not provide for participation by the U.S.S.R., China, and other centrally planned economies.

Decisions will have to be made in the immediate future by both developed and developing countries concerning new and reformed international institutions to discuss and reach decisions on global economic, social, and political issues. It will be important to ensure that in their totality these institutions leave no major group of nations with the feeling that their interests are not being accommodated. Not every nation need be a participant; but all must be satisfied that their interests are represented at the discussions. Second, the institutions, both old and new, will have to grapple with the difficult problem of reconciling the imperatives of national sovereignty and the reality that increased political, economic, and social interdependence has made a modification of sovereignty a necessity. Finally, it will be necessary to create organizations that somehow can accomplish the difficult task of overseeing and coordinating decisions that cut across a variety of issue areas. In the next few years, the developed and developing countries will be discussing, in a variety of forums, issues of trade, raw materials, oceans, technology, aid, food, and energy. Agreements reached in one area are liable to have an impact on others. In addition, some countries will gain from one set of agreements but pay costs in another.

Clearly an institution is needed to provide a central overview of these issues, as the CIEC was originally designed to do. The potential of the Development Committee of the International Monetary Fund and the World Bank merits consideration in this connection. Formally entitled the "Committee on the Transfer of Real Resources to the Developing Countries," the Development Committee was established in 1975. It has the advantages of having a permanent secretariat and representation from both the United Nations agencies and the regional development banks. It thus brings together a number of different groups concerned with the development process, including some which involve the U.S.S.R. and China, as well as the development and international financial institutions.

Finally, there is a need for more effective private mechanisms, both within the United States and internationally, for discussion and analysis of North-South and development issues. There is widespread recognition that the extensive private participation that paralleled world conferences such as those on environment, population, food, women, and human settlements contributed substantially to the usefulness of those conferences. As in domestic fields, the participation of these groups contributed both to pressure on governments to produce results and to improved communications between different nongovernmental groups. Similarly, the Pugwash and Dartmouth series of meetings (initially with only U.S. and Soviet participation) and the meetings of the more recently formed Trilateral Commission (composed of leading private citizens from Western Europe, North America, and Japan) are also illustrations of useful efforts to improve the participation and contribution of private groups to the dialogue on major international issues.

Some encouraging steps have been taken recently to stimulate citizen participation in comprehensive discussion of North-South and other development issues. These include the establishment of "New Directions"—a U.S. citizens' lobby on international issues—in late 1976; the broadening of the work of such organizations as Pugwash and the Club of Rome to specifically encompass North-South and development issues; and the reorganization of the Society for International Development to enhance its capacity to contribute to the dialogue on North-South issues and alternative development strategies. Such efforts need to be encouraged and multiplied.

Major changes also appear to be required with respect to internal U.S. governmental organization to deal with these issues. In recent years, the U.S. government has dealt with the new global or "interdependence" issues through already existing departments and agencies. Some overall coordinating mechanisms such as the Council on International Economic Policy, were established in the White House in the early years of President Nixon's tenure, and, more recently, the powerful interdepartmental body dominated by Treasury and known as the Economic Policy Board, which encompassed both national and international issues. At various times, ad hoc coordination mechanisms also have been created, such as the appointment of a coordinator responsible to the Secretary of State for the U.S. position at the 1974 World Food Conference. Another coordinative body established by Congress in recent years is the largely powerless Development Coordination Committee (chaired by the Administrator of the Agency for International Development), which has a mandate to assure intragovernmental awareness of various U.S. governmental actions affecting the developing countries. This Committee is also responsible for analyzing and reporting annually on all development-related activities of the U.S. government. At the same time, a number of governmental departments have a voice in development cooperation programs—including the Agency for International Development; Action (which now includes the Peace Corps); the Departments of Agriculture, Treasury, Labor, and Health, Education, and Welfare; the Overseas Private Investment Corporation; and the Export-Import Bank. The only overall coordination is handled by the Office of Management and Budget in the context of formulating the annual budget. This process does not, however, provide any overall central view or analysis of either U.S. actions that affect North-South issues or of the various components that make up U.S. development assistance policies.

The new Administration faces several key questions in 1977 in organizing itself to deal with the global issues outlined in this *Agenda*.[35] First among these is the need to coordinate the various branches of the government that must and will have a voice in decisions on international economic and social issues. Food policy, for instance, falls at a minimum within the purview of Agriculture, State, AID, and Treasury. Trade policy is within the aegis of State, Treasury, Commerce, and Labor. And so on. Creating mechanisms that will allow these diverse interests to be represented without paralyzing the policy process will be difficult at best.

Second, the Administration should create some coherence in the multiplicity of government entities involved in programs of development cooperation and should assign to some organization within the government the responsibility of analyzing the impact of actions of the U.S. government on the developing countries.

Finally, fresh attention needs to be given to how the U.S. government can increase the effectiveness of its relationships with and support of the growing number of American private organizations involved in development issues. These encompass both business and private organizations and the private voluntary organizations engaged in supporting development programs in the poor countries.

Recommendations

1. The U.S. government should, at an early date, assume an active role in seeking to improve the effectiveness of international mechanisms for negotiating on North-South issues and for improving consultation and cooperation on development assistance and related issues.

2. Early action also is required for a similar effort within the U.S. government to improve its effectiveness in dealing with both North-South and development issues.

3. Private organizations need a) to increase their contribution to furthering analysis and dialogue on North-South issues and b) to improve their ability to contribute to the evolution of alternative approaches to development that deal more effectively than is generally the case today with issues such as the more effective address of basic human needs, population stabilization, rural development, appropriate technology, and low-cost delivery systems for health and education.

---

[35]For an analysis of these issues and specific proposals on measures to ensure their more comprehensive handling, see Robert H. Johnson, *Managing Interdependence: Restructuring the U.S. Government*, Development Paper 23 (Washington, D.C.: Overseas Development Council, 1977).

STATISTICAL ANNEXES

Florizelle B. Liser

Statistical Annexes

NOTE TO THE ANNEXES

A Physical Quality of Life Index (PQLI)*

In recent years, international development agencies and economic planners in many countries have become increasingly concerned with the task of meeting the "basic human needs" of the very poorest groups of people. As development strategies have shifted their emphasis toward addressing these minimum human needs, there has been a growing recognition of the need to devise an indicator that more effectively measures the degree of progress along these lines than is possible with GNP indicators. The U.S. Foreign Assistance Act of 1973 (and its subsequent amendments)—which mandated that an increasing amount of U.S. bilateral assistance be directed toward the improvement of the lot of the poor majority in developing countries—requires that appropriate criteria be established to assess the progress of countries in meeting this objective. Also in 1973, the Secretary General of the United Nations, in the first overall review and appraisal of progress in Development Decade II, recognized the need for a supplement to per capita GNP as a unit for measuring progress in addressing human needs problems. And in 1976, the report *Reshaping the International Order,* prepared under the guidance of Professor Jan Tinbergen for the Club of Rome, called for the development of a quality of life index to be used in conjunction with the per capita GNP indicator.

The traditional measure of national economic progress—the gross national product (GNP) and its component elements—cannot very satisfactorily measure the extent to which the human needs of individuals are being met, nor should it be expected to do so. There is no automatic policy relationship between any particular level or rate of growth of GNP and improvement in such indicators as life expectancy, death rates, infant mortality, literacy, etc. A nation's economic product at any particular level may be allocated in a variety of ways, both among areas of activities and among social groups; or national policies may emphasize the growth of military power and of sectors of the economy that do not contribute in any obvious way to improving the health and physical well-being of that country's people. Nor does the growth of average per capita GNP or personal disposable income necessarily improve the well-being of large portions of a country's population since that income may flow to social groups in very unequal proportions. The very poorest groups of the society may not benefit much, if at all, from rising incomes and some may even suffer declines in real income. Moreover, even if rising incomes are shared with the poorest groups, there is no guarantee that these increases in income will be spent in ways that improve physical well-being. For example, in some societies in which rising income has led to a decline in breast feeding and an

*The PQLI concept is being developed at the Overseas Development Council under the direction of Morris David Morris, as part of a major project exploring alternative development strategies. A publication on the PQLI index will be issued by the ODC in late 1977.

increase in the use of breast-milk substitutes, higher infant mortality rates have resulted.

Thus the need for new measures of development progress arises from the facts that:

(1) GNP and per capita GNP say nothing about the *distribution* of income;

(2) the conceptual problems inherent in measuring income distribution in any society are compounded in the case of the developing countries, with their largely rural and non-monetary economies; and

(3) money measures do not in themselves indicate anything about the levels of physical well-being of individuals—which is what national and international development planners are seeking to achieve.

Most of the efforts to develop measures of human progress have used a variety of separate indicators such as per capita income, calorie intake, life expectancy, literacy, etc.—all of which improve or deteriorate at varying rates. Use of these disaggregated indicators makes it difficult for national policymakers or administrators of development assistance to determine the combined effectiveness of separate programs addressing different social conditions.

What is needed is not a variety of indicators but some *composite* measure that will summarize the different rates of improvement (or deterioration) in various categories and that will make it possible to estimate the extent to which the basic human needs of all people have or have not been equitably met. The few attempts at devising such a composite measure that have been made have tended to suffer from one or more of three defects:

(1) too close tying of the composite measure to the per capita GNP measure;

(2) use of components (e.g., urbanization, number of telephones per 1,000 people, number of homes with piped water) that assume that the poor countries must inevitably develop along lines followed by developed countries. This assumption, however, fails to take into consideration the long-run implications of the emerging labor-intensive strategy that is being supported by the U.S. Agency for International Development, the World Bank, and the International Labour Office;

(3) the setting of targets that may be excessively ethnocentric (as in the case of nutritional standards).

For the past year, the Overseas Development Council has been exploring the implications of alternative development strategies. One of the concerns in this effort has been to measure how effectively various development strategies distribute the most basic benefits of development progress to all parts of society. Out of this study has come a "Physical Quality of Life Index" (PQLI) that promises to serve as a useful measure of a country's general progress toward more equitably meeting basic human requirements for the majority of its population.

The PQLI does not attempt to measure the many other social and psychological characteristics suggested by the term "quality of life"—justice, political freedom, or a sense of participation. It is based on the assumption that the needs and desires of individuals initially and at the most basic level are for longer life expectancy, reduced illness, and greater opportunity. The index does not measure the amount or the type of effort put into achieving these goals, but the extent to which they are being met—that is, it measures *results.* It acknowledges that improvements in meeting these minimum needs can be achieved in a variety of ways—by better nutrition, improved medical care, better income distribution, increased levels of education, and increased employment.

Developed countries—as a result of improvements made over long periods of time—are today generally able to provide reasonable levels of these basic features of human existence to most of their people. But the poor countries cannot provide better diets, sanitation, medical care, education, etc., all at one time. Moreover, it should not be important that they provide a specific kind of medical organization, a particular type of sanitary facility, or a specific pattern of nutrition, for these are not in themselves ends. They are *means* and must be chosen to suit the resources and cultures of the individual countries. What is important is that, whatever the type of techniques and policies chosen, greater opportunities are made available to those who have the least of these. Thus policymakers are free to apply any mix of policies that will bring about the desired ends. Different policymakers in different countries will choose differently.

Although the Council's analysis is still in its early stages, it seems clear that three indicators—life expectancy, infant mortality, and literacy—can be used to measure the results of a wide range of policies. The PQLI consolidates these into a simple, composite index. Life expectancy, infant mortality, and literacy figures are each rated on an index of 1-100, within which individual countries are ranked according to their performance. For the life expectancy index, for example, the most favorable figure achieved by any country in 1973 (75 years in Sweden) was assigned the upper limit of 100 and the most unfavorable performance in 1950 (28 years in Guinea Bissau) was assigned the lower limit of one (1).[1] Similarly, for infant mortality, the best performance in 1973 (9 per thousand in Sweden) was rated 100 and the worst performance in 1950 was rated 1 (229 in Gabon). Actual literacy figures (being percentages) are nearly identical to their index ratings.

A *composite* index was calculated by averaging the three indexes, giving equal weight to each of the three indicators. The composite rating for

---

[1] Use of the worst performance in 1950 as the lower limit of the index rather than current worst performance (38 years for life expectancy) allows for comparisons across time without resulting in negative ratings.

each country appears in Table A-3 of Annex A. The data below show a comparison of performance as measured by GNP and performance as measured by the Physical Quality of Life Index for income groups as well as for selected countries.

	Average Per Capita GNP ($)	PQLI Achievement
Lower-Income Countries	152	39
India	140	41
Kerala, India	110	69
Sri Lanka	130	83
Lower Middle-Income Countries	338	59
Malaysia	680	59
Korea, Rep. of	480	80
Cuba	640	86
Upper Middle-Income Countries	1,091	67
Gabon	1,960	21
Iran	1,250	38
Algeria	710	42
Taiwan (ROC)	810	88
High-Income Countries	4,361	95
Kuwait	11,770	76
United States	6,670	96
Netherlands	5,250	99

The data for the countries of the world when grouped by income (as shown here as well as in Tables A-1 and A-3) show the expected direct relationship between the level of per capita GNP and PQLI. On the other hand, the correlation for individual countries is not as clear. For example, Cuba, Korea, and Taiwan (with per capita GNPs of more than $300) as well as Sri Lanka and the Indian state of Kerala (with per capita GNPs well below $300) all have PQLIs above the average of countries with incomes between $700 and $2,000. In fact, their PQLI performances are well above those of Gabon, Iran, and Kuwait (with per capita GNPs of $1,960, $1,250, and $11,770, respectively). These divergences from what the expected relationship might be indicate that significant improvements in basic quality of life levels can be attained before there is any great rise in per capita GNP; conversely, a rapid rise in per capita GNP is not in itself a guarantee of good levels of literacy, life expectancy, or infant mortality.

A major advantage of the PQLI is not only that it measures the current *level* of achievement, but that it appears to be a fairly sensitive measure of change over time as well. The data below show quality of life changes over the last two decades for a number of countries.

	1950s	1960s	1970s
Algeria	35	38	42
India	28	36	42
Egypt	32	41	45
Brazil	53	–	66
Sri Lanka	62	77	83
Poland	72	86	93
United States	92	94	96
France	87	94	97
Norway	–	–	99

Similarly, the index can be used for intra-country as well as inter-country comparisons. The data below reveal interesting regional contrasts within the United States; it also suggests that comparisons can be made for various ethnic and other social groups as well. The sensitivity of the PQLI index suggests that policymakers can set appropriate targets for improvement in PQLI ratings not only for developing countries, but for developed countries and for regions and specific groups within countries.

	1900	1939	1950	1973
All U.S. Population	63	85	91	96
White Population	65	87	92	97
Other Races	30	71	81	89
Selected States				
Mississippi		81	87	92
New Mexico		69	85	94
Texas		81	87	95
Wisconsin		89	93	97
Minnesota		91	95	98

The PQLI seems to be fairly free of the major difficulties that in one way or another afflict most other measures of human progress. Because it is not weighted at all by the level of GNP, it avoids all problems of monetary measurement. It avoids ethnocentric biases about as much as is possible. While it does assume that almost all people everywhere would choose improvements in life expectancy, infant mortality, and literacy, the PQLI does not specify how these improvements ought to be achieved. Moreover, it

151

avoids dependence on absolute technical standards (such as a fixed calorie requirement) about which there is no genuine agreement.

The PQLI has a number of advantages. It uses three indicators which apparently do reflect distributional characteristics within countries, for countries cannot achieve high national averages of literacy, life expectancy, and infant mortality unless majorities of their populations are receiving the benefits of progress in each of these areas. It also recognizes that there can be very complex tradeoffs among the inputs that would yield equivalent quality of life results; thus it enables the setting of targets that permit considerable flexibility without suffering from the GNP insensitivity to equity considerations. Moreover, the PQLI automatically narrows the range of data required to measure the extent to which a country is meeting basic human needs objectives; it can help planners decide what specific improvements in types and quality of data collection are immediately necessary.

Further work on the development of the PQLI is needed in refining it and in determining its limitations as well as where and how it can most usefully be employed. But in the meantime, the simplicity of the measure permits it to be easily understood by both lay people and policymakers interested in measuring the progress being made in meeting the most basic needs in particular countries and regions and groups within countries. This is a case in which use of "the good"—the PQLI—should not be precluded because of continuing pursuit of "the best." The PQLI—even in its present form—already serves as a useful measurement of progress in the address of basic human needs.

While there is the danger that the measure may be accepted with too much faith, this problem affects every effort to aggregate complex behavior into a more simple indicator. Future work at the Council will seek to establish methods to use the PQLI along with GNP. If these two can be used in tandem, many of the dangers of misuse and misinterpretation will be eliminated or at least minimized.

Explanatory Notes

Within the Statistical Annexes, and in line with current thinking at the Overseas Development Council, the term "developed" refers to those countries with per capita incomes in 1974 of $2,000 or more that have also attained high standards of living as reflected in a Physical Quality of Life Index rating of 90 or more. Thus not all "high income" countries are considered "developed"; those which are, are so identified in Table A-3 in the Annexes that follow. The term "developed market economies" represents the same group of countries—excluding the developed centrally planned economies of Czechoslovakia, Democratic Republic of Germany, Hungary, Poland, and the U.S.S.R.

The term "developing" refers to all countries that had per capita incomes under $2,000 in 1974 and/or PQLI achievements of less than 90.

"Developing market economies" represents the same group minus the developing centrally planned economies of Albania, Bulgaria, People's Republic of China, Democratic Republic of Korea, Romania, and Democratic Republic of Vietnam. (Because sufficient data are not yet available for the Socialist Republic of Vietnam, the Statistical Annexes still provide data for both the Democratic Republic of Vietnam and the Republic of Vietnam.)

The developing countries identified as "low-income" in Table A-3 (with 1974 per capita incomes under $300) have severe development problems. Most of them are on one or both of two United Nations lists: 1) those twenty-nine countries considered to be "least developed" (LLDCs), and 2) those forty-five countries "most seriously affected" by high oil prices, inflation, and balance-of-payments deficits (MSAs). In previous issues of the *Agenda* series, the category "Fourth World" was composed solely of the combined U.N. lists of LLDCs and MSAs. All other developing countries fell into the "Third World" category.

A clear distinction has been made within the Statistical Annexes between "OPEC countries" and "oil-exporting countries." The Organization of Petroleum Exporting Countries (OPEC) has thirteen members—Algeria, Ecuador, Gabon, Indonesia, Iran, Iraq, Libya, Nigeria, Qatar, Saudi Arabia, United Arab Emirates, and Venezuela. The "oil-exporting countries" is a broader group that encompasses the thirteen OPEC members plus Angola, Bahrain, Brunei, Oman, and Trinidad and Tobago.

The members of the Organisation for Economic Co-operation and Development (OECD) are Australia, Austria, Belgium, Canada, Denmark, Finland, France, the Federal Republic of Germany, Greece, Iceland, Ireland, Italy, Japan, Luxembourg, the Netherlands, New Zealand, Norway, Portugal, Spain, Sweden, Switzerland, Turkey, the United Kingdom, and the United States. The Development Assistance Committee (DAC) is a specialized committee of the OECD whose members consult each other on their development assistance policies and annually review the amounts and natures of their aid programs. Except for Greece, Iceland, Ireland, Luxembourg, Portugal, Spain, and Turkey, all members of the OECD are presently members of DAC.

The various agencies that are the sources of the data provided in the Statistical Annexes that follow differ in their classifications of countries. The World Bank, the United Nations, the General Agreement on Tariffs and Trade (GATT), the U.S. Agency for International Development (AID), and DAC (of the OECD) do not agree in all instances on whether to call particular countries "developed" or "developing." Inclusion of a country in one category or the other will often depend upon the purposes of the compiling organization. For example, the DAC list of developing countries includes all countries, territories, or other geographic designations that receive official development assistance or other resource flows from DAC members. Thus while Portugal was a member of DAC it was considered "developed," but since leaving the Committee in October 1974 and itself becoming a recipient of aid from DAC members, it is considered by that body to be "developing." Similarly, U.N. trade data are compiled according to the more useful trade breakdown of "developed market economies," "developing market economies," and "centrally planned economies"—and countries are classified accordingly.

Examples of the developed-developing variations among different organizations are provided by the cases of Greece, Spain, Turkey, Yugoslavia, Malta, and Israel. The United Nations considers the first four to be "developed" and the latter two "developing." The GATT considers only Israel a developing country. In contrast, the World Bank, AID, and DAC classify all of them as developing. Differences among the various sources also arise from the fact that some provide data for more nations than do others; for example, data on debt and international reserves published by the World Bank and the International Monetary Fund (IMF) do not include most centrally planned economies and, in fact, rarely include more than 75 to 100 countries worldwide. In spite of variations among the data sources, efforts were made where possible to be consistent throughout these Annexes with the classifications set out in Table A-3.

Official development assistance (ODA) is defined by DAC as "those flows to developing countries and multilateral institutions provided by official agencies, including state and local governments, or by their executive agencies, each transaction of which meets the following tests: a) it is administered with the promotion of the economic development and welfare of developing countries as its main objective and b) it is concessional in character and contains a grant element of at least 25 per cent." ODA is comprised of 1) soft (low-interest) bilateral loans, 2) bilateral grants, and 3) multilateral flows in the form of grants, capital subscriptions, and concessional or soft loans to multilateral agencies.

Aid commitments are obligations or pledges; disbursements are actual payments. Gross disbursements minus amortization (i.e., repayment of principal) paid on past loans are equal to "net disbursements" or "net flows."

As a result of rounding, the "totals" shown may not always be equal to the sum of the other figures. An entry of "n.a." signifies that information was not available. Where figures are negligible or less than the smallest unit it is so stated.

The Global
Poverty-Affluence
Spectrum

Annex A: Facts of Interest

The gap between the world's poor and its affluent is wide and—as measured by many indicators of well-being—growing wider. It is a gap in wealth and opportunity that exists between as well as within nations. The discrepancies in the distribution of global wealth are depicted from a variety of perspectives by the tables in Annex A.

1. In 1974, over 100 developing countries in Africa, Asia, and Latin America (with 67 per cent of world population) accounted for only 14 per cent of the global world product; in contrast, the 25 or so developed countries in Europe and North America (with only 25 per cent of world population) accounted for nearly 72 per cent of global GNP in 1974 (Table A-6).

2. Despite varying definitions and estimates of poverty in the developing countries, it is clear that the magnitude and extent of poverty in these countries is severe, with some 920 million to 1.2 billion people living in a state of serious or absolute poverty (Tables A-7 and A-8).

3. Per capita and national income figures alone are not adequate indicators of the gap between the world's affluent and its poor. Other considerations such as birth and death rates, levels of literacy and education, life expectancy, availability of natural resources, and access to trade with other countries must also enter into any assessment of relative advantage and disadvantage. Thus even though Algeria's petroleum revenues have raised its per capita income to $710 in 1974, its infant mortality rate is still high (126 infant deaths per 1,000 live births). Similarly, although India and Sri Lanka have nearly equal per capita incomes ($140 for the former and $130 for the latter), they have markedly different rates of infant mortality, literacy, and life expectancy. These differences are reflected in the "Physical Quality of Life Index" (PQLI). Sri Lanka, for instance, has a PQLI of 83, while India has a PQLI of 41 (Tables A-1 through A-8).

4. While the total number of persons in the developing countries unable to read or write increased from 701 million in 1960 to 756 million in 1970, this represents a decrease in the percentage of illiterate persons in the developing countries from 59 per cent of their population in 1960 to 50 per cent in 1970. In spite of this overall improvement, however, for women the problem of illiteracy remains a major one. In 1970, some 60 per cent of all women (compared to 40 per cent of men) in the developing countries were unable to read or write (Table A-9).

A-1. The Development Gap, by Groups of Countries

	Low-Income Countries	Lower Middle-Income Countries	Upper Middle-Income Countries	High-Income Countries
Mid-1976 Population (millions)	1,341.3	1,145.4	470.6	1,057.0
Average per capita GNP (1974)	$152	$338	$1,091	$4,361
Average PQLI[a]	39	59	67	95
Average Birth Rate (per 1,000)	40	30	36	17
Average Death Rate (per 1,000)	17	11	10	9
Average Life Expectancy (years)	48	61	61	71
Average Infant Mortality Rate (per 1,000 live births)	134	70	82	21
Average Literacy Rate[b]	33%	34%	65%	97%
Average per capita Education Expenditures	$3	$10	$28	$217
Average per capita Military Expenditures	$6	$17	$31	$232

[a]Each country's Physical Quality of Life Index (PQLI) is based on an average of life expectancy, infant mortality, and literacy rates in the mid-1970s. (See pp. 147-54.)

[b]Represents proportion of adult population (15 years of age and over) able to read and write.

NOTES: All averages are weighted by the mid-1976 populations of the countries included in each group. Table A-3 defines the low-income countries as being those with a per capita GNP under $300; the lower middle-income countries as those with a per capita GNP of $300-$699; the upper middle-income countries as those with a per capita GNP of $700-$1,999; and the high-income countries as those with a per capita GNP of $2,000 or more.

SOURCE: This volume, "Statistical Annexes," Table A-3.

A-2. Indicators of Development in Selected Countries

Indicators measuring well-being and development performance that are as traditional as per capita GNP or as new as the Physical Quality of Life Index (see pp. 147-54) reflect wide variations not only between developed and developing countries as groups, but also within each group of countries. Moreover, performance on

PER CAPITA GNP, 1974

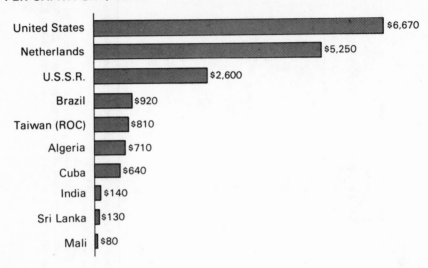

United States	$6,670
Netherlands	$5,250
U.S.S.R.	$2,600
Brazil	$920
Taiwan (ROC)	$810
Algeria	$710
Cuba	$640
India	$140
Sri Lanka	$130
Mali	$80

PHYSICAL QUALITY OF LIFE INDEX [a]

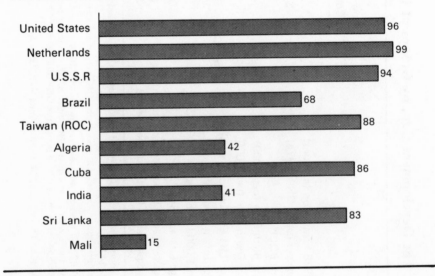

United States	96
Netherlands	99
U.S.S.R	94
Brazil	68
Taiwan (ROC)	88
Algeria	42
Cuba	86
India	41
Sri Lanka	83
Mali	15

[a]See notes on pp. 147-54 for explanation.

such measures of well-being as infant mortality do not necessarily correlate with the level of per capita GNP; some countries with very low per capita GNP (e.g., Cuba and Sri Lanka) have achieved much lower levels of infant mortality than other countries with equally low or even higher per capita GNP.

INFANT MORTALITY PER 1,000 LIVE BIRTHS

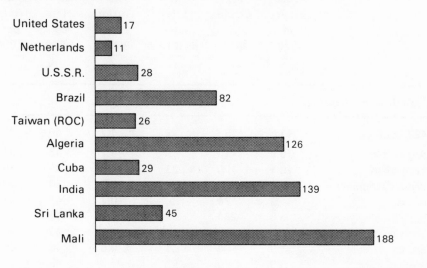

DEATH AND BIRTH RATES PER 1,000

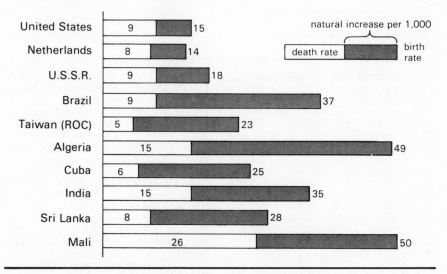

SOURCE: Based on this volume, Statistical Annexes, Table A-3.

A-3. Economic and Social Indicators of Development, by Groups of Countries

	Popu-lation, mid-1976	Per Capita GNP, 1974	Physical Quality of Life Index (PQLI)[a]	Per Capita GNP Growth Rate, 1965-74	Birth Rate per 1,000	Death Rate per 1,000
	(mil.)	($)		(%)		

Low-Income Countries

49 Countries	1,341.3	152	39	1.7	40	17
*+Afghanistan	19.5	110	19	1.1	43	21
*+Bangladesh	76.1	100	33	-1.9	47	20
*+Benin (Dahomey)	3.2	120	23	0.8	50	23
*Bhutan	1.2	70	n.a.	-0.2	44	21
Bolivia	5.8	280	45	2.2	44	18
*Botswana	0.7	290[b]	38	6.2[b]	46	23
+Burma	31.2	100	51	0.8	40	16
*+Burundi	3.9	90	23	1.3	48	25
*+Central African Rep.	1.8	210	18	0.8	43	22

+Considered by the United Nations to be one of the 45 countries "most seriously affected" (MSA) by recent adverse economic conditions.
*Considered by the United Nations to be one of the 29 least developed (LLDC) countries.
oConsidered to be a developed country because of its per capita income of $2,000 or more and PQLI rating of 90 or more.
□Member of the Organization of Petroleum Exporting Countries (OPEC).

[a]Each country's PQLI (Physical Quality of Life Index) rating is based on an average of its index ratings for life expectancy, infant mortality, and literacy in the mid-1970s. See pp. 147-54 for further explanation.
[b]Tentative estimate.
[c]June 1976 figure.
[d]1973 figure.
[e]International Monetary Fund, *International Financial Statistics*, Vol. 29, No. 12, December 1976.
[f]Figure is for 1961-74 or 1962-74.
[g]*World Bank Atlas, 1975: Population, Per Capita Product, and Growth Rates* (Washington, D.C.: World Bank Group, 1975).
[h]Figure is for 1965-73.
[i]f.o.b.
[j]U.S. Agency for International Development, Bureau for Population and Humanitarian Assistance, *Population Program Assistance:*

Annual Report, FY 1973 (Washington, D.C.: U.S. Government Printing Office, 1973).
[k]Figure is for mainland Tanzania.
[l]Mid-1975 figure.
[m]Population Reference Bureau, *World Population Growth and Response, 1965-1975: A Decade of Global Action* (Washington, D.C.: April 1976).
[n]1974 figure.
[o]Figure for People's Republic of China includes Dem. Rep. of Korea, Mongolia, and Dem. Rep. of Vietnam.
[p]Figure is for 1969-74.
[q]Population Reference Bureau, Inc., "1975 World Population Data Sheet" (Washington, D.C.)
[r]UNESCO, *Statistical Yearbook, 1965.*
[s]March 1976 figure.
[t]U.S. Central Intelligence Agency, *National Basic Intelligence Factbook* (Washington,

Life Expectancy at Birth (years)	Infant Mortality per 1,000 Live Births	Literacy (%)	Per Capita Public Education Expend's, 1973 ($)	Per Capita Military Expend's, 1973 ($)	Total Exports, f.o.b., 1975 ($ mil.)	Total Imports, c.i.f., 1975 ($ mil.)	International Reserves, Sept. 1976 ($ mil.)
48	**134**	**33**	**3**	**6**	**27,143**	**32,809**	**13,869**
40	182	8	1	1	205	290	118
43	132	22	1	1	350	1,200	256
41	185	20	5	2	50	170	17
44	n.a.	n.a.	n.a.	n.a.	n.a.	n.a.	n.a.
47	108	40	8	4	450	350	219
44	97	20	9	0	90	140	n.a.
50	126	60	3	5	190	125	129
39	150	10	2	2	27	62	29
41	190	5-10	6	4	48	50	12^c

D.C.: July 1976).   ^vFigure is for 1971-74.
^uFigure is for 1970-75.   ^wFigure is for Belgium and Luxembourg.

NOTES: Low-income countries: those with per capita GNP under $300; lower middle-income countries: those with per capita GNP of $300-$699; upper middle-income countries: those with per capita GNP of $700-$1,999; high-income countries: those with per capita GNP of $2,000 or more.

Bold summary lines for each income-group are cumulative totals for population, exports, imports, and international reserve figures, and averages weighted by mid-1976 populations for all other indicators.

SOURCES: Unless otherwise indicated, population, birth rate, death rate, and life expectancy figures are from Population Reference Bureau, Inc., "1976 World Population Data Sheet" (Washington, D.C.); infant mortality figures are from "1976 World Population Data Sheet" and from United Nations, *Demographic Yearbook, 1974;* all data are the latest available. Per capita GNP and per capita GNP growth rate figures are from *World Bank Atlas, 1976: Population, Per Capita Product, and Growth Rates* (Washington, D.C.: World Bank Group, 1976); literacy figures are from UNESCO, *Statistical Yearbook, 1973* and from U.S. Agency for International Development, Bureau for Population and Humanitarian Assistance, *Population Program Assistance: Annual Report, FY 1973* (Washington, D.C.: U.S. Government Printing Office, 1973); per capita public education expenditure figures are from Ruth Leger Sivard, *World Military and Social Expenditures, 1976* (WMSE Publications, Box 1003, Leesburg, Virginia 22075); per capita military expenditures are from U.S. Arms Control and Disarmament Agency, *World Military Expenditures and Arms Transfers, 1965-1974* (Washington, D.C.: U.S. Government Printing Office, 1976); export and import figures are from UNCTAD, *Handbook of International Trade and Development Statistics, 1976;* international reserves figures are from International Monetary Fund, *International Financial Statistics,* Vol. 29, No. 12, December 1976.

Low-Income Countries (Continued)

	Popu-lation, mid-1976	Per Capita GNP, 1974	Physical Quality of Life Index (PQLI)[a]	Per Capita GNP Growth Rate, 1965-74	Birth Rate per 1,000	Death Rate per 1,000
	(mil.)	($)		(%)		
*+Chad	4.1	100	20	-1.5	44	24
Comoro Is.	0.3	230[b]	40	1.6[b]	44	20
+Egypt	38.1	280	46	1.0	38	15
Equatorial Guinea	0.3	290	28	-3.7[f]	37	20
*+Ethiopia	28.6	100	16	1.5	49	26
*+Gambia, The	0.5	170	22	3.2	43	24
*+Guinea	4.5	120	20	0.1	47	23
*+Haiti	4.6	170	31	0.6	36	16
+India	620.7	140	41	1.3	35	15
□Indonesia	134.7	170	50	4.1	38	17
+Kenya	13.8	200	40	3.5	49	16
+Khmer Rep.	8.3	70[b]	41	-6.2	47	19
*+Laos	3.4	70[b]	32	2.0	45	23
*+Lesotho	1.1	140	50	3.7	39	20
Macao	0.3	270[dg]	n.a.	-4.6[gh]	25	7
+Malagasy Rep.	7.7	180	44	0.2	50	21
*Malawi	5.1	130	29	4.7	48	24
*Maldive Is.	0.1	100[b]	n.a.	0.4[b]	50	23
*+Mali	5.8	80	15	0.4	50	26
+Mauritania	1.3	290	15	1.3	39	25
*+Nepal	12.9	100	25	0.0	43	20
*+Niger	4.7	120	14	-3.8	52	25
□Nigeria	64.7	290	25	8.4	49	23
+Pakistan	72.5	130	37	2.5	44	15
*+Rwanda	4.4	80	27	1.4	50	24
+Sierra Leone	3.1	190	29	1.4	45	21
*Sikkim	0.2	90[b]	n.a.	0.1[b]	48[j]	29[j]
*+Somalia	3.2	90	19	1.1	47	22
+Sri Lanka	14.0	130	83	2.0	28	8
*+Sudan	18.2	230	33	4.3	48	18
*+Tanzania	15.6	160[k]	28	2.3[k]	50	22
Togo	2.3	250	28	2.8	51	23
Tonga	0.1[lm]	210[dg]	70	-0.9[gh]	35[m]	10[m]
*+Uganda	11.9	240	33	0.7	45	16

Life Expectancy at Birth	Infant Mortality per 1,000 Live Births	Literacy	Per Capita Public Education Expend's, 1973	Per Capita Military Expend's, 1973	Total Exports, f.o.b., 1975	Total Imports, c.i.f., 1975	International Reserves, Sept. 1976
(years)		(%)	($)	($)	($ mil.)	($ mil.)	($ mil.)
38	160	5-10	3	5	52	115	3c
42	160	58	n.a.	n.a.	5de	15de	n.a.
52	98	26	11	49	1,500	3,300	448c
44	165	20	10	15	n.a.	n.a.	n.a.
38	181	5	2	2	270	300	333
40	165	10	4	0	55	56	26
41	175	5-10	7	5	130	80	n.a.
50	150	10	1	1	65	110	23
50	139	34	2	4	4,200	6,000	2,686
48	125	60	3	3	6,200	5,000	1,202
50	119	20-25	10	3	550	960	296
45	127	41	4	15	30	100	n.a.
40	123	20-25	1	7	10	80	n.a.
46	114	59	4	0	15	80	n.a.
n.a.	78	79	n.a.	n.a.	120	150	n.a.
44	102	39	12	3	260	390	51
41	148	22	3	1	130	260i	28
n.a.	n.a.	n.a.	n.a.	n.a.	2de	3de	n.a.
38	188	5	2	2	47	160	5c
38	187	1-5	8	5	190	220	88
44	169	13	1	1	55	100	123
39	200	5	2	1	75	100	75
41	180	25	3	11	7,420	5,000	5,776
50	124	16	2	8	1,005	2,125	648
41	133	10	2	2	40	80	39
44	136	10	7	2	130	200	28
n.a.	208	16	n.a.	n.a.	n.a.	n.a.	n.a.
41	177	5	2	5	50	110	78
68	45	81	7	2	500	770	74
49	141	10-15	6	7	380	850	23
44	162	15-20	4	3	350	950	72
41	127	5-10	5	3	200	127	48
56j	107j	90-95	n.a.	n.a.	7en	17en	n.a.
50	160	20	5	5	290	210	n.a.

Low-Income Countries (Continued)

	Popu-lation, mid-1976	Per Capita GNP, 1974	Physical Quality of Life Index (PQLI)[a]	Per Capita GNP Growth Rate, 1965-74	Birth Rate per 1,000	Death Rate per 1,000
	(mil.)	*($)*		*(%)*		
*+Upper Volta	6.2	90	17	-0.5	49	26
Vietnam, Dem. Rep.	24.8	130[g]	n.a.	-0.5[gh]	32	14
Vietnam, Rep. of	21.6	170[g]	60	-0.7[gh]	42	16
*+Yemen, Arab Rep.	6.9	180	27	n.a.	50	21
*+Yemen, People's Rep.	1.7	220	27	-4.3[p]	50	21
Zaire	25.6	150	28	2.9	45	20

Lower Middle-Income Countries

	Popu-lation, mid-1976	Per Capita GNP, 1974	Physical Quality of Life Index (PQLI)[a]	Per Capita GNP Growth Rate, 1965-74	Birth Rate per 1,000	Death Rate per 1,000
39 Countries	**1,145.4**	**338**	**59**	**4.4**	**30**	**11**
Albania	2.5	530[g]	76	4.9[b]	30	8
+Cameroon	6.5	300	28	4.2	40	22
+Cape Verde Is.	0.3	470[b]	46	4.7[b]	33	10
China, People's Rep.	836.8	300[g]	59	4.6[b]	27	10
Colombia	23.0	500	71	3.4	41	9
Congo, People's Rep.	1.4	470	25	4.0	45	21
Cuba	9.4	640[g]	86	0.3[b]	25	6
Dominican Rep.	4.8	650	64	5.5	46	11
□Ecuador	6.9	500	68	3.1	42	10
+El Salvador	4.2	410	67	1.0	40	8
+Ghana	10.1	430	31	0.3	49	22
Grenada	0.1	330	80	1.6	26	8
+Guatemala	5.7	580	53	3.8	43	15
+Guinea-Bissau	0.5	390	10	5.2	40	25
+Guyana	0.8	500	84	1.1	36	6
+Honduras	2.8	340	50	2.2	49	14
+Ivory Coast	6.8	460	28	2.7	46	21
Jordan	2.8	430	48	-2.5	48	15
Korea, Dem. Rep.	16.3	390[g]	n.a.	3.5[b]	36	9
Korea, Rep. of	34.8	480	80	8.7	29	9
Liberia	1.6	390	26	4.1	50	21
Malaysia	12.4	680	59	3.8	39	10
Mauritius	0.9	580	75	1.9	28	7
Mongolia	1.5	620[g]	n.a.	1.8[b]	40	10

Life Expectancy at Birth (years)	Infant Mortality per 1,000 Live Births	Literacy (%)	Per Capita Public Education Expend's, 1973 ($)	Per Capita Military Expend's, 1973 ($)	Total Exports, f.o.b., 1975 ($ mil.)	Total Imports, c.i.f., 1975 ($ mil.)	International Reserves, Sept. 1976 ($ mil.)
38	182	5-10	2	1	30	114	71
48	n.a.	65	3	12	n.a.°	n.a.°	n.a.
40	37	65	6	21	60	700	n.a.
45	152	10	1	4	10	250	651
45	152	10	7	19	300	200	106°
44	160	15-20	6	6	1,000	1,140	88
61	70	34	10	17	37,828	48,835	13,015
71	87	72	20	51	n.a.	n.a.	n.a.
41	137	10-15	10	4	430	600	49°
50	91	27	n.a.	n.a.	13	41	n.a.
62	55^q	25	9	19	6,600°	10,400°	n.a.
61	76	73	10	5	1,400	1,600	832
44	180	20	28	18	95	168	5°
70	29	78	31	36	2,200	1,550	n.a.
58	98	68	10	8	900	840^i	83
60	78	67	14	8	1,077	1,000	303
58	54	57	11	4	570	600	206
44	156	25	10	3	850	800	174
63	32	76	n.a.	n.a.	12^e	24^e	n.a.
53	79	38	11	4	720	730	448
38	208	1^r	n.a.	n.a.	3	55	n.a.
68	40	80	22	5	335	320	37
54	117	45	9	4	270	400	130
44	164	20	36	6	1,100	1,130	54
53	97	32	9	50	170	610	509
61	n.a.	n.a.	10	40	n.a.°	n.a.°	n.a.
61	47	88	10	14	4,670	7,200	2,374
45	159	10	7	2	400	330	24
59	75	41	31	25	4,200	4,200	1,933°
66	46	61	11	1	400	370	83
61	n.a.	95	24	39	n.a.°	n.a.°	n.a.

Lower Middle-Income Countries (Continued)

	Popu-lation mid-1976	Per Capita GNP, 1974	Physical Quality of Life Index (PQLI)[a]	Per Capita GNP Growth Rate, 1965-74	Birth Rate per 1,000	Death Rate per 1,000
	(mil.)	*($)*		*(%)*		
Morocco	17.9	430	40	2.8	46	16
+Mozambique	9.3	340	23	3.5	43	20
Nicaragua	2.2	670	53	1.5	48	14
Papua New Guinea	2.8	470	34	4.1	41	17
Paraguay	2.6	510	74	2.5	40	9
Philippines	44.0	330	73	2.7	41	11
Rhodesia	6.5	520	42	3.5	48	14
Sao Tome & Principe	0.1	470	n.a.	-1.0	45	11
+Senegal	4.5	330	22	-0.9	48	24
Swaziland	0.5	390[b]	36	6.1[b]	49	22
Syria	7.6	560	52	4.2	45	15
Thailand	43.3	310	70	4.3	36	11
Tunisia	5.9	650	44	5.4[f]	38	13
*+Western Samoa	0.2[lm]	300[b]	86	1.3[b]	37[m]	7[m]
Zambia	5.1	520	28	1.0	51	20

Upper Middle-Income Countries

	Popu-lation mid-1976	Per Capita GNP, 1974	Physical Quality of Life Index (PQLI)[a]	Per Capita GNP Growth Rate, 1965-74	Birth Rate per 1,000	Death Rate per 1,000
35 Countries	**470.6**	**1,091**	**67**	**4.7**	**36**	**10**
□Algeria	17.3	710	42	3.5	49	15
Angola	6.4	710	15	3.2	47	24
Argentina	25.7	1,520	84	2.9	22	9
Barbados	0.2	1,200	88	5.2	21	9
Brazil	110.2	920	68	6.3	37	9
Bulgaria	8.8	1,890[b]	94	3.6[b]	17	10
Chile	10.8	830	77	1.3	28	8
Costa Rica	2.0	840	87	3.7	28	5
Cyprus	0.7	1,320	87	5.1	18	10
Fiji	0.6	840[b]	83	5.4[b]	28	5
□Gabon	0.5	1,960	21	6.4	32	22
Guadeloupe	0.4	1,240[b]	85	2.6[b]	28	7
Hong Kong	4.4	1,610	88	5.4	19	5
□Iran	34.1	1,250	38	7.7	45	16

Life Expectancy at Birth (years)	Infant Mortality per 1,000 Live Births	Literacy (%)	Per Capita Public Education Expend's, 1973 ($)	Per Capita Military Expend's, 1973 ($)	Total Exports, f.o.b., 1975 ($ mil.)	Total Imports, c.i.f., 1975 ($ mil.)	International Reserves, Sept. 1976 ($ mil.)
53	130	21	19	11	1,600	2,500	666
44	165	7	n.a.	n.a.	270	320	n.a.
53	123	58	12	8	402	520	145
48	159	29	n.a.	n.a.	500	530[i]	n.a.
62	65	75	7	6	180	210[i]	153
58	74	83	7	4	2,214	3,600	1,626
52	122	25-30	14	7	500[n]	500[in]	n.a.
n.a.	64	n.a.	n.a.	n.a.	10	12	n.a.
40	159	5-10	11	6	380	530	19
44	149	36	15	0	150	110	n.a.
54	93	40	14	54	1,000	1,500	632[s]
58	81	79	7	7	2,400	3,200	1,989
54	128	32	28	7	800	1,400	424
63[j]	41	97	n.a.	n.a.	7	35	4
44	160	15-20	28	15	1,000	900[i]	113
61	**82**	**65**	**28**	**31**	**104,821**	**114,129**	**39,193**
53	126	26	43	9	3,900	5,400	2,009
38	203	10-15	n.a.	n.a.	850	430	n.a.
68	64	93	28	18	3,200	4,000	772[c]
69	38	91	n.a.	n.a.	106	200	40
61	82	66	20	15	8,355	13,558	3,716[c]
72	25	95	66	152	4,614	5,324	n.a.
63	78	88	28	16	1,450	2,050	410
69	45	89	42	0	470	630	70
71	28	76	38	16	151	306	294
70	21	64	n.a.	n.a.	180	270	116
41	178	12	50	19	920	500	109[c]
69	44	83	n.a.	n.a.	85	290	n.a.
71	18	77	n.a.	n.a.	6,019	6,757	n.a.
51	139	23	29	73	19,865	10,900	9,642

Upper Middle-Income Countries (Continued)

	Popu-lation, mid-1976	Per Capita GNP, 1974	Physical Quality of Life Index (PQLI)[a]	Per Capita GNP Growth Rate, 1965-74	Birth Rate per 1,000	Death Rate per 1,000
	(mil.)	($)		(%)		
□Iraq	11.4	1,160	46	4.8	48	15
Jamaica	2.1	1,190	87	4.5	31	7
Lebanon	2.7	1,070[b]	80	3.7	40	10
Malta	0.3	1,220	89	8.4	18	9
Martinique	0.3	1,540[b]	88	3.9[b]	22	7
Mexico	62.3	1,090	75	2.8	46	8
Netherland Antilles	0.2	1,590[b]	n.a.	0.6[b]	25	7
Oman	0.8	1,660	n.a.	19.2	50	19
Panama	1.7	1,000	81	3.7	31	5
Peru	16.0	740	58	1.8	41	12
Portugal	8.5	1,630	79	6.5	19	11
Reunion	0.5	1,550[b]	74	3.5[b]	28	7
Romania	21.5	1,960[t]	92	6.8[tu]	20	9
South Africa	25.6	1,210	48	2.5	43	16
Surinam	0.4	1,120	85	2.2	41	7
Taiwan (ROC)	16.3	810	88	6.9	23	5
Trinidad & Tobago	1.1	1,680	88	2.2	26	7
Turkey	40.2	750	54	4.3	39	12
Uruguay	2.8	1,190	88	0.8	21	10
□Venezuela	12.3	1,970	80	1.7	36	7
Yugoslavia	21.5	1,310	85	5.4	18	8

High-Income Countries

37 Countries	1,057.0	4,361	95	4.0	17	9
○Australia	13.8	5,330	96	3.4	18	9
○Austria	7.5	4,410	95	5.0	13	12
Bahamas	0.2	2,460	87	-1.7	22	6
Bahrain	0.2	2,330[b]	60	21.2[bv]	44	15
○Belgium	9.8	5,670	95	4.9	13	12
○Canada	23.1	6,190	97	3.5	15	7
○Czechoslovakia	14.9	3,590[b]	95	2.5[b]	20	12
○Denmark	5.1	6,430	98	3.4	14	10

Life Expectancy at Birth	Infant Mortality per 1,000 Live Births	Literacy	Per Capita Public Education Expend's, 1973	Per Capita Military Expend's, 1973	Total Exports, f.o.b., 1975	Total Imports, c.i.f., 1975	International Reserves, Sept. 1976
(years)		(%)	($)	($)	($ mil.)	($ mil.)	($ mil.)
53	99	26	27	54	8,180	4,000	3,410
68	26	82	45	7	707	1,207	73
63	59	86	24	21	613[de]	1,283[de]	n.a.
70	21	83	62	5	164[e]	375[e]	585
69	32	88	n.a.	n.a.	95	340	n.a.
63	61	74	23	6	2,850	6,400	1,501[s]
73	28	n.a.	n.a.	n.a.	2,600	2,800	118
47[j]	138	n.a.	n.a.	155	1,443[e]	668[e]	n.a.
66	44	78	40	1	300	840	n.a.
56	110	61	24	23	1,360	2,500	312[c]
68	38	65	24	79	2,000	4,000	1,291[c]
63	47	63	n.a.	n.a.	90	400	n.a.
69	35	98-99	48	88	4,872[en]	5,553[en]	n.a.
52	117	42	17	31	5,411	7,630	887
66	30	84	n.a.	n.a.	256	216	124
69	26	85	9	53	5,292[e]	5,915[e]	1,629
66	26	89	49	4	1,900	1,700	928
57	119	51	16	23	1,401	4,640	1,059
70	45	90	32	22	320	500	236[c]
65	54	82	63	27	10,741	4,850[i]	7,891
68	40	84	52	38	4,061	7,697	1,971
71	**21**	**97**	**217**	**232**	**687,478**	**680,253**	**175,967**
72	16	98	227	121	11,575	9,811[i]	3,257
71	23	98	181	35	7,518	9,301	4,221
66	32	89	n.a.	n.a.	2,250	1,900	49
61	78	40	n.a.	20	1,107[e]	1,189[e]	392
71	16	97	323	129	32,230[w]	30,450[w]	4,714
73	16	98	452	109	31,881	34,306[i]	5,838
70	20	100	111	188	8,659	8,970[i]	n.a.
73	12	99	420	114	8,721	10,335	613

High-Income Countries (Continued)

	Popu- lation, mid- 1976	Per Capita GNP, 1974	Physical Quality of Life Index (PQLI)[a]	Per Capita GNP Growth Rate, 1965-74	Birth Rate per 1,000	Death Rate per 1,000
	(mil.)	*($)*		*(%)*		
oFinland	4.7	4,700	95	5.2	13	10
oFrance	53.1	5,440	97	4.8	15	10
oGermany, Dem. Rep.	16.8	3,950[b]	96	2.2[b]	11	14
oGermany, Fed. Rep.	62.1	6,260	95	3.9	10	12
oGreece	9.0	2,090	91	6.5	16	8
oHungary	10.6	2,370	92	2.9	18	12
oIceland	0.2	5,430	99	2.4	20	7
oIreland	3.1	2,320	96	3.6	22	11
oIsrael	3.5	3,460	90	5.8	28	7
oItaly	56.3	2,820	94	4.0	16	10
oJapan	112.3	4,070	98	8.5	19	6
□Kuwait	1.1	11,770	76	2.2	45	8
□Libya	2.5	4,640	42	4.5	45	15
oLuxembourg	0.4	6,050	96	3.2	11	12
oNetherlands	13.8	5,250	99	4.1	14	8
oNew Zealand	3.2	4,310	96	1.8	19	8
oNorway	4.0	5,860	99	3.4	15	10
oPoland	34.4	2,750[b]	94	4.5[b]	18	8
oPuerto Rico	3.2	2,230	92	4.7	23	6
□Qatar	0.1	8,560	32	7.1	50	19
□Saudi Arabia	6.4	2,870	29	9.7	49	20
Singapore	2.3	2,240	85	10.0	20	5
oSpain	36.0	2,490	94	5.4	19	8
oSweden	8.2	7,240	100	2.8	13	11
oSwitzerland	6.5	7,870	98	2.9	13	9
oU.S.S.R.	257.0	2,600[b]	94	3.4[b]	18	9
□United Arab Emirates	0.2	11,710	34	9.2	50	19
oUnited Kingdom	56.1	3,590	97	2.2	13	12
oUnited States	215.3	6,670	96	2.4	15	9

Life Expectancy at Birth	Infant Mortality per 1,000 Live Births	Literacy	Per Capita Public Education Expend's, 1973	Per Capita Military Expend's, 1973	Total Exports, f.o.b., 1975	Total Imports, c.i.f., 1975	International Reserves, Sept. 1976
(years)		(%)	($)	($)	($ mil.)	($ mil.)	($ mil.)
69	10	99	231	54	5,487	7,609	497
73	12	97	286	181	52,214	54,247	9,371
71	16	99	126	183	8,748[n]	9,646[in]	n.a.
71	21	99	254	193	90,026	74,263	35,034
72	24	84	34	72	2,100	5,480	948
70	34	98	70	114	6,091	7,176	n.a.
74	11	99	219	0	308	487	91
72	17	98	93	29	3,177	3,768	1,680
71	23	84	110	1,110	1,826	4,128	1,313
72	23	93-95	119	75	34,216	38,366	5,080
73	11	98	166	33	55,844	57,881	16,489
69	44	55	239	156	7,830	2,200	1,828
53	130	27	186	69	6,000	3,900	2,792
71	14	98	220	44	32,230[w]	30,450[w]	9
74	11	98	331	150	35,180	34,740	6,466
72	16	98	169	64	2,100	3,300	441
74	12	99	263	152	6,825	9,718	2,197
70	24	98	83	116	10,253	12,568[i]	n.a.
72	23	89	n.a.	n.a.	n.a.	n.a.	n.a.
47[j]	138	10-15	n.a.	279	1,791[e]	413[e]	118[c]
45	152	15	56	171	26,000	4,800	26,222
67	16	75	49	95	5,360	8,260	3,227[c]
72	14	90	35	54	7,691	16,097	5,530
75	9	99	489	212	17,439	17,874	2,904
73	13	98	282	125	12,887	13,265	10,959
70	28	100	172	368	27,405[n]	24,890[in]	n.a.
47[j]	138	20	n.a.	106	6,822[e]	2,669[e]	n.a.
72	16	98-99	181	154	43,760	53,262	5,217
71	17	99	348	374	106,157	102,984	18,470

A-4. Two Measures of the Gap Between Developed and Developing Countries, 1960-1975 ($ and per thousand)

While some indicators measuring well-being (such as per capita GNP) reflect a widening gap over time between developed and developing countries, other indicators (such as death rates per 1,000) reflect a diminishing gap between the two groups of countries. From 1960 to 1974, the gap in per capita GNP between developed and developing countries grew from a ratio of 12-1 to 13-1. By 1975, the number of deaths per 1,000 in the developing countries was only one-and-one-half times that in the developed countries; in 1960, the death rate had been twice as high in the developing as in the developed countries.

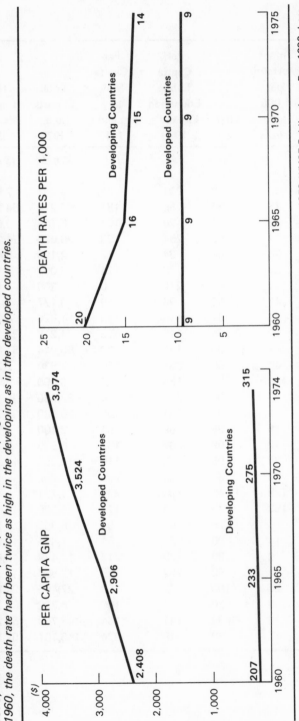

SOURCES: Per capita GNP figures are from Ruth Leger Sivard, *World Military and Social Expenditures, 1976*, WMSE Publications, Box 1003, Leesburg, Virginia 22075, p. 14; death rate figures are from United Nations, Department of Economic and Social Affairs, Population Division, *Selected World Demographic Indicators by Countries, 1950-2000*, Doc. No. ESA/P/WP.55, May 28, 1975.

A-5. Comparison of Health and Education Resources Available in Developed and Developing Countries, 1973

In 1973, the gap between developed and developing countries in both human and capital resources available for health and education remained substantial. More than twice as many teachers were available per 1,000 school-age children in developed than in developing countries, for example; and nearly 45 times as much was spent per person on health care in the richer, developed countries than in the poorer, developing nations.

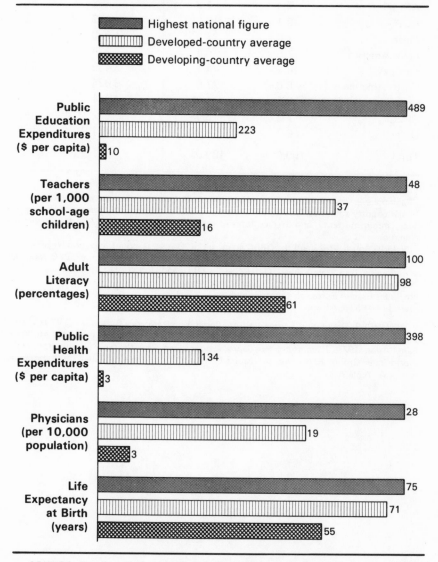

Highest national figure
Developed-country average
Developing-country average

Public Education Expenditures ($ per capita)
489
223
10

Teachers (per 1,000 school-age children)
48
37
16

Adult Literacy (percentages)
100
98
61

Public Health Expenditures ($ per capita)
398
134
3

Physicians (per 10,000 population)
28
19
3

Life Expectancy at Birth (years)
75
71
55

SOURCE: Based on Ruth Leger Sivard, *World Military and Social Expenditures, 1976*, WMSE Publications, Box 1003, Leesburg, Virginia 22075, pp. 16 and 17.

A-6. Population, GNP, and Physical Quality of Life Index (PQLI), by Region, 1974

	Population[a]	GNP[a]	Average Per Capita GNP[b]	Average POLI[bc]
	(percentages)	(percentages)	($)	
Africa[d]	7.4	1.3	258	46
Asia[e]	49.1	8.1	252	52
Japan	2.8	7.9	4,070	98
Latin America[f]	7.6	4.8	923	71
Europe[g]	18.6	44.1	3,435	94
North America	6.0	27.5	6,624	96
Oceania	0.5	1.6	4,311	87
OPEC	7.3	3.4	632	44
Other	0.7	1.3	1,481[h]	53[h]
Total	100.0	100.0		

[a] In 1974, world GNP was $5.6 trillion; population was 3.9 billion.
[b] Regional averages are weighted by mid-1976 populations of the countries included.
[c] Each country's Physical Quality of Life Index (PQLI) is based on an average of life expectancy, infant mortality, and literacy rates in the mid-1970s. See pp. 147-54 for further explanation.
[d] Excludes South Africa and the OPEC countries of Algeria, Gabon, Libya, and Nigeria.
[e] Includes the People's Republic of China, but excludes Israel, Japan, and the OPEC countries of Indonesia, Iran, Iraq, Kuwait, Qatar, Saudi Arabia, and United Arab Emirates.
[f] Excludes the OPEC countries of Ecuador and Venezuela.
[g] Includes Eastern European countries and the U.S.S.R.
[h] Israel and South Africa.

SOURCES: Population figures are from Population Reference Bureau, Inc., "1975 World Population Data Sheet: Supplement" (Washington, D.C.); GNP figures are based on *World Bank Atlas, 1976: Population, Per Capita Product, and Growth Rates* (Washington, D.C.: World Bank Group, 1976); and per capita GNP and PQLI figures are based on this volume, Annex A, Table A-3.

A-7. Disparities Between Groups of Countries, 1975 (millions and $)

	Population (millions)			Per Capita Income[a] (in constant 1975 U.S. $)			
	Total	Absolute Poor	Under-nourished	1965	1975	1985[bc]	2000[bd]
Poorest Countries (under $200 per capita GNP)	1,200	750[e]	600	130	150	160–180	180–230
Middle-Income Developing Countries (over $200 per capita GNP)	900	170[e]	140	630	950	1,130–1,350	1,510–2,400
Developed Countries	700	<20[f]	<20[f]	4,200	5,500	6,700–8,100	9,000–14,600

[a]Based on official exchange rates rather than purchasing power comparisons and therefore represents only broad orders of magnitude.

[b]Long-term projections of economic growth are, of course, highly speculative; they are presented here not as predictions, but only to call attention to problems that may develop if present trends continue.

[c]The higher figures are World Bank projections based on 1975-1985 annual per capita growth rates of 1.6% for the poorest countries, 3.9% for the middle-income countries, and 4% for the developed countries. The lower figures are ODC projections based on annual per capita growth rates only half that good. ODC derived the higher figures by projecting a continuation of the 1975-1985 growth rates assumed by the World Bank and the lower figures by projecting a continuation of growth rates half that high.

[e]In the developing countries, defined as those with annual per capita incomes of less than $100 in 1975 U.S. dollars. They are considered to have only a slight chance of being able to increase their incomes by more than $2 annually over the next decade. In addition, there are hundreds of millions more with incomes that are somewhat above this minimum level of poverty but still less than one third the national average.

[f]Even in the rich countries, there are millions who suffer from poverty and undernourishment.

NOTE: Data for centrally planned economies are not included in this table.

SOURCES: Adapted, with revision, from Robert S. McNamara, "Address to the Board of Governors," Manila, Philippines, October 4, 1976 (Washington, D.C.: World Bank, 1976), pp. 3, 5, and 15.

A-8. Poverty in Developing Countries, by Region, 1972 (millions and percentages)

	Total Population (millions)	Seriously Poor[a]		Destitute[b]	
		(millions)	(percentage of population)	(millions)	(percentage of population)
Africa	345	239	69	134	39
Asia[c]	1,196	853	71	499	42
Latin America	274	118	43	73	27
Total[d]	1,815	1,210	67	706	39

[a]The "seriously poor" are defined as those with annual per capita incomes of U.S. $115 in Africa, U.S. $100 in Asia, and U.S. $180 in Latin America.
[b]The "destitute" are defined as that portion of the seriously poor with annual per capita incomes of U.S. $59 in Africa, U.S. $50 in Asia, and U.S. $90 in Latin America.
[c]Excludes People's Republic of China, with a 1972 population of approximately 800 million.
[d]Total of only the above. Excludes People's Republic of China; also excludes developing countries in Europe and Oceania with a 1972 population of about 25 million.

SOURCE: ILO International Labour Office, *Employment, Growth, and Basic Needs: A One-World Problem.* Originally published by the International Labour Office (Geneva: 1976). Also published for the Overseas Development Council by Praeger Publishers, Inc. (New York: 1977), p. 22.

A-9. Illiteracy in Developing Countries, by Region and Sex, 1960 and 1970
(millions and percentages)

	1960		1970	
	(millions)	*(percentages)*	*(millions)*	*(percentages)*
Africa	124	81	143	74
Male	56	73	61	63
Female	68	88	82	84
Asia[a]	542	55	579	47
Male	224	45	231	37
Female	318	63	348	57
Latin America	40	33	39	24
Male	17	28	16	20
Female	23	37	23	27
Total	**701**	**59**	**756**	**50**
Male	295	50	306	40
Female	406	69	450	60

[a]Excludes the People's Republic of China.

NOTES: Illiteracy is generally defined as that proportion of the adult population 15 years or older unable to read or write. It is estimated that, by 1980, the number of illiterate adults in the developing world will increase to some 865 million.

SOURCE: *The Assault on World Poverty: Problems of Rural Development, Education and Health.* Published for the World Bank. (Baltimore: Johns Hopkins University Press, 1975), p. 295. Based on UNESCO data.

A-10. Estimated Population Unemployed and Underemployed in Developing and Developed Countries, by Region, 1975 (millions and percentages)

In the developing countries, underemployment—especially in the form of inadequate income—poses in both numbers and intensity the main employment problem. In the developed countries, where the concept of underemployment has not yet been fully explored or defined, the unemployment data alone provide a "meaningful indication of the underutilization of labor."

Whereas in developing countries employment problems of all kinds are primarily rural, in developed countries they are concentrated in urban areas. In both groups of countries, employment problems are particularly acute among some groups, for example, women, youth, and migrants.

	All Sectors		Urban Sector	
	(millions)	*(percentage of labor force)*	*(millions)*	*(percentage of labor force)*
Africa	63	45.0	10	35.9
Unemployed	10	7.1	3	10.8
Underemployed	53	37.9	7	25.1
Asia	186	40.3	26	30.1
Unemployed	18	3.9	6	6.9
Underemployed	168	36.4	20	23.2
Latin America	33	34.0	19	29.3
Unemployed	5	5.1	5	6.5
Underemployed	28	28.9	14	22.8
Oceania	1	49.0	n.a.	n.a.
Unemployed	—	—	n.a.	n.a.
Underemployed	1	49.0	n.a.	n.a.
Developing Countries	283	40.4	55	31.3
Unemployed	33	4.7	14	8.0
Underemployed	250	35.7	41	23.3
Developed Countries[a]	17.1[b]	5.2	n.a.	n.a.
Unemployed	17.1	5.2	n.a.	n.a.
Underemployed	n.a.	n.a.	n.a.	n.a.

[a]Australia, Austria, Belgium, Canada, Denmark, Finland, France, Federal Republic of Germany, Greece, Ireland, Italy, Japan, Netherlands, New Zealand, Norway, Portugal, Spain, Sweden, Switzerland, Turkey, United Kingdom, United States, and Yugoslavia.
[b]Of this number, 8.1 million unemployed are in North America (the United States and Canada); this represents about 8.1 per cent of their combined labor force.

NOTES: Centrally planned economies are not included in this table.
The unemployed are defined as those "persons without a job and looking for work"; the underemployed are defined as those "persons who are in employment of less than normal duration and who are seeking or would accept additional work" as well as those "with a job yielding inadequate income."

SOURCE: Adapted from ILO International Labour Office, *Employment, Growth, and Basic Needs: A One-World Problem.* Originally published by the International Labour Office (Geneva: 1976). Also published for the Overseas Development Council by Praeger Publishers, Inc. (New York: 1977), pp. 18 and 26.

A-11. Income Distribution Within Selected Developing and Developed Countries
(percentages)

| | Share of National Income of Population Groups | | | | |
	Richest 20%	2nd 20%	3rd 20%	4th 20%	Poorest 20%
Developing Countries					
Argentina (1961)	52.0	17.6	13.1	10.3	7.0
Ecuador (1970)	73.5	14.5	5.6	3.9	2.5
Egypt (1964-65)	47.0	23.5	15.5	9.8	4.2
India (1963-64)	52.0	19.0	13.0	11.0	5.0
Kenya (1969)	68.0	13.5	8.5	6.2	3.8
Korea, Rep. of (1970)	45.0	22.0	15.0	11.0	7.0
Mexico (1969)	64.0	16.0	9.5	6.5	4.0
Sri Lanka (1969-70)	46.0	20.5	16.5	11.0	6.0
Tanzania (1967)	57.0	17.0	12.0	9.0	5.0
Developed Countries					
Australia (1967-68)	38.7	23.4	17.8	13.5	6.6
France (1962)	53.7	22.8	14.0	7.6	1.9
Germany, Dem. Rep. (1970)	30.7	23.3	19.8	15.8	10.4
Germany, Fed. Rep. (1970)	45.6	22.5	15.6	10.4	5.9
Hungary (1967)	33.5	23.5	19.0	15.5	8.5
Japan (1968)	43.8	23.4	16.8	11.3	4.6
Sweden (1970)	42.5	24.6	17.6	9.9	5.4
United Kingdom (1968)	39.2	23.8	18.2	12.8	6.0
United States (1970)	38.8	24.1	17.4	13.0	6.7

NOTES: Income distribution data are incomplete and deficient, and inter-country comparisons should be made with caution. A completely equal distribution of national income would show the richest 20% and the poorest 20% of the population (as well as all other quintiles) each receiving 20% of that country's income.

SOURCE: Montek S. Ahluwalia, "Inequality, Poverty and Development," *Journal of Development Economics* 3 (1976).

Food, Fertilizer, Energy, and Raw Materials

Annex B: Facts of Interest

In an increasingly interdependent world, a rapidly growing world population as well as affluent consumption patterns affect both present and future generations. Each person added to the world's population, as well as any one person's excessive consumption, exerts an increasing claim and burden on the world's scarce food, energy, minerals, and other resources.

1. While U.S. earnings from its agricultural exports rose nearly fivefold from $4.5 billion in FY 1960 to $22.1 in FY 1976, food assistance under Public Law 480 (the Food for Peace Program) as a percentage of total agricultural exports has rapidly decreased over the same period—from 25 per cent in FY 1960 to only 4 per cent in FY 1976 (Table B-5).

2. North America, Western Europe, and Japan—which together comprise about 20 per cent of the world's population—consume nearly 58 per cent of the world's energy; in contrast, the developing countries, with nearly three quarters of the world's people, consume only 15 per cent of world energy (Table B-8).

3. The United States depends heavily on imports of a number of crucial minerals in order to satisfy consumption needs. In 1974, the United States depended on imports for 84 per cent of its tin consumption; 73 per cent of its consumption came from the developing market economies alone. Nonetheless, the United States is at somewhat more of an advantage than other developed countries in the minerals area. While the European Communities and Japan are completely dependent on imports of such crucial industrial raw materials as nickel, tungsten, and to a lesser degree copper, the United States depends on imports for 72 per cent of its nickel consumption, 64 per cent of its tungsten needs, and only 20 per cent of its copper needs (Tables B-11 and B-12).

4. The developing countries are the major world suppliers of many vital raw materials whose prices tend to fluctuate. In recent years, fluctuations in the terms of trade of many of these raw materials, such as metals and minerals, also have been particularly extreme (Tables B-13, B-14, and B-15).

B-1. Indexes of Total Food Production and Per Capita Food Production in Developed and Developing Countries, 1955-1976 (1961-1965=100)

Population growth has a crucial effect on the amount of food available in the developing countries. While total food production of the developing countries has increased 49 per cent in the last 10-15 years, per capita food production has risen only 9 per cent in the same period.

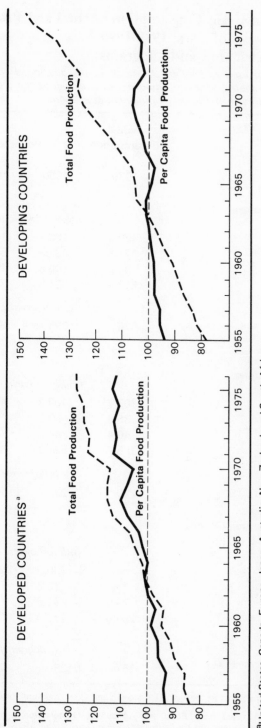

[a]United States, Canada, Europe, Japan, Australia, New Zealand, and South Africa.

NOTES: Data for 1976 are preliminary. Centrally planned economies are not included in this table. Data do not include non-food commodities such as coffee, fibers, or rubber.

SOURCE: Informal estimates from U.S. Agency for International Development, Office of Financial Management, Statistics and Reports Division, December 1976.

B-2. Annual Grain Consumption (Actual and Projected), by Main Types of Uses, 1970-1990 (million metric tons and kilograms)

In 1970, grain used as feed for livestock in the developed countries totalled 371.5 million metric tons—an amount which exceeded the grain consumed as food by the more than 100 developing market economies.

	Actual Consumption	Projected Demand[a]		
	1970	1980	1985	1990
Developed Countries	*(million metric tons)*			
Food	160.9	163.1	164.1	164.6
Feed	371.5	467.9	522.7	565.7
Other uses	84.9	100.6	109.5	116.4
Total	617.3	731.6	796.3	846.7
	(kilograms)			
Per Capita	576	623	649	663
Developing Market Economies	*(million metric tons)*			
Food	303.7	409.3	474.5	547.2
Feed	35.6	60.9	78.6	101.9
Other uses	46.4	64.1	75.4	88.5
Total	385.7	534.3	628.5	737.6
	(kilograms)			
Per Capita	220	233	240	246
Developing Centrally Planned Economies	*(million metric tons)*			
Food	164.1	200.5	215.2	225.3
Feed	15.3	38.7	48.7	61.4
Other uses	24.6	32.6	36.0	39.1
Total	204.0	271.8	299.9	325.8
	(kilograms)			
Per Capita	257	290	298	304

[a]FAO projections based on "trend" GDP growth and U.N. "medium" population projections.

SOURCE: Adapted from Food and Agriculture Organization of the United Nations, *Population, Food Supply and Agricultural Development* (Rome: 1975), p. 28.

B-3. Indicators of World Food Security, 1961-1976 (million metric tons and days)

	Reserve Stocks of Grain[a]	Grain Equivalent of Idled U.S. Cropland	Total World Reserves	Reserves as Days of Annual Grain Consumption
	(million metric tons)			
1961	163	68	231	105
1962	176	81	257	105
1963	149	70	219	95
1964	153	70	223	87
1965	147	71	218	91
1966	151	78	229	84
1967	115	51	166	59
1968	144	61	205	71
1969	159	73	232	85
1970	188	71	259	89
1971	168	41	209	71
1972	130	78	208	69
1973	148	24	172	55
1974	108	0	108	33
1975	111	0	111	35
1976[b]	100	0	100	31

[a]Based on carry-over stocks of grain at beginning of crop year in individual countries for year shown. Stock levels now include reserve stocks of importing as well as of exporting countries and thus are slightly higher than previous figures.
[b]Estimate.

SOURCE: Lester R. Brown, *The Politics and Responsibility of the North American Breadbasket,* Worldwatch Paper 2, October 1975, p. 8.

B-4. World Net Grain Trade, by Groups of Countries and by Region, 1960-1963 Average and 1973-1977 (million metric tons)

Although preliminary estimates indicate a decrease in North America's exports of grain for the 1976-77 crop year, North America will remain the "breadbasket" of the world—supplying most of the world's exports of grain to the grain-importing areas of Western Europe, the Soviet Union and Eastern Europe, Africa, the Middle East, and Asia.

	1960/61-1962/63 Average	1973/74	1974/75	1975/76	1976/77[a]
Developed Market Economies	20.3	58.9	54.8	75.0	49.3
North America	42.4	87.7	77.5	98.7	91.7
Western Europe	-25.7	-22.5	-19.2	-18.8	-34.7
Australia and New Zealand	6.6	9.4	11.6	12.7	9.4
Other Developed[b]	- 3.1	-15.6	-15.0	-17.6	-17.1
Centrally Planned Economies	- 3.2	-16.2	-13.3	-34.7	-23.0
People's Republic of China	- 3.9	- 5.7	- 4.5	- 1.3	- 1.3
U.S.S.R. and Eastern Europe	0.7	-10.6	- 8.8	-33.4	-21.7
Developing Countries	-11.7	-29.9	-35.1	-30.8	-25.9
Africa and Middle East	- 6.2	-14.7	-17.7	-15.3	-17.2
Latin America[c]	1.0	- 0.2	- 1.4	1.1	6.1
Asia	- 6.4	-15.2	-16.0	-16.6	-14.8
Other	- 0.9	- 2.7	- 1.8	- 1.8	- 1.7
Total Interregional Exports	50.7	97.1	89.1	112.5	107.2
Total World Exports	n.a.	139.5	133.7	149.1	144.4

[a]Preliminary estimate.

[b]Japan and South Africa.

[c]Excluding Argentina (a large net grain exporter) would show Latin America to be a grain-importing region. Figures above would be –4.2, –10.4, –9.3, –8.8, and –6.4, respectively.

NOTE: "World grain" includes wheat and wheat flour, milled rice, the major coarse grains—corn, barley, rye, oats, sorghum, and millet—as well as minor coarse grains. Neither the minor coarse grains nor millet were included in the grain trade tables in previous issues of *The U.S. and World Development: Agenda for Action.*

SOURCES: U.S. Department of Agriculture, Economic Research Service, *World Agricultural Situation,* Publication No. WAS-11, October 1976, p. 18, and U.S. Department of Agriculture, Foreign Agricultural Service, "World Grain Situation: 1976/77 Crop and Trade Developments," *Foreign Agriculture Circular: Grains,* Doc. No. FG-29-76, December 15, 1976, pp. 2 and 9.

B-5. U.S. Agricultural Exports, FYs 1960 and 1970-1976 ($ millions)

| | Public Law 480 | | | | | Other Agricultural Exports | | Total Agricultural Exports[e] | Public Law 480 as Percentage of Total |
| | Title I | | Title II[a] | Title III[b] | Total | Mutual Security Programs[c] | Commercial Sales[d] | | |
	Sales for foreign currency	Long-term dollar credit sales							
1960	824	—	143	149	1,116	167	3,236	4,519	25
1970	309	506	241	—	1,056	12	5,650	6,718	16
1971	204	539	280	—	1,023	56	6,674	7,753	13
1972	143	535	380	—	1,058	66	6,922	8,046	13
1973	6	661	287	—	954	84	11,864	12,902	7
1974	—	575	292	—	867	76	20,350	21,293	4
1975	—	762	339	—	1,101	123	20,354	21,578	5
1976[f]	—	615	216	—	831	216	21,000	22,147	4
Total[fg]	**12,292**	**5,561**	**5,502**	**1,732**	**25,087**	**2,868**	**149,199**	**177,154**	**14**

[a]Transfers of commodities for emergency relief or to promote economic development, as well as donations to the World Food Program and voluntary relief agencies.

[b]Barter and, for 1960, some shipments in exchange for goods and services for U.S. agencies.

[c]Sales for foreign currency, economic aid, and expenditures under development loans.

[d]Commercial sales for dollars include, in addition to unassisted commercial transactions, shipments of some commodities with government assistance in the form of barter shipments for overseas procurement for U.S. agencies, short-term credit and credit guarantees, sales of government-owned commodities at less than domestic market prices, and export payments in cash or kind.

[e]Figures do not include furskins or bulk tobacco and, from 1966 to 1971, also exclude citric acid, fatty acids, glues, and adhesives. Some non-food agricultural products such as cotton are included.

[f]Preliminary.

g1955-1976.

SOURCE: U.S. Department of Agriculture, Economic Research Service, *Foreign Agricultural Trade of the United States (FATUS)*, October 1976, p. 26.

187

B-6. Developing-Country Imports of Manufactured Fertilizers, 1971-1974
($ millions and million metric tons)

In 1971, the developing countries imported 4.6 million metric tons of fertilizer for $533 million. Three years later, only slightly more fertilizer (4.9 million metric tons) cost the developing countries $1,450 million—more than two-and-one-half times as much.

	1971	1972[a]	1973[a]	1974[a]
	($ millions)			
Nitrogenous	311	341	462	900
Phosphate	126	183	275	380
Potash	96	101	138	170
Total	**533**	**625**	**875**	**1,450**
	(million metric tons)			
Nitrogenous	2.3	2.5	2.6	2.0
Phosphate	1.0	1.2	1.4	1.1
Potash	1.3	1.5	1.8	1.8
Total	**4.6**	**5.2**	**5.8**	**4.9**

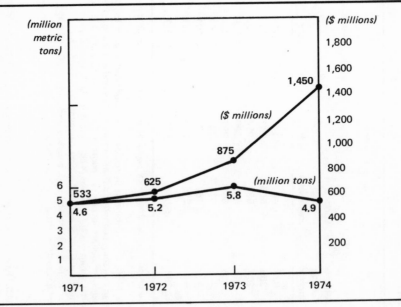

[a]Estimate.

NOTE: The oil-exporting developing countries and the People's Republic of China are not included in data.

SOURCE: *CERES: FAO Review on Development,* March-April 1975, p. 7.

B-7. World Energy Production, by Groups of Countries and Types of Energy, 1960, 1970, 1972, and 1973 (as percentage of world production of energy type)

		Developed Market Economies					Centrally Planned Economies	Developing Market Economies		
		North America	Europe[a]	Japan	Other[b]	Total		OPEC	Non-OPEC	Total
Coal and Lignite	1960	18.2	22.6	2.3	3.0	46.1	50.0	0.1	3.5	3.6
	1970	23.5	15.8	1.6	4.6	45.7	49.5	—	4.8	4.8
	1972	22.9	13.9	1.1	5.0	43.0	52.1	—	4.6	4.8
	1973	22.2	13.9	0.9	5.2	42.3	52.6	—	4.9	5.0
Crude Petroleum	1960	36.3	1.4	0.1	0.0	37.7	15.6	40.3	6.2	46.6
	1970	25.8	1.0	—	0.3	27.5	16.6	48.6	7.4	56.0
	1972	23.5	0.9	—	0.6	25.4	17.0	50.8	6.8	57.7
	1973	21.6	0.8	—	0.7	23.4	17.3	53.0	6.3	59.4
Natural Gas	1960	80.4	2.6	0.2	0.0	82.9	12.0	1.7	3.2	5.0
	1970	62.8	7.5	0.2	0.1	70.8	22.5	3.5	3.0	6.6
	1972	55.4	10.8	0.3	0.3	69.5	22.4	4.6	3.2	7.9
	1973	56.1	11.8	0.2	0.3	68.5	22.8	5.1	3.4	8.5
Hydro and Nuclear Electricity	1960	37.2	33.7	8.1	1.1	80.2	10.4	1.0	19.8	21.0
	1970	34.3	29.9	7.0	1.9	73.2	14.0	0.6	11.5	12.1
	1972	36.3	29.6	6.7	1.6	74.3	13.4	1.1	11.2	12.3
	1973	37.5	29.1	5.8	2.1	74.6	12.6	1.1	11.6	12.7

[a]Includes Israel.
[b]Australia, New Zealand, South Africa.

SOURCE: United Nations, Department of Economic and Social Affairs, *World Energy Supplies, 1970-1973*, Statistical Papers Series J, Nos. 7 (1965) and 18 (1975).

B-8. World Energy Consumption, by Region, 1960, 1970, 1980, and 1990 (quadrillion Btus[a] and percentages)

	1960		1970		1980		1990	
	quad. Btus	*percentages*	*quad. Btus*	*percentages*	*quad. Btus*	*percentages*	*quad. Btus*	*percentages*
United States	44.6	33.9	67.0	30.9	86.3	29.1	121.9	29.3
Western Europe	26.4	20.1	46.0	21.2	62.6	21.1	87.2	20.9
Japan	3.7	2.8	12.0	5.5	20.4	6.9	34.0	8.2
Centrally Planned Economies[b]	39.0	29.6	58.3	26.9	82.0	27.7	109.0	26.2
Rest of world	18.0	13.7	33.6	15.5	45.0	15.2	64.4	15.4
Total	**131.7**	**100.0**	**216.9**	**100.0**	**296.3**	**100.0**	**416.5**	**100.0**

[a]British thermal unit. One quadrillion Btus is equivalent to 500,000 barrels of petroleum per day for a year; 40 million tons of bituminous coal; 1 trillion cubic feet of natural gas; or 100 billion kilowatt hours.
[b]U.S.S.R., Eastern Europe, People's Republic of China, Cuba.

SOURCE: Based on U.S. Department of the Interior, *Energy Perspectives: A Presentation of Major Energy and Energy Related Data* (Washington, D.C.: U.S. Government Printing Office, February 1975), p. 6.

B-9. World Energy Consumption, by Types of Energy, 1960, 1970, 1980, and 1990 (quadrillion Btus[a] and percentages)

	1960 quad. Btus	1960 percentages	1970 quad. Btus	1970 percentages	1980 quad. Btus	1980 percentages	1990 quad. Btus	1990 percentages
Coal	61.5	46.7	66.8	30.8	79.2	26.7	92.0	22.1
Petroleum	45.3	34.4	96.9	44.7	132.3	44.7	165.0	39.6
Natural Gas	18.0	13.7	40.6	18.7	56.8	19.2	77.1	18.5
Hydropower and Geothermal	6.9	5.2	11.8	5.4	15.4	5.2	18.8	4.5
Nuclear	—	—	0.8	0.4	12.6	4.3	63.6	15.3
Total	131.7	100.0	216.9	100.0	296.3	100.0	416.5	100.0

[a]British thermal unit. One quadrillion Btus is equivalent to 500,000 barrels of petroleum per day for a year; 40 million tons of bituminous coal; 1 trillion cubic feet of natural gas; or 100 billion kilowatt hours.

SOURCE: Based on U.S. Department of the Interior, Energy Perspectives: A Presentation of Major Energy and Energy Related Data (Washington, D.C.: U.S. Government Printing Office, February 1975), p. 8.

B-10. World Crude Petroleum Production and Consumption, 1975
(million barrels per day)

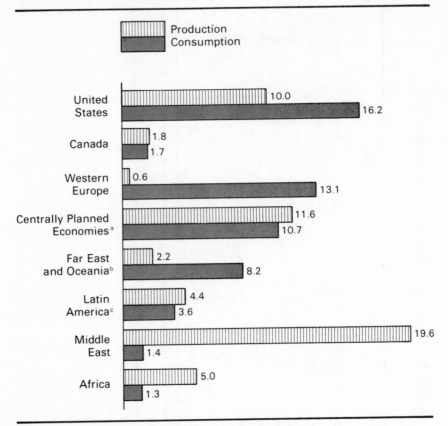

Legend:
- Production
- Consumption

	Production	Consumption
United States	10.0	16.2
Canada	1.8	1.7
Western Europe	0.6	13.1
Centrally Planned Economies[a]	11.6	10.7
Far East and Oceania[b]	2.2	8.2
Latin America[c]	4.4	3.6
Middle East	19.6	1.4
Africa	5.0	1.3

[a]U.S.S.R., Eastern Europe, People's Republic of China, and Cuba.
[b]1973 figure.
[c]Excluding Mexico.

NOTE: Total world production of crude petroleum in 1975 amounted to 55.2 million barrels per day or 20.2 billion barrels per year.

SOURCE: Based on *International Economic Report of the President*, transmitted to Congress, March 1976 (Washington, D.C.: U.S. Government Printing Office, 1976), p. 15.

B-11. U.S. Mineral Import Dependence, 1974 (net imports as percentage of consumption)

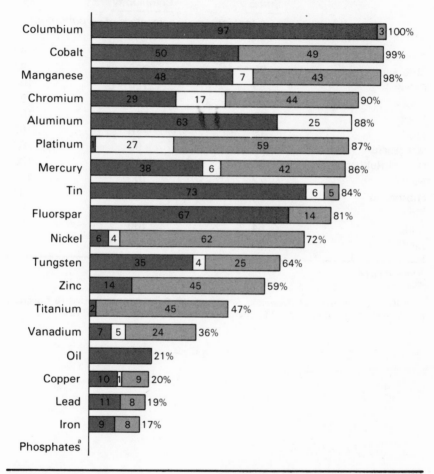

Imports from Developing Market Economies

Imports from Centrally Planned Economies

Imports from Developed Market Economies

Columbium	97	3	100%
Cobalt	50	49	99%
Manganese	48	7	43	98%
Chromium	29	17	44	90%
Aluminum	63	25	88%
Platinum	1	27	59	87%
Mercury	38	6	42	86%
Tin	73	6	5	84%
Fluorspar	67	14	81%
Nickel	6	4	62	72%
Tungsten	35	4	25	64%
Zinc	14	45	59%
Titanium	2	45	47%
Vanadium	7	5	24	36%
Oil			21%
Copper	10	1	9	20%
Lead	11	8	19%
Iron	9	8	17%
Phosphates[a]			

[a]The United States is a net exporter of phosphates; domestic production accounts for all (100%) U.S. consumption.

NOTE: Figures are based on metal and metal content of ores and scrap.

SOURCE: Adapted from *International Economic Report of the President*, transmitted to Congress, March 1976 (Washington, D.C.: U.S. Government Printing Office, 1976), p. 96.

B-12. U.S., European Communities, and Japanese Import Dependence on Selected Industrial Raw Materials, 1974 (net imports as percentage of consumption)

	United States	European Community	Japan
	(net imports as percentage of consumption)		
Aluminum[a]	88	31	93
Chromium	90	100	90
Cobalt	99	100	100
Copper	20	76	93
Iron[a]	17	59	100
Lead	19	70	67
Manganese	98	99	87
Natural Rubber	100	100	100
Nickel	72	100	100
Phosphates	b	100	100
Tin	84	87	90
Tungsten	64	100	100
Zinc	59	73	74

[a]Ore and metal.
[b]Net exporter.

SOURCE: *International Economic Report of the President,* transmitted to Congress, March 1976 (Washington, D.C.: U.S. Government Printing Office, 1976), p. 184.

B-13. Terms of Trade of Nine Minerals Exports from Developing Countries, 1950-1975 (1973=100)

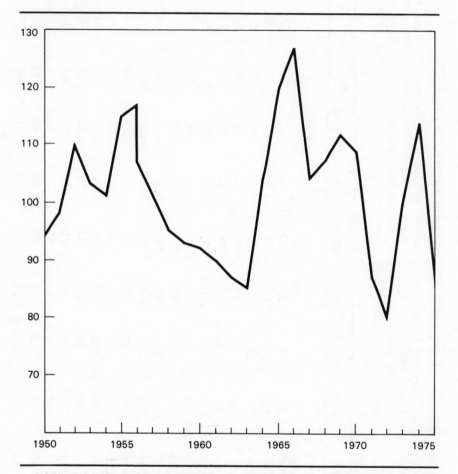

NOTE: The index has been weighted by the 1967-1969 value of the exports of the nine commodities included (bauxite, copper, iron ore, lead, manganese, phosphate rock, silver, tin, and zinc) and the World Bank index of prices of manufactured goods.

SOURCE: World Bank, Commodities and Export Projections Division.

B-14. Prices of Selected Primary Commodities, 1972-1976 (Annual and Quarterly)

World prices of many of the raw materials of which the developing countries are the major exporters fluctuate widely and severely affect the earnings of these countries from year to year. The average world price of sugar, for example, increased from 7 cents per pound in 1972 to 30 cents per pound in 1974 and, by the third quarter of 1976, had fallen again to 11 cents per pound. Such drastic fluctuations of price adversely affect both developing-country producers and developed-country consumers.

	1972	1973	1974	1975	1976[a]	1975 (iii)	1975 (iv)	1976 (i)	1976 (ii)	1976 (iii)
Bananas[b] (cents/kg.)	14	15	17	22	22	19	20	22	21	n.a.
Cocoa[c] (cents/lb.)	32	65	98	75	96	75	72	76	97	117
Coconut Oil[d] ($/met. ton)	234	513	998	394	387	376	338	339	357	463
Coffee[e] (cents/lb.)	51	63	68	71	130	84	86	95	137	159
Copper[f] (cents/lb.)	49	81	93	56	65	56	53	57	69	70
Copra[g] ($/met. ton)	141	353	662	256	247	237	207	203	222	317
Cotton[h] (cents/lb.)	36	59	63	54	74	58	60	67	72	83
Fishmeal[i] ($/met. ton)	239	542	372	245	351	230	287	303	335	416
Groundnut Oil[j] ($/met. ton)	426	546	1,077	857	690[k]	n.a.	n.a.	392	402	419
Groundnuts[j] ($/met. ton)	261	393	607	452	404	n.a.	n.a.	22	22	n.a.
Iron Ore[l] ($/met. ton)	11	17	20	23	22	23	23	22	22	n.a.
Jute[m] ($/met. ton)	299	289	353	371	297	318	304	308	301	284
Maize[n] ($/met. ton)	69	99	132	120	116	125	112	112	117	118
Natural Rubber[o] (cents/lb.)	18	33	36	28	37	29	28	34	39	38
Palm Oil[p] ($/met. ton)	217	378	669	434	391	429	386	365	363	446
Petroleum[q] ($/barrel)	1.9	2.7	9.8	10.7	11.5	10.5	11.5	11.5	11.5	11.5
Phosphate rock[r] ($/met. ton)	12	14	55	67	45	68	65	47	44	44
Rice[s] ($/met. ton)	116	350	542	363	252	344	331	260	245	250

Sisal[t] ($/met. ton)	240	527	1,056	580	457	358	427	430	457	485
Sugar[i] (cents/lb.)	7	10	30	20	13	17	14	14	14	11
Tea[u] (cents/kg.)	105	106	140	139	148	132	129	131	145	168
Timber[v] (logs) ($/m^3)	44	81	83	74	97	72	79	90	98	104
Tin[w] (cents/lb.)	175	220	375	318	345	310	294	307	348	381
Wheat[x] ($/met. ton)	71	142	193	160	144	163	156	154	145	133

[a] January-September.
[b] Ecuador.
[c] Ghana.
[d] Sri Lanka for 1972; 1973 and later, average of Philippines and Indonesia.
[e] Average of Colombia, Guatemala, Brazil, Angola.
[f] London Metal Exchange.
[g] Philippines.
[h] Average of United States and Mexico.
[i] World.
[j] Nigeria.
[k] January-June.
[l] Sweden for 1972; 1973 and later, Europe.
[m] Bangladesh.
[n] Average of Argentina and United States for 1972; 1973 and later, United States.
[o] Average of Singapore and New York markets.
[p] Malaysia.
[q] Saudi Arabia.
[r] Morocco.
[s] Average of Burma and Thailand for 1972; 1973 and later, Thailand.
[t] East Africa.
[u] London auctions.
[v] Average of Ivory Coast and Philippines.
[w] Average of London Metal Exchange and New York market for 1972; 1973 and later, average of Malaysia, United Kingdom, and United States markets.
[x] Average of United States and Canada.

SOURCES: Annual figures for 1972 are from World Bank/International Development Association, *Commodity Trade and Price Trends (1976 Edition)*, Report No. EC-166/76, August 1976; all other figures are from World Bank, Economic Analysis and Projections Department, "Commodity Price Data," February 18, 1976, and October 20, 1976.

B-15. Developing-Country Exports of Selected Primary Commodities, 1975 and 1972-1974 Average ($ millions and percentages)

	Developing-Country Exports, 1975	Developing-Country Exports, 1972-1974 Average		Major Developing-Country Suppliers, 1972-1974, with Percentage of World Exports Supplied by Each
	($ millions)	($ millions)	(as percentage of world exports of commodity)	
Bananas	730	599	93	Ecuador, 17% Costa Rica, 14% Honduras, 13% Panama, 9%
Cocoa	1,606	1,059	98	Ghana, 29% Nigeria, 18% Ivory Coast, 15% Brazil, 11%
Coconut Oil	329	277	78	Philippines, 58% Malaysia, 6%
Coffee	3,953	3,772	94	Brazil, 26% Colombia, 15%
Copper	5,411[a]	3,848	59	Chile, 17% Zambia, 16% Zaire, 10% Peru, 5%
Copra	263	214	99	Philippines, 65% Papua-New Guinea, 10%
Cotton	2,165	2,146	52	Egypt, 13% Sudan, 5% Brazil, 4% Mexico, 4%
Fishmeal	305[a]	283	45	Peru, 30% Angola, 4% Chile, 4%
Groundnut oil	243	176	72	Senegal, 27% Argentina, 14% Brazil, 10% Nigeria, 10%
Groundnuts	270	200	59	Sudan, 12% Nigeria, 11% India, 7% Brazil, 6%

Commodity				Major exporters
Iron Ore	1,666[a]	1,309	37	Brazil, 11%; Venezuela, 6%; Liberia, 6%; India, 5%
Jute	157	229	48	Bangladesh, 32%; Thailand, 10%
Maize	1,048	668	15	Argentina, 9%; Thailand, 4%
Natural Rubber	1,536	1,667	98	Malaysia, 52%; Indonesia, 21%
Palm Oil	911	412	80	Malaysia, 50%; Indonesia, 18%; Ivory Coast, 6%; Zaire, 4%
Petroleum	129,858[a]	66,327	77	Saudi Arabia, 17%; Iran, 12%; Venezuela, 7%; Kuwait, 6%
Phosphate Rock	1,063[a]	552	61	Morocco, 33%; Gilbert/Ellice Is., 8%
Rice	989	697	45	Thailand, 13%; Pakistan, 5%; Egypt, 3%
Sisal	154	182	98	Brazil, 35%; Tanzania, 21%; Angola, 15%; Kenya, 12%
Sugar	8,810	4,132	73	Cuba, 21%; Brazil, 13%; Philippines, 7%
Tea	823	629	81	India, 26%; Sri Lanka, 25%
Timber	2,734[a]	2,241	26	Malaysia, 6%; Indonesia, 6%
Tin	1,265[a]	891	84	Malaysia, 42%; Bolivia, 15%; Indonesia, 11%; Thailand, 10%
Wheat/Meslin	299	273	4	Argentina, 3%

[a] 1974 figure.

NOTE: The data do not include the exports of centrally planned developing economies or of Taiwan; except for petroleum products, the exports of Hong Kong and Singapore—because of their substantial re-exports—are also excluded.

SOURCES: World Bank/International Development Association, *Commodity Trade and Price Trends (1976 Edition)*, Report No. EC-166/76, August 1976; export figures for 1975 are informal preliminary estimates from World Bank, Economic Analysis and Projections Department.

World Trade

Annex C: Facts of Interest

Trade is a more crucial factor in the development prospects of the poor nations than either aid or investment. The tables in Annex C reflect the importance of trade to developing countries as well as the differences among these countries, and between them and developed countries, in the amount of foreign exchange available to them as a result of different resource endowments and export capabilities.

1. In 1975, the total exports of the developed market economies amounted to $580.5 billion and represented 66 per cent of the value of world exports. In contrast, the exports of the developing market economies in that year amounted to $211.2 billion, or only 24 per cent of world exports; and the OPEC countries alone accounted for over half ($113.9 billion) of the value of total developing-country exports. In fact, the share of OPEC exports in total world value of exports has nearly doubled from 6.7 per cent in 1960 to 13.0 per cent in 1975—a share greater than that of the centrally planned economies, which had only 9.9 per cent of world exports in 1975 (Tables C-4 and C-5).

2. The composition of trade differs among various groups of countries. Although the developed market economies account for 38 per cent of world exports of primary products (including fuels), these products represent only 24 per cent of the total value of their own exports; manufactured products comprise nearly 75 per cent of the exports of developed market economies and they comprise 57 per cent of those of the centrally planned economies. In contrast, nearly 83 per cent of the exports of developing market economies are primary products. For all three groups, manufactured products represent the greatest portion of imports (Tables C-1 through C-3).

3. Fuel products as a share of total value of the developing market economies' exports more than doubled between 1960 and 1974, going from 28 per cent in 1960 to 60 per cent in 1974 (Table C-3).

4. In 1976, the United States had an $11 billion deficit with the OPEC countries; it had a $1 billion surplus with the low-income countries; and a $762 million deficit with the middle-income countries. Worldwide the United States had a trade deficit of nearly $6 billion in 1976 (Table C-8).

C-1. Composition of World Exports and Imports, by Groups of Countries and Types of Products, 1974 (percentages)

	Developed Market Economies	Developing Market Economies	Centrally Planned Economies	World
EXPORTS				
Primary Products	**24.1**	**82.9**	**35.6**	**40.7**
Food, beverages, and tobacco	10.9	12.5	11.4	11.3
Crude materials excluding fuels; oils and fats	8.3	10.2	10.3	9.0
Mineral fuels and related materials	4.9	60.2	13.9	20.4
Manufactured Products	**74.6**	**16.8**	**57.4**	**57.7**
Chemicals	10.4	1.5	5.4	7.6
Machinery and transport equipment	33.1	3.0	27.8	24.6
Other manufactured goods	31.1	12.3	24.2	25.5
Miscellaneous	**1.3**	**0.3**	**7.0**	**1.6**
Total	100.0	100.0	100.0	100.0
IMPORTS				
Primary Products	**43.4**	**35.3**	**28.6**	**40.7**
Food, beverages, and tobacco	10.8	12.5	13.1	11.3
Crude materials excluding fuels; oils and fats	9.7	6.0	9.8	9.0
Mineral fuels and related materials	22.9	16.8	5.7	20.4
Manufactured Products	**55.5**	**61.9**	**68.3**	**57.7**
Chemicals	7.2	9.1	7.7	7.6
Machinery and transport equipment	22.2	29.5	33.1	24.6
Other manufactured goods	26.1	23.3	27.5	25.5
Miscellaneous	**1.1**	**2.8**	**3.1**	**1.6**
Total	100.0	100.0	100.0	100.0

SOURCE: United Nations, *Monthly Bulletin of Statistics,* Vol. 30, No. 8, August 1976, Special Table C.

C-2. Composition of Exports, 1960 and 1974
($ millions and percentages)

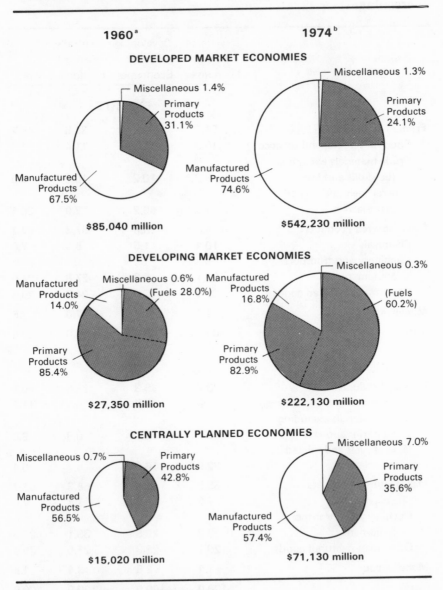

1960[a]

1974[b]

DEVELOPED MARKET ECONOMIES

Miscellaneous 1.4%
Primary Products 31.1%
Manufactured Products 67.5%

$85,040 million

Miscellaneous 1.3%
Primary Products 24.1%
Manufactured Products 74.6%

$542,230 million

DEVELOPING MARKET ECONOMIES

Manufactured Products 14.0%
Miscellaneous 0.6%
(Fuels 28.0%)
Primary Products 85.4%

$27,350 million

Miscellaneous 0.3%
Manufactured Products 16.8%
(Fuels 60.2%)
Primary Products 82.9%

$222,130 million

CENTRALLY PLANNED ECONOMIES

Miscellaneous 0.7%
Primary Products 42.8%
Manufactured Products 56.5%

$15,020 million

Miscellaneous 7.0%
Primary Products 35.6%
Manufactured Products 57.4%

$71,130 million

[a]World trade in 1960 totalled $127,410 million.
[b]World trade in 1974 totalled $835,490 million.

SOURCES: For this and for figure on the following page, 1960 data are based on *U.N. Monthly Bulletin of Statistics*, Vol. 19, No. 3, March 1965, Special Table E; 1974 data are based on *U.N. Monthly Bulletin of Statistics*, Vol. 30, No. 8, August 1976, Special Table C.

C-3. Composition of Imports, 1960 and 1974
($ millions and percentages)

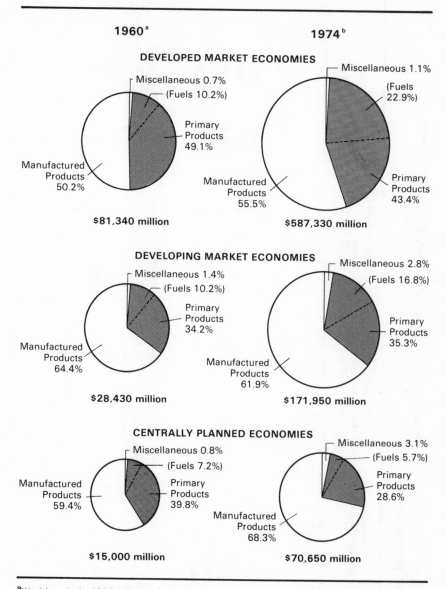

1960[a] **1974**[b]

DEVELOPED MARKET ECONOMIES

1960:
Miscellaneous 0.7%
(Fuels 10.2%)
Primary Products 49.1%
Manufactured Products 50.2%
$81,340 million

1974:
Miscellaneous 1.1%
(Fuels 22.9%)
Primary Products 43.4%
Manufactured Products 55.5%
$587,330 million

DEVELOPING MARKET ECONOMIES

1960:
Miscellaneous 1.4%
(Fuels 10.2%)
Primary Products 34.2%
Manufactured Products 64.4%
$28,430 million

1974:
Miscellaneous 2.8%
(Fuels 16.8%)
Primary Products 35.3%
Manufactured Products 61.9%
$171,950 million

CENTRALLY PLANNED ECONOMIES

1960:
Miscellaneous 0.8%
(Fuels 7.2%)
Primary Products 39.8%
Manufactured Products 59.4%
$15,000 million

1974:
Miscellaneous 3.1%
(Fuels 5.7%)
Primary Products 28.6%
Manufactured Products 68.3%
$70,650 million

[a]World trade in 1960 totalled $127,410 million; this figure includes certain imports which, because their regions of destination could not be determined, are not otherwise included.
[b]World trade in 1974 totalled $835,490 million; this figure includes certain imports which, because their regions of destination could not be determined, are not otherwise included.

SOURCE: See previous page.

C-4. Destination of Exports, by Groups of Countries, 1960, 1970, and 1973-1975 ($ billions and percentages)

From: / To:	Developed Market Economies		Developing Market Economies (including OPEC)		Centrally Planned Economies		World[a]		Exports as Percentage of Total World Exports
	($ billions)	(percentages)	($ billions)	(percentages)	($ billions)	(percentages)	($ billions)	(percentages)	
Developed Market Economies									
1960	58.8	69.2	21.2	24.9	3.0	3.5	85.0	100.0	66.7
1970	172.5	77.0	41.9	18.7	8.4	3.8	224.1	100.0	71.8
1973	312.0	76.7	73.7	18.1	18.4	4.5	406.9	100.0	70.7
1974	398.5	73.5	113.7	21.0	26.6	4.9	542.2	100.0	64.9
1975	404.1	69.6	138.3	23.8	35.1	6.1	580.5	100.0	66.1
OPEC									
1960	n.a.	n.a.	n.a.	n.a.	n.a.	n.a.	8.5	n.a.	6.7
1970	14.3	80.3	3.2	18.0	0.3	1.7	17.8	100.0	5.7
1973	33.5	77.2	8.4	19.4	0.7	1.6	43.4	100.0	7.5
1974	95.6	78.2	24.5	20.0	1.3	1.1	122.3	100.0	14.6
1975	88.0	77.3	23.8	20.9	1.6	1.4	113.9	100.0	13.0
Non-OPEC Developing Market Economies									
1960	19.8[b]	72.3[b]	6.0[b]	21.9[b]	1.2[b]	4.4[b]	18.9	100.0	14.8
1970	26.4	70.6	7.8	20.9	2.9	7.8	37.4	100.0	12.0

1973	48.4	71.1	14.5	21.3	4.4	6.5	68.1	100.0	11.8
1974	70.7	70.8	22.1	22.1	6.4	6.4	99.9	100.0	12.0
1975	66.0	67.8	23.7	24.4	6.7	6.9	97.3	100.0	11.1
Centrally Planned Economies									
1960	2.8	18.7	1.2	8.0	10.8	72.0	15.0	100.0	11.8
1970	7.8	23.7	5.2	15.8	19.9	60.5	32.9	100.0	10.5
1973	15.4	26.9	8.8	15.4	32.4	56.6	57.2	100.0	9.9
1974	22.6	31.8	11.6	16.3	36.4	51.2	71.1	100.0	8.5
1975	24.4	28.1	13.2	15.2	48.4	55.8	86.8	100.0	9.9
World									
1960	81.4	63.9	28.4	22.3	15.0	11.8	127.4	100.0	100.0
1970	221.0	68.8	58.1	18.1	31.5	10.1	312.3	100.0	100.0
1973	409.3	71.1	105.4	18.3	55.9	9.7	575.6	100.0	100.0
1974	587.3	70.3	171.9	20.6	70.7	8.5	835.5	100.0	100.0
1975	582.5	66.3	199.0	22.7	91.8	10.5	878.5	100.0	100.0

[a] Includes certain exports which, because their regions of destination could not be determined, are not included elsewhere in the table.
[b] Includes OPEC exports.

NOTE: The table does not include the exports of Southern Rhodesia. Figures for 1960 and 1970 do not include trade between the Federal Republic of Germany and the German Democratic Republic. All figures represent f.o.b. (free on board) values.

SOURCES: Figures for 1960 are based on *U.N. Monthly Bulletin of Statistics*, Vol. 19, No. 3, March 1965, Special Table E; those for 1970, 1973, and 1974 are based on *U.N. Monthly Bulletin of Statistics*, Vol. 30, No. 8, August 1976, Special Table C; and 1975 figures are based on *U.N. Monthly Bulletin of Statistics*, Vol. 30, No. 6, June 1976, Special Table C.

C-5. Shares of World Exports, by Groups of Countries, 1960, 1970, and 1975
($ billions and percentages)

While the dollar amount of the non-OPEC developing countries' exports has increased from $18.9 billion in 1960 to $97.3 billion in 1975, their share of total world exports has declined from 14.8 per cent in 1960 to 12.0 per cent in 1970 to 11.1 per cent in 1975.

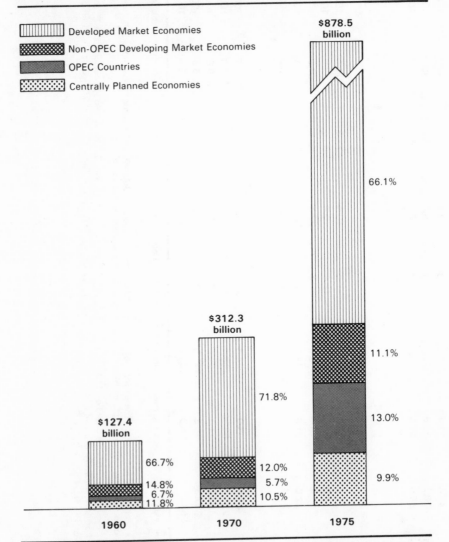

SOURCES: Figures for 1960 are from *U.N. Monthly Bulletin of Statistics*, Vol. 19, No. 3, March 1965, Special Table E; those for 1970 are from *U.N. Monthly Bulletin of Statistics*, Vol. 30, No. 8, August 1976, Special Table C; and those for 1975 are from *U.N. Monthly Bulletin of Statistics*, Vol. 30, No. 6, June 1976, Special Table C.

C-6. Terms of Trade Index, by Groups of Countries, 1960 and 1970-1975 (1970=100)

While the purchasing power of the exports of the developed countries increased 19 per cent between 1970 and 1975, that of the developing countries as a group increased 75 per cent. However, excluding the major petroleum exporters and the fast-growing exporters of manufactures reveals that the purchasing power of all other developing countries' exports in fact declined 5 per cent between 1970 and 1975; that of the poorest countries declined 24 per cent.

	1960	1970	1971	1972	1973	1974	1975
Developed Market Economies	**42**	**100**	**106**	**117**	**130**	**122**	**119**
Developing Countries							
Major petroleum exporters[a]	62	100	102	**108**	**132**	**199**	**175**
Fast-growing exporters of manufactures[b]	59	100	118	123	158	402	334
All others	47	100	107	125	159	156	142
of which, countries with 1974 per capita GNP:	67	100	90	95	110	106	95
over $400	61	100	89	96	115	114	107
$200-$400	66	100	94	102	118	122	110
under $200	79	100	88	89	92	79	76

[a] "Major petroleum exporters" are those countries for which petroleum and petroleum products accounted for more than 50% of their total exports in 1974. These countries are the OPEC countries of Algeria, Ecuador, Gabon, Indonesia, Iran, Iraq, Kuwait, Libya, Nigeria, Qatar, Saudi Arabia, United Arab Emirates, and Venezuela, plus Angola, Bahrain, Brunei, Oman, and Trinidad and Tobago.

[b] "Fast-growing exporters of manufactures" are countries whose exports of manufactures amounted to more than $50 million and accounted for more than one third of their total exports in 1972 and whose manufactured exports grew at an average annual rate higher than the world average of 16% during the period 1967-1972. These countries are Hong Kong, Israel, Republic of Korea, Lebanon, Malta, Mexico, and Singapore.

NOTE: "Terms of trade" is defined as the purchasing power of exports and is calculated by deflating the value index of exports by the unit value of imports.

SOURCE: UNCTAD, *Handbook of International Trade and Development Statistics, 1976,* U.N. Publications Sales No. E/F.76.II.D.3, p. 59.

C-7. U.S. Trade, by Trading Partners and by Composition, 1975 ($ billions and percentages)

In 1975, 37 per cent of U.S. exports went to the developing countries—more than to the European Communities countries, Japan, the Soviet Union, Eastern Europe, and all other centrally planned economies combined.

The kinds of products the United States exports are different from those it imports. For example, while fuels and nonagricultural raw materials comprise only 9 per cent of total U.S. exports, they comprise 35 per cent of U.S. imports.

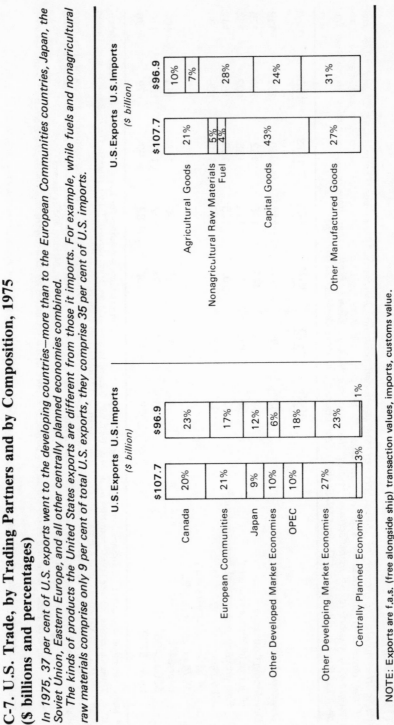

NOTE: Exports are f.a.s. (free alongside ship) transaction values; imports, customs value.

SOURCE: Adapted from *International Economic Report of the President*, transmitted to Congress, March 1976 (Washington, D.C.: U.S. Government Printing Office, 1976), pp. 26 and 27. Based on U.S. Department of Commerce data.

C-8. U.S. Trade, 1973-1976
($ millions)

	1973	1974	1975	1976[a]
U.S. Trade with All Countries				
Exports	71,339	98,506	107,652	104,264
Imports	69,475	100,972	96,940	110,255
Trade Balance	+1,864	-2,466	+10,712	-5,991
U.S. Trade with Developing Countries				
Exports	22,404	34,973	40,940	38,005
Imports	21,050	40,708	40,723	48,882
Trade Balance	+1,354	-5,735	+217	-10,877
With Low-Income Countries[b]				
Exports	1,941	3, 512	4,001	3,061
Imports	1,197	1,535	1,408	1,898
Trade Balance	+744	+1,977	+2,593	+1,163
With Middle-Income Countries[c]				
Exports	16,843	24,738	26,172	23,742
Imports	15,263	23,530	22,234	24,504
Trade Balance	+1,580	+1,208	+3,938	-762
With OPEC Countries				
Exports	3,620	6,723	10,767	11,202
Imports	4,590	15,643	17,082	22,480
Trade Balance	-970	-8,920	-6,315	-11,278
U.S. Trade Balance with Developing Countries, by Region				
Africa	-277	-2,958	-3,350	-6,632
(Africa excl. OPEC)	(+374)	(+809)	(+1,073)	(+497)
East and South Asia	+180	-376	-27	-4,096
(East and South Asia excl. OPEC)	(+243)	(+782)	(+1,385)	(-2,285)
Near East	+984	-147	+2,134	-556
(Near East excl. OPEC)	(+474)	(+791)	(+1,184)	(+847)
Latin America	+322	-2,608	+1,039	-37
(Latin America excl. OPEC)	(+1,088)	(+450)	(+2,469)	(+898)
Oceania	-27	-26	-5	-34
Europe	+172	+379	+425	+477

[a]Preliminary

[b]Those countries identified as "low-income" in Table A-3 of this volume (with the exception of Indonesia and Nigeria).

[c]Those countries identified as "lower middle-income" and "upper middle-income" in Table A-3 (with the exception of Algeria, Ecuador, Gabon, Iran, Iraq, and Venezuela) plus the Bahamas, Bahrain, and Singapore, which are identified as "high-income" in Table A-3.

NOTE: Exports are f.a.s. (free alongside ship); imports, customs value.

SOURCES: Based on U.S. Department of Commerce, *Highlights of U.S. Export and Import Trade,* December 1974, and *Highlights of U.S. Export and Import Trade,* December 1975; 1976 figures are preliminary ones from U.S. Department of Commerce, Trade Reference Center.

World Military Expenditures

Total world military and arms expenditures have risen in only a decade from $198 billion in 1963 to $286 billion in 1974 (in constant 1973 dollars).

1. Even at a time when they have been severely affected by increases in the cost of essential imports and/or foreign exchange shortages, many developing nations are allocating 1-5 per cent of their GNP for military expenditures. In fact, developing-country military expenditures in 1974 amounted to $50.2 billion (in constant 1973 dollars) and accounted for 18 per cent of global military expenditures (Tables D-1 and D-2).

2. In 1973, 25 countries had military expenditures of $1 billion or more; many of these had per capita military expenditures that exceeded those for education and for health. Total U.S. military expenditures in 1973 were $78 billion (ranking it second largest military spender after the U.S.S.R.). U.S. per capita military expenditures of $374 exceeded per capita public expenditures on education ($348) and on health ($171) (Table D-3).

3. Between 1968 and 1974, the proportion of global arms transfers delivered to the countries of the Middle East and North Africa increased from 12 per cent to 35 per cent. Of the $8.4 billion of weapons transferred worldwide in 1974, the United States provided 45 per cent (Table D-4).

D-1. Shares of World Military Expenditures, 1963-1974 ($ billions)

Total world military expenditures increased in only a decade from $197.7 billion to $285.5 billion. While the United States and the Soviet Union together still account for the majority of world military expenditures, their share declined from 68 per cent in 1963 to 60 per cent in 1974; during that same period, the developing countries' share of world military expenditures doubled from 9 per cent to 18 per cent.

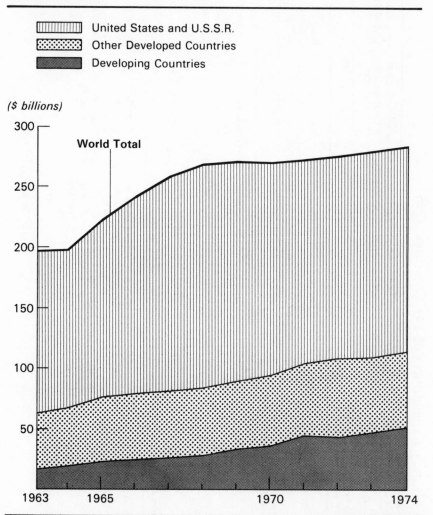

United States and U.S.S.R.
Other Developed Countries
Developing Countries

($ billions)

World Total

1963 1965 1970 1974

NOTES: Figures for 1963 and 1964 are in constant 1972 dollars; all others are in constant 1973 dollars. World military expenditures in 1974, which in constant dollars amounted to $285.5 billion, amounted to $315.4 in current dollars.

SOURCE: Based on U.S. Arms Control and Disarmament Agency, *World Military Expenditures and Arms Transfers, 1965-1974* (Washington, D.C.: U.S. Government Printing Office, 1976), Publication No. 84, Tables I and II, pp. 14-53.

D-2. Relative Military Expenditures of 141 Countries, 1975

Military Expenditures more than 10 per cent of GNP

Per Capita GNP under $100	Per Capita GNP $100–$199	Per Capita GNP $200–$299	Per Capita GNP $300–$499	Per Capita GNP $500–$999	Per Capita GNP $1,000–$1,999	Per Capita GNP $2,000–$2,999	Per Capita GNP $3,000 and up
Khmer Rep.	Vietnam, S.	China (PRC)	Jordan	Syria	Iran	Israel	U.S.S.R.
Vietnam, N.		Egypt	Korea, N.		Iraq	Oman	

Military Expenditures 5–10 per cent of GNP

Per Capita GNP under $100	Per Capita GNP $100–$199	Per Capita GNP $200–$299	Per Capita GNP $300–$499	Per Capita GNP $500–$999	Per Capita GNP $1,000–$1,999	Per Capita GNP $2,000–$2,999	Per Capita GNP $3,000 and up
Chad	Pakistan	Yemen,	Albania	Cuba	Bulgaria	Greece	Czechoslovakia
Laos	Yemen,	People's Rep.	Korea, S.	Malaysia	Portugal	Hungary	Germany (GDR)
Somalia	Arab Rep.			Mongolia	Romania	Poland	Qatar
				Taiwan (ROC)		Singapore	Saudi Arabia
							United States

Military Expenditures 2–4.9 per cent of GNP

Per Capita GNP under $100	Per Capita GNP $100–$199	Per Capita GNP $200–$299	Per Capita GNP $300–$499	Per Capita GNP $500–$999	Per Capita GNP $1,000–$1,999	Per Capita GNP $2,000–$2,999	Per Capita GNP $3,000 and up
Burundi	Burma	Equatorial	Bolivia	Algeria	Argentina	Bahrain	Australia
Ethiopia	Central	Guinea	Congo	Angola	Cyprus	Italy	Belgium
Mali	African Rep.	Mauritania	Morocco	Brazil	Lebanon	Spain	Canada
Rwanda	Guinea	Sudan	Nigeria	Chile	South Africa	Venezuela	Denmark
Upper Volta	India	Uganda	Philippines	Guyana	Yugoslavia		France
	Indonesia		Rhodesia	Nicaragua			Germany (FRG)
	Tanzania		Thailand	Peru			Kuwait
	Zaire			Turkey			Netherlands
				Uruguay			Norway
				Zambia			Sweden
							United Kingdom

Military Expenditures 1–1.9 per cent of GNP

Afghanistan	Benin	Cameroon	Colombia	Dominican	Gabon	Austria
	Haiti	Honduras	El Salvador	Rep.	Ireland	Finland
		Kenya	Ghana	Ecuador		Libya
		Malagasy Rep.	Senegal	Guatemala		Luxembourg
		Togo		Ivory Coast		New Zealand
				Paraguay		Switzerland
				Tunisia		

Military Expenditures less than 1 per cent of GNP

Bangladesh	Sri Lanka	Botswana	Costa Rica	Trinidad &	Barbados	Iceland
Gambia		Liberia	Fiji	Tobago	Jamaica	Japan
Lesotho		Mozambique	Mauritius		Malta	United Arab
Malawi		Swaziland	Mexico		Surinam	Emirates
Nepal			Panama			
Niger						
Sierra Leone						

NOTE: In 1975, total world military expenditures amounted to $339.8 billion in constant 1974 dollars and $371.3 in current dollars. The total value of arms transferred worldwide in 1975 is estimated to be about $9 billion in constant 1974 dollars.

SOURCE: Adapted from U.S. Arms Control and Disarmament Agency, *World Military Expenditures and Arms Transfers, 1966-1975* (Washington, D.C.: U.S. Government Printing Office, 1976), Publication No. 90, p. 6.

D-3. Performance of Major Military Powers in Education and Health, 1973

Countries by Rank in Total Military Expenditures[a]	Total Military Expenditures ($ millions)	Per Capita Military Expenditures ($)	(rank[b])	Per Capita Public Education Expenditures ($)	(rank[b])	Rank in Literacy[c]	Per Capita Public Health Expenditures ($)	(rank[b])	Rank in Life Expectancy[c]
U.S.S.R.	92,000	368	3	172	19	1	82	18	27
United States	78,000	374	2	348	4	1	171	10	20
China (PRC)	17,000	19	23	9	87	88	2	87	53
Germany (FRG)	11,900	193	5	254	10	1	259	3	20
France	9,500	181	8	286	7	1	209	5	5
United Kingdom	8,610	154	9	181	17	13	131	13	10
Italy	4,100	75	18	119	23	27	29	32	10
Poland	3,860	116	14	83	27	13	62	21	27
Israel	3,650	1,110	1	110	25	42	16	43	20
Japan	3,600	33	22	166	21	1	130	14	5
Germany (GDR)	3,110	183	7	126	22	13	181	19	5
Czechoslovakia	2,740	188	6	111	24	13	99	17	36
Iran	2,450	73	19	29	49	80	9	55	81
Canada	2,410	109	16	452	2	26	319	2	10
India	2,160	4	25	2	118	83	1	105	81
Netherlands	2,010	150	11	331	5	1	206	6	1

Spain	1,870	54	20	—	35	44	26	—	17	40	10
Romania	1,830	88	17	—	48	37	31	—	34	29	45
Sweden	1,730	212	4	—	489	1	1	—	398	1	1
Egypt	1,710	49	21	—	11	74	88	—	6	63	78
Australia	1,580	121	13	—	227	13	13	—	79	20	10
Brazil	1,550	15	24	—	20	63	62	—	2	87	55
Bulgaria	1,310	152	10	—	66	29	31	—	31	31	10
Belgium	1,260	129	12	—	323	6	13	—	191	7	5
Hungary	1,180	114	15	—	70	8	13	—	56	24	27

[a]All countries with military expenditures of more than $1 billion.

[b]Rank according to per capita expenditures among 132 countries.

[c]Rank among 132 countries.

NOTES: The rank order number is repeated if more than one country has the same figure.

In 1973, world military expenditures of $280 billion were slightly more than the total amount of $251 billion spent by governments on education and nearly twice the $142 billion spent by governments on medical care and other health services. In the developing countries as a whole, more public revenue was devoted to military programs ($46.6 billion) than to education and health care combined ($35.9 billion).

SOURCES: Adapted from Ruth Leger Sivard, *World Military and Social Expenditures, 1976,* WMSE Publications, Box 1003, Leesburg, Virginia 22075, pp. 15 and 24-29; military expenditures figures and ranking are based on U.S. Arms Control and Disarmament Agency, *World Military Expenditures and Arms Transfers, 1965-1974* (Washington, D.C.: U.S. Government Printing Office, 1976), Publication No. 84, Table II, pp. 19-53.

D-4. World Arms Transfers, by Recipient Regions and Supplying Countries, 1968 and 1974 ($ millions and percentages)

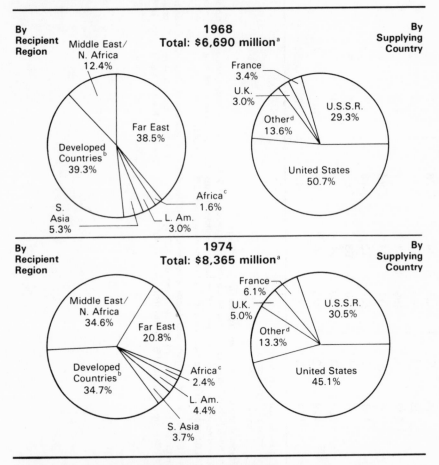

aAll data in constant 1973 dollars and inflation corrected.

bIncludes the 22 NATO and Warsaw Pact countries plus Albania, Australia, Austria, Finland, Ireland, Japan, New Zealand, Spain, Sweden, Switzerland, and Yugoslavia.

cBlack Africa (including the Republic of South Africa, which accounted for 0.2% in 1968 and 0.5% in 1974).

dThe major "other" suppliers in 1968 were Poland, the People's Republic of China, Canada, and the Federal Republic of Germany; in 1974, they were the People's Republic of China, the Federal Republic of Germany, Italy, and Canada.

NOTE: "Arms transfers" indicates actual *deliveries* (through either sales or aid), as distinguished from sales orders, contracts, or agreements, or the value of aid programs that may result in a future transfer of goods. The data include deliveries of military equipment only and exclude the value of training, technical and other services, and consumables.

SOURCE: Based on U.S. Arms Control and Disarmament Agency, *World Military Expenditures and Arms Transfers, 1965-1974* (Washington, D.C.: U.S. Government Printing Office, 1976), Publication No. 84, Tables III and IV, pp. 54-72.

Resource Flows

The severe impact of the recent international economic crises on the non-oil-exporting developing countries has been apparent in their deteriorating balance-of-payments situation and their rapidly rising external indebtedness.

1. The current account deficit of the developing-country primary producers (that is, the excess of their imports of goods and services and private transfer payments over their exports and private transfer receipts) amounted to some $32 billion in 1976. Although this represented a small decline from their 1975 current account deficit of $37 billion, it was still more than three times their $10 billion deficit in 1973 (Table E-1).

2. At the end of 1974, the outstanding public debt of the non-OPEC developing countries (including both disbursed and undisbursed debt) totalled $113.9 billion ($77.8 billion of which was already disbursed or drawn on). Total public debt at the end of 1975 for this group is estimated to have been some $138.6 billion; rapidly rising debt service payments (principal and interest), totalling $9.1 billion in 1974 and $11.3 billion in 1975, have placed an increasing claim on the already declining export earnings of these countries (Tables E-2 and E-3).

3. The low-income non-OPEC developing countries accounted for none of the $25.3 billion in bonds floated worldwide in the first three quarters of 1976 and received less than 1 per cent of worldwide publicized Eurocurrency credits in the same period (Tables E-5 and E-6).

4. In 1975, the total net disbursement of official development assistance (ODA) from all DAC members was $13.6 billion or 0.36 per cent of their combined GNP and represented 80 per cent of worldwide official development assistance to the developing countries and multilateral institutions (Tables E-8, E-9, E-14, and E-22).

5. Commitments of official development assistance from OPEC members totalled $4.7 billion in 1975. Of the $4.1 billion committed bilaterally, over 60 per cent was pledged to Arab League countries. Net disbursements of official development assistance from OPEC members in 1975 were, however, only $2.7 billion; this constituted some 1.35 per cent of their combined GNP and accounted for 16 per cent of worldwide ODA (Tables E-8, E-20, E-21, and E-22).

6. Of the $1.9 billion in aid commitments from the Soviet Union, the Eastern European countries, and the People's Republic of China to developing countries in 1975, two nations alone—Turkey and Afghanistan—received 59 per cent of the pledges. Net disbursements of ODA from the centrally planned economies totalled $750 million, or approximately 0.06 per cent of their GNP, and accounted for only 4 per cent of worldwide ODA to developing countries (Tables E-8, E-19, and E-22).

7. Between 1973 and 1975, more than half of the official development assistance of all three donor groups—DAC, OPEC, and the centrally planned economies—was to middle-income rather than low-income developing countries. The low-income countries received 37 per cent, 23 per cent, and 41 per cent, from the DAC countries, the OPEC countries, and the centrally planned economies, respectively (Table E-23).

E-1. Current Account Balances, by Groups of Countries, 1973-1976
($ billions)

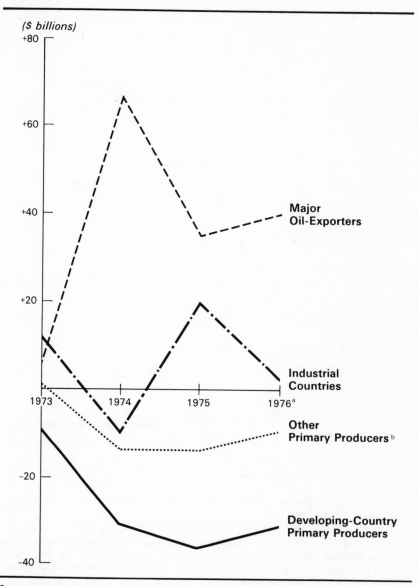

aPreliminary.

bAustralia, Finland, Greece, Iceland, Ireland, Malta, New Zealand, Portugal, Romania, South Africa, Spain, Turkey, and Yugoslavia.

NOTE: Centrally planned economies are not included in this table.

SOURCE: Based on International Monetary Fund, *Annual Report, 1976*, p. 15.

E-2. Debt, Debt Service, and Export Earnings of Non-OPEC Developing Countries, 1967-1975 ($ billions)

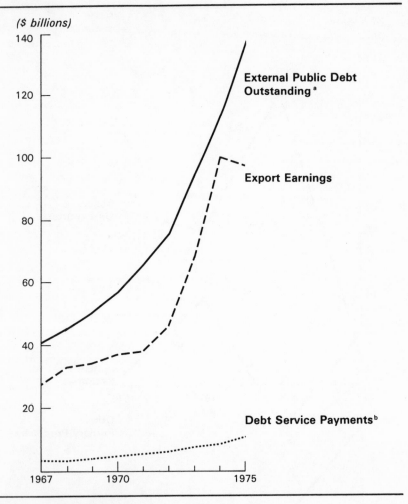

(\$ billions)

External Public Debt Outstanding [a]

Export Earnings

Debt Service Payments [b]

[a]Disbursed and undisbursed debt.
[b]Payments of principal (amortization) plus interest payments.

NOTE: Debt and debt service figures include only those 75 non-OPEC developing countries (plus the East African Community) that report to the World Bank. The 1975 figures for debt and debt service are ODC estimates based on World Bank and IMF data. Export earnings data are for all developing countries.

SOURCES: Debt and debt service figures are based on World Bank, *World Debt Tables: External Public Debt of LDCs*, Doc. No. EC-167/76, Vol. 1, October 31, 1976, pp. 35-36, 47-48, and 106-11; export figures are based on various issues of *U.N. Monthly Bulletin of Statistics* and on United Nations Conference on Trade and Development, *Handbook of International Trade and Development Statistics, 1976*, U.N. Publication Sales No. E/F.76.II.D.3, Table 1.1.

E-3. External Public Debt Outstanding (Disbursed and Undisbursed) of Developing Countries, by Income Groups, 1974 ($ millions and percentages)

	($ millions)	(percentages)
Low-Income Countries[a]	**38,770.2**	**100.0**
Official Sources	34,100.0	88.0
Bilateral	25,221.4	65.1
Multilateral	8,878.6	22.9
Private Sources	4,670.2	12.0
Suppliers' credits	1,894.0	4.9
Banks	2,322.7	6.0
Other private	453.5	1.1
Middle-Income Countries[b]	**75,145.0**	**100.0**
Official Sources	42,099.8	56.0
Bilateral	25,072.3	33.4
Multilateral	17,027.5	22.6
Private Sources	33,045.2	44.0
Suppliers' credits	8,919.3	11.9
Banks	18,806.5	25.0
Other private	5,319.4	7.1
Total, Non-OPEC Countries	**113,915.2**	**100.0**
Official Sources	76,199.8	66.9
Private Sources	37,715.4	33.1
OPEC Countries[c]	**26,081.6**	**100.0**
Official Sources	16,306.9	62.5
Bilateral	12,855.3	49.3
Multilateral	3,451.6	13.2
Private	9,774.7	37.5
Suppliers' credits	4,839.8	18.6
Banks	4,030.1	15.4
Other private	904.8	3.5
Total, OPEC and Non-OPEC	**139,996.8**	**100.0**
Official Sources	**92,506.7**	**66.1**
Private Sources	**47,490.1**	**33.9**

[a]Those 32 non-OPEC low-income countries (as determined by classfication in Table A-3 of this volume) that report to the World Bank plus the East African Community.
[b]Those 43 non-OPEC middle-income countries (as determined by classification in Table A-3 of this volume) that report to the World Bank.
[c]Those 8 OPEC countries that report to the World Bank.

NOTES: Debt figures—from both official and private sources—in this table include only that debt owed or guaranteed by the public sector (governments or public bodies) of the recipient developing countries. It does not include unguaranteed loans to private entities or persons—amounts which are not included in World Bank published data but constitute a substantial amount of additional developing-country debt. Figures include only those 83 developing countries (plus the East African Community) that report to the World Bank.

SOURCE: Based on World Bank, *World Debt Tables: External Public Debt of LDCs,* Doc. No. EC-167/76, Vol. 1, October 31, 1976, pp. 114-15.

E-4. Distribution of International Reserves, by Groups of Countries, 1950, 1960, 1970, and 1976 ($ billions and percentages)

A country's international reserves serve rather like a bank account does for individuals. Between 1950 and September 1976, the share of world reserves of the major oil-exporting countries rose from 3 per cent to 26 per cent; during that time, the share of the developing-country primary producers decreased from 17 per cent to 15 per cent of total international reserves.

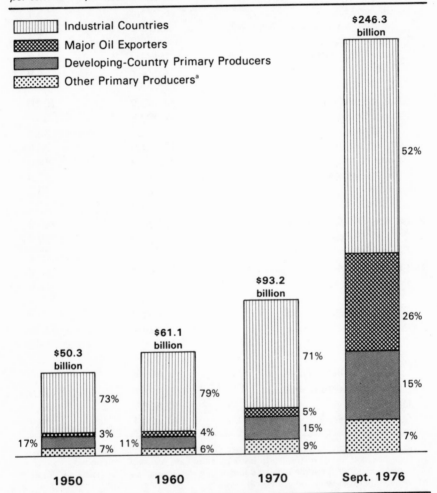

Industrial Countries
Major Oil Exporters
Developing-Country Primary Producers
Other Primary Producers[a]

$246.3 billion

$93.2 billion

$61.1 billion

$50.3 billion

| 1950 | 1960 | 1970 | Sept. 1976 |

[a]Australia, Finland, Greece, Iceland, Ireland, Malta, New Zealand, Portugal, Romania, South Africa, Spain, Turkey, and Yugoslavia.

NOTE: Centally planned economies are not included in this table.

SOURCE: Figures for 1950, 1960, and 1970 are based on International Monetary Fund, *Annual Report, 1976*, p. 35; those for September 1976 are based on International Monetary Fund, *International Financial Statistics*, December 1976, p. 18.

226

E-5. Foreign and International Bonds Floated by Developed and Developing Countries and International Organizations, 1976[a]
($ millions and percentages)

	($ millions)	(percentage of total)
Developed Countries (24)[b]	17,521.2	69.3
Developing Countries		
Oil-Exporting Countries (2)[c]	139.3	0.5
Upper Middle-Income Countries (6)[d]	670.3	2.6
Lower Middle-Income Countries (5)[e]	446.7	1.8
Low-Income Countries (0)	0	0.0
Socialist Organizations	0	0.0
International Organizations	6,073.8	24.1
Others	442.9	1.7
Total	25,294.2	100.0

[a]Figure is for first nine months of the year.
[b]Australia, Austria, Belgium, Canada, Denmark, Finland, France, Federal Republic of Germany, Hungary, Iceland, Ireland, Israel, Italy, Japan, Luxembourg, Netherlands, New Zealand, Norway, Poland, Spain, Sweden, Switzerland, United Kingdom, United States.
[c]Algeria, Iran.
[d]Brazil, Mexico, Singapore, South Africa, Turkey, Yugoslavia.
[e]Republic of Korea, Malaysia, Morocco, Philippines, Tunisia.

NOTE: The figures in this table include both public and private bonds.

SOURCE: International Bank for Reconstruction and Development, *Borrowing in International Capital Markets,* Doc. No. EC-181/762, Second Quarter 1976, and *Borrowing in International Capital Markets,* Doc. No. EC-181/763, Third Quarter 1976.

E-6. Recipients of Publicized Eurocurrency Credits, 1976[a] ($ millions and percentages)

	($ millions)	(percentage of total)
Developed Countries[b] (21)	7,575.5	41.8
Developing Countries		
Oil-Exporting Countries (7)	2,117.1	11.7
Upper Middle-Income Countries[c] (13)	4,481.6	24.7
Lower Middle-Income Countries[c] (13)	2,207.1	12.2
Low-Income Countries[c] (2)	162.0	0.9
Socialist Organizations	600.0	3.3
International Organizations	377.0	2.1
Others	592.7	3.3
Total	18,113.0	100.0

[a]Figure is for first nine months of the year.
[b]Those countries identified as "high-income" in Table A-3 of this volume (except for the Bahamas, Bahrain, Kuwait, Libya, Qatar, Saudi Arabia, Singapore, and the United Arab Emirates) with publicized Eurocurrency credits.
[c]Except for the oil-exporting countries, those countries listed in this category in Table A-3 of this volume with publicized Eurocurrency credits in the first nine months of 1976.

SOURCE: International Bank for Reconstruction and Development, *Borrowing in International Capital Markets,* Doc. No. EC-181/763, Third Quarter 1976, Tables 5.1, 5.2, and 5.3.

E-7. Official and Private Export Credits from DAC Countries to Developing Countries, 1972-1975
($ millions)

	Net Export Credits Extended				Stock of Export Credits Outstanding
	1972	1973	1974	1975	1975 (end)
Australia	38	-65	-38	2	166
Austria	15	44	74	87	515
Belgium	81	160	222	360	1,449
Canada	101	48	253	148	1,003
Denmark	6	48	5	32	336
Finland	14	7	21	37	97[a]
France	271	354	268	552	6,651
Germany	-31	-223	573	1,029	5,693
Italy	134	72	43	1,170	4,448
Japan	457	694	157	422	6,356
Netherlands	68	44	52	56	640
New Zealand	3	n.a.	2	1[a]	6
Norway	-24	-13	9	9	50
Sweden	-4	3	142	64	402
Switzerland	-20	115	107	40	1,601
United Kingdom	535	281	353	415	7,637
United States	**529**	**745**	**929**	**1,015**	8,446
Total	2,173	2,314	3,172	5,438	45,646
of which:					
Official	724	1,117	691	1,371	

[a]Estimate

NOTES: Except in the case of the United States, the figures include nonguaranteed export credits. Negative figures result from repayments on old credits exceeding new credit extensions.

Major beneficiaries of net export credits (those countries receiving more than $100 million) in 1975 were Portugal, Spain, Turkey, and Yugoslavia in Europe; Algeria, Liberia, Morocco, Sudan, Zaire, and Zambia in Africa; Argentina, Brazil, Cuba, Mexico, and Panama in Latin America; and Iraq, Indonesia, Republic of Korea, and Taiwan in Asia. In 1975, these 19 countries accounted for 97% of total net export credits extended from DAC to developing countries.

SOURCE: Report by the Chairman of the Development Assistance Committee, *Development Co-operation, 1976 Review* (Paris: OECD, 1976), p. 75.

E-8. Net Flow of Official Development Assistance from All DAC Countries, the United States, OPEC Countries, and Centrally Planned Economies, 1975 ($ billions and percentages)

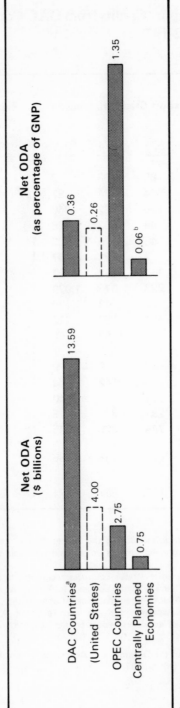

aIncluding the United States.
bBased on the GNP of the U.S.S.R. and the People's Republic of China only.

SOURCE: Based on Report by the Chairman of the Development Assistance Committee, *Development Co-operation, 1976 Review* (Paris: OECD, 1976), p. 59.

E-9. Net Flow of Official Development Assistance (ODA) from DAC Countries as a Percentage of Gross National Product, 1960, 1970, and 1975-1980

	1960	1970	1975	1976[a]	1977[a]	1978[a]	1979[a]	1980[a]
Australia	.38	.59	.61	.55	.56	.57	.57	.58
Austria	n.a.	.07	.17	.16	.16	.17	.17	.18
Belgium	.88	.46	.59	.57	.61	.64	.65	.68
Canada	.19	.42	.58	.58	.61	.65	.68	.70
Denmark	.09	.38	.58	.62	.64	.67	.70	.70
Finland	n.a.[b]	.07	.19	.20	.22	.24	.27	.29
France	1.38	.66	.62	.61	.59	.60	.61	.62
Germany	.31	.32	.40	.32	.29	.28	.27	.26
Italy	.22	.16	.12	.11	.12	.12	.12	.12
Japan	.24	.23	.24	.23	.22	.22	.21	.20
Netherlands	.31	.61	.75	.85	.88	.89	.88	.88
New Zealand	n.a.[c]	.23	.52	.42	.41	.44	.46	.47
Norway	.11	.32	.66	.74	.86	.96	.97	.97
Portugal[d]	1.45	.67	n.a.	n.a.	n.a.	n.a.	n.a.	n.a.
Sweden	.05	.38	.82	.86	.89	.92	.96	1.00
Switzerland	.04	.15	.19	.16	.15	.14	.14	.14
United Kingdom	.56	.37	.39	.37	.37	.39	.40	.41
United States[e]	**.53**	**.31**	**.27**	**.26**	**.24**	**.23**	**.22**	**.21**

DAC TOTAL

	1960	1970	1975	1976	1977	1978	1979	1980
ODA ($ billions)								
current prices	4.6	6.8	13.6	14.6	16.2	18.3	20.5	22.8
1975 prices	11.0	11.5	13.6	13.6	14.1	14.6	15.3	15.9
GNP ($ billions)								
current prices	900	2,000	3,800	4,200	4,800	5,500	6,200	6,900
ODA as % of GNP	.52	.34	.36	.35	.34	.34	.33	.33

[a]Estimate.
[b]Finland became a member of DAC in 1975; ODA figures for 1960 are not available.
[c]New Zealand became a member of DAC in 1973; ODA figures for 1960 are not available.
[d]Portugal withdrew from DAC in October 1974; figures later than 1973 are not available.
[e]U.S. ODA amounted to 2.79% of GNP at the beginning of the Marshall Plan in 1949.

NOTE: Countries included are (or were) members of the OECD Development Assistance Committee and account for 80% of the world's total concessional aid (ODA). Figures for 1975 and earlier years are based on actual data. Those for 1976-1980 are based on OECD and World Bank estimates of growth of GNP, on information about budget appropriations for aid, and on aid policy statements by governments. They are projections—not predictions—of what will occur unless action not now planned takes place.

SOURCES: Adapted from Robert S. McNamara, "Address to the Board of Governors," Manila, Philippines, October 4, 1976 (Washington, D.C.: World Bank, 1976), p. 40, and Report by the Chairman of the Development Assistance Committee, *Development Cooperation, 1976 Review* (Paris: OECD, 1976), Table 2.

E-10. U.S. Official Development Assistance in Comparison with All Other DAC Countries, 1965-1975
($ billions)

From 1965 to 1975, net U.S. official development assistance (ODA) only increased from $3.4 billion to $4.0 billion (with a low point of $3.0 billion in 1973). In contrast, the ODA of all other DAC countries increased nearly fourfold, from $2.5 billion in 1965 to $9.6 billion in 1975.

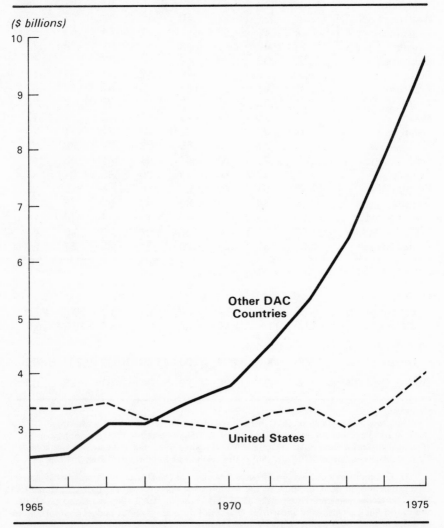

($ billions)

Other DAC Countries

United States

1965   1970   1975

NOTE: Finland and New Zealand not included until 1970. Portugal not included after 1972.

SOURCES: Based on Report by the Chairman of the Development Assistance Committee, *Development Co-operation, 1973 Review* (Paris: OECD, 1973), pp. 181 and 189; *Development Co-operation, 1975 Review* (Paris: OECD, 1975), pp. 195 and 256-57; and *Development Co-operation, 1976 Review* (Paris: OECD, 1976), pp. 207 and 268.

E-11. U.S. Official Development Assistance in Comparison with All Other DAC Countries, 1965-1975 (as percentage of GNP)

From 1965 to 1975, net U.S. official development assistance (ODA) as a percentage of GNP decreased by nearly half—going from 0.49 per cent to 0.26 per cent. The ODA of all other countries as a percentage of their combined wealth has remained fairly constant.

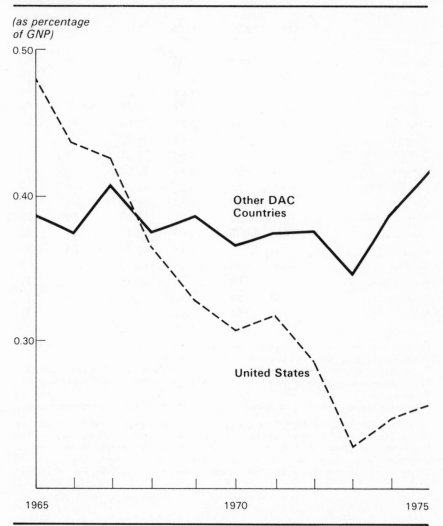

(as percentage of GNP)

Other DAC Countries

United States

1965   1970   1975

NOTE: Finland and New Zealand not included until 1970. Portugal not included after 1972.

SOURCES: Based on Report by the Chairman of the Development Assistance Committee, *Development Co-operation, 1973 Review* (Paris: OECD, 1973), pp. 181 and 189; *Development Co-operation, 1975 Review* (Paris: OECD, 1975), pp. 195 and 256-57; and *Development Co-operation, 1976 Review* (Paris: OECD, 1976), pp. 207 and 268.

E-12. Net Flow of Official Development Assistance from DAC Countries, 1960 and 1975 ($ millions, $, and percentages)

Countries Listed by 1975 Rank[a]	Total Contribution ($ millions)		Per Capita Contribution ($)		Contribution as Percentage of GNP	
	1960	1975	1960	1975	1960	1975
Sweden	7	566	.94	69.06	.05	.82
Netherlands	35	604	3.05	44.24	.31	.75
Norway	5	184	1.39	45.92	.11	.66
France	823	2,091	18.07	39.65	1.38	.62
Australia	59	507	5.74	37.54	.38	.61
Belgium	101	378	11.04	38.57	.88	.59
Denmark	5	205	1.09	40.51	.09	.59
Canada	75	880	4.21	38.54	.19	.58
New Zealand	n.a.[b]	66	n.a.[b]	21.26	n.a.[b]	.52
Germany	223	1,689	4.18	27.32	.31	.40
United Kingdom	407	863	7.75	15.40	.56	.38
United States	**2,702**	**4,007**	**14.96**	**18.76**	**.53**	**.26**
Japan	105	1,148	1.13	10.26	.24	.24
Finland	n.a.[c]	48	n.a.[c]	10.20	n.a.[c]	.19
Switzerland	4	104	.75	16.24	.04	.19
Austria	3[d]	64	.43[d]	8.50	.04[d]	.17
Italy	77	182	1.56	3.26	.22	.11
Portugal	37	n.a.[e]	4.15	n.a.[e]	1.45	n.a.[e]

[a]Rank according to 1975 ODA as a percentage of 1975 GNP.
[b]New Zealand became a member of DAC in 1973; ODA figures for 1960 are not available.
[c]Finland became a member of DAC in 1975; ODA figures for 1960 are not available.
[d]Figure is for 1961.
[e]Portugal withdrew from DAC in October 1974; figures for 1975 are not available.

SOURCES: Based on Report by the Chairman of the Development Assistance Committee, *Development Co-operation, 1971 Review* (Paris: OECD, 1971), pp. 165 and 175; Report by the Chairman of the Development Assistance Committee, *Development Co-operation, 1976 Review* (Paris: OECD, 1976), Tables 2 and 44; and United Nations, Department of Economic and Social Affairs, *Demographic Yearbook, 1961,* Table 4, pp. 126-37.

E-13. Net Flow of Private Voluntary Assistance from DAC Countries, 1970 and 1975 ($ millions, $, and percentages)

Countries Listed by 1975 Rank[a]	Total Contribution ($ millions)		Per Capita Contribution ($)		Contribution as Percentage of GNP	
	1970	1975	1970	1975	1970	1975
Switzerland	11	32	1.74	5.01	.05	.06
Sweden	25	39	3.13	4.73	.08	.06
United States	**598**	**804**	**2.92**	**3.76**	**.06**	**.05**
New Zealand	1	6[b]	.50	2.06	.02	.05
Germany	78	205	1.28	3.32	.04	.05
Canada	52	67	2.42	2.91	.06	.04
Australia	16	34	1.26	2.50	.05	.04
Norway	4	11	1.01	2.65	.03	.04
Belgium	15	20[b]	1.54	2.04	.06	.03
Austria	4	11	.49	1.47	.03	.03
Netherlands	5	24	.40	1.72	.02	.03
United Kingdom	34	53	.61	.95	.03	.02
Denmark	3	6	.61	1.23	.02	.02
Finland	1	2	.17	.47	.01	.009
France	6	15	.12	.29	.004	.005
Japan	3	10	.03	.09	.002	.002
Italy	5	3	.09	.05	.009	.002
Portugal	1	n.a.[c]	.09	n.a.[c]	.01	n.a.[c]

[a]Rank according to 1975 grants by voluntary agencies as a percentage of 1975 GNP.
[b]Estimate of OECD Secretariat.
[c]Portugal withdrew from DAC in October 1974; figures for 1975 are not available.

SOURCES: Based on Report by the Chairman of the Development Assistance Committee, *Development Co-operation, 1975 Review* (Paris: OECD, 1975), pp. 206-17, and Report by the Chairman of the Development Assistance Committee, *Development Co-operation, 1976 Review* (Paris: OECD, 1975), Tables 10 and 44.

E-14. Net Flow of Resources from DAC Countries to Developing Countries and Multilateral Institutions, 1964-1966 Average, 1970, and 1973-1975 ($ millions)

	1964-1966[a] Average	1970[a]	1973	1974	1975
Official	**6,146.9**	**7,929.2**	**11,813.6**	**13,499.9**	**16,608.9**
Official Development Assistance (ODA)	5,913.0	6,790.5	9,350.7	11,316.8	13,585.3
Bilateral	5,550.0	5,666.7	7,082.3	8,257.1	9,815.5
Grants and grant-like contributions[b]	3,732.6	3,309.2	4,461.7	5,335.9	6,268.0
Development lending and capital[c]	1,817.1	2,357.4	2,620.8	2,921.1	3,547.3
Contributions to multilateral institutions	363.1	1,123.8	2,268.2	3,059.6	3,769.6
Grants	204.2	551.7	1,055.1	1,464.0	2,028.7
Capital subscription payments	157.3	540.6	1,126.6	1,535.8	1,731.6
Concessional lending	1.6	31.5	86.4	59.7	9.3
Other official flows[d]	233.9	1,138.7	2,462.9	2,183.1	3,023.6
Private, at market terms	**3,928.1**	**6,875.1**	**11,449.5**	**13,266.0**	**21,962.0[e]**
Private investment and lending[f]	3,016.6	4,733.2	10,253.8	10,785.1	17,894.6
Private export credits	911.4	2,141.9	1,195.7	2,480.8	4,067.3[e]
Grants by Private Voluntary Agencies	**n.a.[g]**	**857.5**	**1,364.5**	**1,217.3**	**1,341.8[e]**
Total	**10,075.0**	**15,662.8**	**24,627.6**	**27,983.2**	**39,912.7[e]**

[a]Figures prior to 1972 exclude New Zealand and Finland
[b]Technical assistance, food aid, and other grants.
[c]New development lending, food aid loans, debt reorganization, and equities and other bilateral assets.
[d]Official export credits, debt relief, equities and other bilateral assets, and contributions to multilateral institutions not on terms concessional enough to qualify as ODA.
[e]Estimate of OECD Secretariat.
[f]Direct investment, bilateral portfolio investment, and multilateral portfolio investment.
[g]Voluntary grants were not recorded by DAC before 1970.

SOURCE: Report by the Chairman of the Development Assistance Committee, *Development Co-operation, 1976 Review* (Paris: OECD, 1976), p. 229.

E-15. Net Flow of Resources from the United States to Developing Countries and Multilateral Institutions, 1964-1966 Average, 1970, and 1973-1975 ($ millions)

	1964-1966 Average	1970	1973	1974	1975
Official	**3,427.9**	**3,218.0**	**3,445.0**	**4,262.0**	**4,927.0**
Official Development Assistance (ODA)	3,453.0	3,050.0	2,968.0	3,439.0	4,007.0
Bilateral	3,366.3	2,657.0	2,337.0	2,557.0	2,941.0
Grants and grant-like contributions[a]	2,274.7	1,381.0	1,438.0	1,742.0	1,705.0
Development lending and capital[b]	1,091.6	1,276.0	899.0	815.0	1,236.0
Contributions to multilateral institutions	86.6	393.0	631.0	882.0	1,066.0
Grants	82.9	160.0	258.0	344.0	412.0
Capital subscription payments	3.7	233.0	373.0	538.0	654.0
Concessional lending	–	–	–	–	–
Other official flows[c]	–25.1[d]	168.0	477.0	823.0	920.0
Private, at market terms	**1,748.1**	**2,394.7**	**3,996.0**	**5,273.0**	**11,635.0**
Private investment and lending[e]	1,705.3	2,312.0	3,721.4	4,832.4	11,418.8
Private export credits	42.8	82.7	274.6	440.6	216.2
Grants by Private Voluntary Agencies	**n.a.[f]**	**598.0**	**905.0**	**735.0**	**804.0**
Total	**5,175.9**	**6,210.7**	**8,346.0**	**10,270.0**	**17,366.0**

[a]Technical assistance, food aid, and other grants.
[b]New development lending, food aid loans, debt reorganization, and equities and other bilateral assets.
[c]Official export credits, debt relief, equities and other bilateral assets, and contributions to multilateral institutions not on terms concessional enough to qualify as ODA.
[d]Negative figure results from repayments on old official export credits exceeding new credit extensions during the 1964-1966 period.
[e]Direct investment, bilateral portfolio investment, and multilateral portfolio investment.
[f]Voluntary grants were not recorded by DAC before 1970.

SOURCE: Report by the Chairman of the Development Assistance Committee, *Development Co-operation, 1976 Review* (Paris: OECD, 1976), p. 229.

E-16. Current Value and Real Value of U.S. Official Development Assistance, 1961-1975
($ billions)

The annual net flow of U.S. official development assistance (ODA) increased by some $1.1 billion (or 38 per cent) between 1961 and 1975. However, when inflation is accounted for, it is apparent that the real value of U.S. aid actually decreased by that amount—falling from $2.9 billion in 1961 to $1.8 billion in 1975.

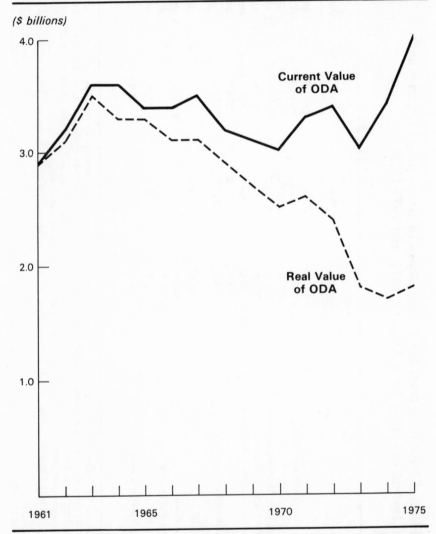

($ billions)

NOTE: The "real value" of ODA is calculated by adjusting for inflation and/or changes in currency values; it reflects the problem of being able to buy fewer and fewer goods for the same or even more U.S. dollars.

SOURCE: Based on data from Report to the Chairman of the Development Assistance Committee, *Development Co-operation, 1973 Review* (Paris: OECD, 1973) and *Development Co-operation, 1975 Review* (Paris: OECD, 1975).

E-17. Selected U.S. Personal Consumption Expenditures and Net ODA Disbursements, 1975 ($ billions)

In 1975, the U.S. government provided $4 billion in official development assistance to the developing countries—a relatively small amount compared to expenditures on other goods. Individual Americans, for example, spent more than twice as much on nondurable toys and sports supplies and over six times as much on alcoholic beverages.

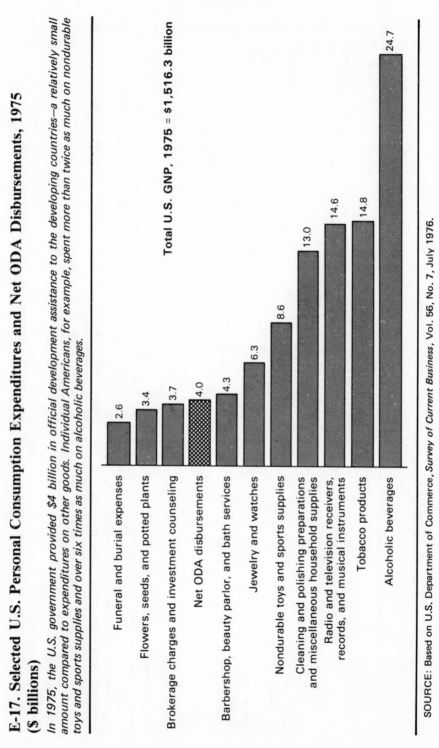

Total U.S. GNP, 1975 = $1,516.3 billion

Category	Value
Funeral and burial expenses	2.6
Flowers, seeds, and potted plants	3.4
Brokerage charges and investment counseling	3.7
Net ODA disbursements	4.0
Barbershop, beauty parlor, and bath services	4.3
Jewelry and watches	6.3
Nondurable toys and sports supplies	8.6
Cleaning and polishing preparations and miscellaneous household supplies	13.0
Radio and television receivers, records, and musical instruments	14.6
Tobacco products	14.8
Alcoholic beverages	24.7

SOURCE: Based on U.S. Department of Commerce, *Survey of Current Business*, Vol. 56, No. 7, July 1976.

E-18. Recipients of U.S. Economic Assistance, FY 1975 ($ millions)

10 Major Recipients	Agency for International Development (AID)			P.L. 480	Other[b]	Total Economic Assistance[c]
	Security Supporting Assistance[a]	Development Assistance	Total			
Egypt	253	—	253	117	—	370
Israel	324	20	344	9	—	353
Bangladesh	—	62	62	242	—	304
India	—	20	20	227	2	249
Vietnam, Rep. of	188	3	191	50	—	241
Pakistan	—	96	96	85	d	181
Cambodia	55	—	55	94	—	149
Syria	83	—	83	22	d	105
Jordan	87	—	87	12	2	99
Chile	—	31	31	62	2	95
Total, 10 Recipients	990	232	1,222	920	4	2,146
Total, All Recipients	1,226	1,293	2,519	1,328	1,061	4,098

[a] Assistance to countries of special interest to the United States under specific programs such as Indochina Postwar Reconstruction, Middle East Special Requirements Fund, and Assistance to Portugal and Portuguese Colonies in Africa.
[b] Consists of Peace Corps, grants to programs such as the Inter-American Foundation and the International Narcotics Control Program, capital subscriptions to international financial institutions, and contributions to international organizations.
[c] U.S. "economic assistance" is equivalent to the aid reported to DAC as "official development assistance" (ODA). However, "economic assistance" figures represent gross commitments in fiscal years, while ODA figures are net disbursements in calendar years.
[d] Less than $1 million.

SOURCE: Based on U.S. Agency for International Development, Office of Financial Management, Statistics and Reports Division, *U.S. Overseas Loans and Grants and Assistance from International Organizations: Obligations and Loan Authorizations, July 1, 1945–June 30, 1975.*

E-19. Economic Aid from U.S.S.R., Eastern Europe, and China to Non-Communist Developing Countries, Gross Commitments, 1971-1975 ($ millions)

	1971	1972	1973	1974	1975
Donors					
U.S.S.R.	992	610	657	563	1,264[a]
Eastern Europe[b]	468	832	484	531	319
People's Republic of China	505	553	428	242	269
Total	**1,965**	**1,995**	**1,569**	**1,336**	**1,852**
Recipients					
Africa (excluding South Africa)	640	426	443	302	313[c]
East Asia (excluding Japan)	57	—	1	25	65[d]
Europe	—	45[e]	—	—	—
Latin America	259	331	5	429	166[f]
Near East and South Asia	1,009	1,193	1,120	580	1,308[g]
Total	**1,965**	**1,995**	**1,569**	**1,336**	**1,852[h]**

[a]Almost 86% of Soviet commitments were given to Turkey ($650 million) and Afghanistan ($437 million).
[b]Bulgaria, Czechoslovakia, Democratic Republic of Germany, Hungary, Poland, and Romania.
[c]Of this amount, $150 million was committed by China, primarily to Mozambique, Malagasy Republic, The Gambia, and Guinea-Bissau.
[d]Of this amount, $59 million was committed to the Philippines, with Eastern Europe and China each donating about one half.
[e]All from China to Malta.
[f]Of this amount, $150 million was committed to Brazil by the Eastern European countries.
[g]Of this amount, Turkey received $650 million and Afghanistan $437 million, all from the U.S.S.R.
[h]Of this total, two nations—Turkey and Afghanistan—received 59%.

NOTES: Aid to the communist countries of Albania, Cambodia, Cuba, Mongolia, Democratic Republic of Korea, North Vietnam, and Romania is excluded from this table. In 1971 (the latest data available), aid *disbursements* to these countries from the U.S.S.R., China, and the Eastern European countries amounted to $1,335.0 million. Soviet aid commitments to other communist countries (including the Eastern European countries) totalled $2,125 million in 1971. Thus the largest part of communist aid goes to other communist countries.

Short-term commitments are also excluded. Only 5% of communist aid is in the form of pure grants, although grants have accounted for about 15% of China's aid commitments, compared with less than 2% in other communist countries. All communist economic aid is characterized by concentration on the public sector and close-tying of credits to the purchase of donor-country goods. However, the terms of aid are softest from China (interest-free loans repayable in developing-country products over 10 to 30 years with a 10-year grace period) and hardest from Eastern Europe and the U.S.S.R. (8 to 10 year loans at 3 to 3.5% interest for the former and 12 year loans at 2.5 to 3% interest for the latter).

SOURCE: Based on *International Policy Report*, Vol. II, No. 1, April 1976. Published by the Institute for International Policy, Washington, D.C.

E-20. Resources from OPEC Members to Developing Countries and Multilateral Institutions, Commitments and Disbursements, 1975 ($ millions and percentages)

| | CONCESSIONAL | | | | | NONCONCESSIONAL | | | | |
| | Commitments ($ millions) | | Net Disbursements ($ millions) | | Total Net Disbursements as Percentage of GNP | Commitments ($ millions) | | Net Disbursements ($ millions) | | Total Net Disbursements as Percentage of GNP |
	Bilateral	Total	Bilateral	Total		Bilateral	Total	Bilateral	Total	
Algeria	5.8	34.5	2.0	18.7	0.14	–	11.7	–	9.7	0.07
Iran	1,267.9	1,272.3	481.0	485.4	0.85	350.0	364.0	155.0	236.0	0.41
Iraq	294.8	320.6	190.0	224.8	1.48	–	–	20.0	24.8	0.16
Kuwait	500.0	612.7	250.0	330.5	2.75	1,748.8	1,768.8	800.0	816.7	6.80
Libya	56.3	132.4	100.0	165.7	1.62	229.0	283.0	170.0	193.0	1.89
Nigeria	20.4	29.7	20.4	29.7	0.15	–	51.5	–	168.5	0.85
Qatar	177.6	203.2	125.0	147.0	6.39	–	0.3	30.0	33.2	1.44
Saudi Arabia	1,438.8	1,676.3	675.0	917.2	2.64	705.7	788.3	670.0	1,097.3	3.16
United Arab Emirates	338.2	399.4	345.0	403.7	4.64	367.6	383.1	225.0	239.2	2.75
Venezuela	–	11.5	–	24.9	0.08	89.0	638.0	150.6	402.6	1.29
Total	4,099.8	4,692.6	2,188.4	2,747.6	1.35	3,490.1	4,288.7	2,220.6	3,221.0	1.58

aEstimates.

NOTE: Figures in this table exclude OPEC contributions to the IMF Oil Facilities and Euro-currency financing. The other three members of OPEC—Ecuador, Gabon, and Indonesia—still need and receive, rather than give, economic aid.

SOURCE: Based on Report by the Chairman of the Development Assistance Committee, *Development Co-operation, 1976 Review* (Paris: OECD, 1976), pp. 101 and 121.

E-21. Recipients of Bilateral Assistance Commitments from OPEC Members, by Region, 1975
($ millions and percentages)

	Concessional		Nonconcessional	
	($ millions)	(as % of total)	($ millions)	(as % of total)
Middle East	**2,089.4**	**51.0**	**2,615.2**	**74.9**
Egypt[a]	985.5	24.0	2,133.1	61.1
Jordan[a]	267.5	6.5	110.4	3.2
Oman[a]	148.9	3.6	—	—
Syria[a]	501.5	12.2	247.9	7.1
Yemen, Arab Rep.[a]	94.1	2.3	100.0	2.9
Yemen, People's Rep.[a]	50.2	1.2	0.3	b
Other	41.7	1.0	23.5	0.7
Africa	**533.2**	**13.0**	**322.2**	**9.2**
Algeria[a]	—	—	50.0	1.4
Mauritania[a]	47.6	1.2	1.3	b
Morocco[a]	87.4	2.1	20.7	0.6
Somalia[a]	89.3	2.2	—	—
Sudan[a]	90.5	2.2	10.0	0.3
Tunisia[a]	71.4	1.7	3.0	0.1
Uganda	67.4	1.6	35.3	1.0
Zaire	—	—	101.3	2.9
Other	79.6	1.9	100.6	2.9
Asia	**1,446.5**	**35.3**	**227.5**	**6.5**
India	930.7	22.7	3.8	0.1
Indonesia	99.5	2.4	200.0	5.7
Pakistan	141.9	3.5	20.0	0.6
Other	274.4	6.7	3.7	0.1
Latin America	**—**	**—**	**108.5**	**3.1**
Peru	—	—	65.0	1.9
Other	—	—	43.5	1.3
Europe	**1.0**	**b**	**216.8**	**6.2**
Yugoslavia	—	—	195.0	5.6
Other	1.0	b	21.8	0.6
Arab countries, unallocated	**29.7**	**0.7**	**—**	**—**
Total	**4,099.8**	**100.0**	**3,490.1**	**100.0**
of which:				
Arab countries	2,468.9	60.2	2,680.2	76.8

[a]Arab country as defined by membership in Arab League.
[b]Negligible.

SOURCE: Report by the Chairman of the Development Assistance Committee, *Development Co-operation 1976 Review* (Paris: OECD, 1976), pp. 101, 116-17, 121, and 124.

E-22. Net ODA and Total Net Flow of Resources to Developing Countries and Multilateral Institutions, by Groups of Countries, 1972-1975 ($ millions and percentages)

	Amount ($ millions)				As Percentage of Total				As Percentage of GNP			
	1972	1973	1974	1975	1972	1973	1974	1975	1972	1973	1974	1975
Official Development Assistance												
DAC Countries	8,538	9,351	11,317	13,585	87	86	76	80	0.33	0.30	0.33	0.36
OPEC Countries	420	480	2,488	2,748	4	4	17	16	0.69	0.52	1.36	1.35
U.S.S.R. and Eastern Europe	600	625	600	375	6	6	4	2	0.08[a]	0.08[a]	0.07[a]	0.04[a]
People's Republic of China	250	375	425	375	3	4	3	2	0.13	0.17	0.19	0.16
Total	9,808	10,831	14,830	17,083	100	100	100	100				
Total Official and Private Flows												
DAC Countries	19,693	24,628	27,983	39,913	93	92	83	85	0.77	0.79	0.82	1.05
OPEC Countries	530	920	4,711	5,969	2	4	14	13	0.87	0.98	2.57	2.94
U.S.S.R. and Eastern Europe	750	775	750	500	4	3	2	1	0.09[a]	0.09[a]	0.08[a]	0.04[a]
People's Republic of China	250	375	425	375	1	1	1	1	0.13	0.17	0.19	0.16
Total	21,223	26,698	33,869	46,757	100	100	100	100				

[a]Refers to U.S.S.R. only.

SOURCE: Adapted from Report by the Chairman of the Development Assistance Committee, *Development Co-operation, 1976 Review* (Paris: OECD, 1976), p. 59.

E-23. Recipients of Official Development Assistance from DAC Countries, OPEC Countries, and Centrally Planned Economies, by Income Level, 1973-1975 Average (percentages)

From: \ To:	Oil-Exporting Countries	Middle-Income Countries[a]	Low-Income Countries[b]	Total
DAC Countries	11	52	37	100
OPEC Countries	—	77	23	100
Centrally Planned Economies	7	52	41	100

[a]Those with per capita incomes of more than $375.
[b]Those with per capita incomes of less than $375.

SOURCE: United Nations, Economic and Social Council, Committee for Development Planning, "New Mechanisms for the Transfer of Resources to Developing Countries," Doc. No. E/AC.54/L.83, p. 51. Prepared by Nurul Islam.

E-24. Net Flow of Resources from Multilateral Institutions to Developing Countries, 1965, 1970, 1974, and 1975 ($ millions)

	1965	1970	1974	1975
World Bank Group	586	739	2,247	3,064
International Development Association	277	163	901	1,086
Other	309	576	1,346	1,978
United Nations	252	498	900	900
Regional Institutions	212	548	1,432	1,841
European Communities	116	221	614	748
Inter-American Development Bank	96	308	510	524
Asian Development Bank	—	17	172	339
African Development Bank	—	2	23	49
Other	—	—	113	181
Total	**1,046**	**1,785**	**4,579**	**5,805**
of which: Concessional	633	845	2,845	3,119

SOURCE: Adapted from Report by the Chairman of the Development Assistance Committee, *Development Co-operation, 1976 Review* (Paris: OECD, 1976), p. 164.

About the Overseas Development Council and the Authors

The Overseas Development Council is an independent, nonprofit organization established in 1969 to increase American understanding of the economic and social problems confronting the developing countries, and of the importance of these countries to the United States in an increasingly interdependent world. The ODC seeks to promote consideration of development issues by the American public, policy makers, specialists, educators, and the media through its research, conferences, publications, and liaison with U.S. mass membership organizations interested in U.S. relations with the developing world. The ODC's program is funded by foundations, corporations, and private individuals; its policies are determined by its Board of Directors. Theodore M. Hesburgh, C.S.C., is Chairman of the Board, and Davidson Sommers is its Vice Chairman. The Council's President is James P. Grant.

The authors of *The United States and World Development: Agenda 1977* are listed here in the sequence of the chapters they contributed.

Theodore M. Hesburgh, C.S.C., ODC's Chairman of the Board of Directors, is President of the University of Notre Dame. He was formerly Chairman of the U.S. Commission on Civil Rights and is on the boards of a number of organizations devoted to meeting America's social needs. Father Hesburgh is the Chairman of the Board of Trustees of the Rockefeller Foundation, a member of the Council of the International Association of Universities, and a member of the Board of Directors of the Chase Manhattan Bank and of the Council on Foreign Relations. His most recent book is *The Humane Imperative: A Challenge for the Year 2000*.

James P. Grant has been President of the Overseas Development Council since its establishment in 1969. He was formerly Assistant Administrator of the U.S. Agency for International Development, and a Deputy Assistant Secretary of State. He is currently on the boards of several public service organizations and is the Vice President of the Society for International Development. Mr. Grant's recent analyses have centered on the world food situation, major structural changes taking place in the international order, and the effectiveness of various development strategies.

John W. Sewell, who directed the preparation of *Agenda 1977*, is the Vice President of the Overseas Development Council. He joined the

Council's staff in 1971 after serving as Assistant to the President of the Brookings Institution and spending ten years as a foreign service officer in the Department of State. Mr. Sewell has written on American public opinion concerning the developing countries, on the ethics of development assistance, and on development in the African Sahel.

Roger D. Hansen is a Senior Fellow at the Council. He is also presently serving as a Senior Research Fellow at the Council on Foreign Relations while working on the Council's 1980s Project. He previously served as U.S. Deputy Assistant Special Trade Representative in the Office of the Special Representative for Trade Negotiations. He is the author of *The Politics of Mexican Development* (1971); *Mexican Economic Development: The Roots of Rapid Growth* (1971); *Central America: Regional Integration and Economic Development* (1967). His recent articles have examined the global distribution of income and economic opportunity, the "political economy" of North-South relations, the official U.S. response to the "new international economic order" issues, and the need for a new policy framework for U.S.-Latin American relations.

Florizelle B. Liser, a Staff Associate at the Council, received her B.A. Degree in political science from Dickinson College in 1973 and her Master's Degree in international affairs from the Johns Hopkins School of Advanced International Studies (SAIS) in 1975. While at SAIS and before joining the Council staff, she was a Research Assistant at the Brookings Institution.

Overseas Development Council
1717 Massachusetts Avenue, N.W.
Washington, D.C. 20036
(202-234-8701)

ODC Staff

James P. Grant, *President*
John W. Sewell, *Vice President and Treasurer*
Michael V. O'Hare, *Controller*
Patricia A. Neace, *Secretary to the Board and Conference Coordinator*

James E. Boyle
Librarian

Guy F. Erb
Senior Fellow

Denis Goulet
Visiting Fellow

Roger D. Hansen
Senior Fellow

James W. Howe
Senior Fellow

Robert H. Johnson
Visiting Fellow

Valeriana Kallab
Executive Editor

William Knowland
Staff Associate

Nancy J. Krekeler
Associate Editor

Kenneth Kugel
Staff Consultant

Florizelle B. Liser
Staff Associate

Martin M. McLaughlin
Senior Fellow

Diana T. Michaelis
Communications Specialist

Morris D. Morris
Visiting Fellow

Rosemarie Philips
Associate Editor

John G. Sommer
Fellow

Stephen M. Taran
Staff Associate

Paul M. Watson
Visiting Fellow

Jayne Millar Wood
Director of Public Education

Research Assistants

James A. Bever
James Dempsey
Bachir Haskouri
John Holtzman
Nadine R. Horenstein
Anthony S. G. Pearce-Batten
Drew D. Reynolds
Patricia Robinson
James J. Tarrant
Kenneth G. Weiss

Support Staff

Patricia K. Abell
K. Sue Croy
Kandi J. Fisher
Mary Scott Gordon
William B. Hager
Ferne M. Horner
Margaret G. Hubbard
Margaret C. Jameson
Louisa P. Kessel
Kathryn M. Lenney
Angela Marie LoRé
Anne McCormally
Thérèse Roy

ODC Board of Directors

Chairman: Theodore M. Hesburgh
Vice-Chairman: Davidson Sommers

RELATED TITLES
Published by
Praeger Special Studies

**Titles published in cooperation with the
Overseas Development Council:**

**BEYOND DEPENDENCY: THE DEVELOPING
WORLD SPEAKS OUT**
    edited by Guy F. Erb and Valeriana Kallab

***EMPLOYMENT, GROWTH AND BASIC NEEDS:
A ONE-WORLD PROBLEM**
    prepared by the ILO International Labour Office
    with an Introduction by James P. Grant,
    Overseas Development Council

**WOMEN AND WORLD DEVELOPMENT:
WITH AN ANNOTATED BIBLIOGRAPHY**
    edited by Irene Tinker, Michèle Bo Bramsen,
    and Mayra Buvinić

Other related titles:

***THE MULTINATIONAL CORPORATION AND
SOCIAL CHANGE**
    edited by David E. Apter and
    Louis Wolf Goodman

*U.S. POLICY TOWARD AFRICA
    edited by Frederick S. Arkhurst

***PLANNING ALTERNATIVE WORLD FUTURES:
VALUES, METHODS, AND MODELS**
    edited by Louis Rene Beres and
    Harry R. Targ

***THE MAKING OF U.S. INTERNATIONAL
ECONOMIC POLICY: PRINCIPLES, PROBLEMS,
AND PROPOSALS FOR REFORM**
    Stephen D. Cohen

***PATTERNS OF POVERTY IN THE THIRD
WORLD: A STUDY OF SOCIAL AND
ECONOMIC STRATIFICATION**
    Charles Elliott, assisted by
    Françoise de Morsier

**THE NATION-STATE AND TRANSNATIONAL
CORPORATIONS IN CONFLICT: WITH SPECIAL
REFERENCE TO LATIN AMERICA**
edited by John P. Gunnemann

**EQUITY, INCOME, AND POLICY: STUDIES IN
THREE WORLDS OF DEVELOPMENT**
edited by Irving Louis Horowitz

**DEVELOPMENT IN RICH AND POOR
COUNTRIES: A GENERAL THEORY WITH
STATISTICAL ANALYSIS**
Thorkil Kristensen

*DEVELOPMENT WITHOUT DEPENDENCE
Pierre Uri

**THE WORLD FOOD CONFERENCE AND
GLOBAL PROBLEM SOLVING**
Thomas G. Weiss and
Robert S. Jordan

*Also available in paperback as a PSS Student Edition.

PRAEGER PUBLISHERS
200 Park Avenue
New York, N.Y. 10017